Discovery House Publishers

Books, music, and videos that feed the soul with the Word of God

Box 3566 Grand Rapids, MI 49501

ELIZABETH R. SKOGLUND

Found FAITHFUL

THE TIMELESS STORIES OF
CHARLES SPURGEON, AMY CARMICHAEL,
C. S. LEWIS, RUTH BELL GRAHAM,
AND OTHERS

Found Faithful
© 2003 by Elizabeth Ruth Skoglund.
All rights reserved.

Library of Congress Cataloging-in-Publication Data

Skoglund, Elizabeth.
    Found faithful : the timeless stories of Charles Spurgeon, Amy Carmichael,
    C. S. Lewis, Ruth Bell Graham, and others who triumphed over pain /
    by Elizabeth R. Skoglund.
        p.   cm.
    Includes bibliographical references.
    ISBN 1-57293-105-1
    1. Suffering—Religious aspects—Christianity. I. Title.
    BV4909.S56 2003

                                                270.8'092'2—dc22

    2003018118

Printed in the United States of America

03 04 05 06 07 08 09 10 11 12 / DP / 10 9 8 7 6 5 4 3 2 1

To Ken and Carolyn Connolly
To Lynn and John Whorrall
Among those found faithful

VIGNETTES

CONTENTS

ACKNOWLEDGMENTS

The genesis of *Found Faithful* goes back to my Aunt Ruth's influence on me when I was about four and she had come back home after a number of years as a missionary in China. Names like Hudson Taylor, D. E. Hoste, and the China Inland Mission became familiar.

Then at the age of fifteen I attended a Christian school where a teacher, Beverly West, a principal, Pamela Reeve, and a Bible teacher, Grace King, introduced me to Amy Carmichael and Bible expositors like H. C. G. Moule. Encountering these greats of the past opened the door to others. All of them helped shape my life.

As if to round out the life cycle of influence, only a few years ago when I researched this book did I find the wealth of teaching in the writings of F. B. Meyer who I then discovered had been a favorite of my maternal grandfather. His signature affixed to many of my books began to explain the rather large library I have of Meyer.

Researching the material for *Found Faithful* was a Herculean task and stretched back over decades. Then condensing and connecting it into something that would not only help the reader but also whet his or her appetite for reading more of the writings of these great saints presented an even greater challenge. Many people helped in this task throughout the various partial editions of this book, for one does not write any book alone.

Few publishers combine godliness with practicality and skill as well as Discovery House. To Carol Holquist I owe my thanks for the vision to see the importance of the people written about in this book. To Tim Gustafson I am indebted for hours of hard work and for sharing a genuine enthusiasm for these people, some of whom have been almost forgotten. Kim Collins is there at the end as she always is to begin the work of promotion. Beth Koops has been once again a valuable resource for all sorts of information and Kathie Schiedel has ably helped in these same areas as the book was being finished. I have appreciated Judith Markham for her insightfulness when several opinions were needed. Much thanks also to Donna Huisjen, Jackie Phillips, and Peggy Willison.

Ken and Carolyn Connolly and John and Lynn Whorrall helped fill in research details and, along with University Bible Church and a substantial group of others who committed to regular prayer, offered consistent prayer support as well. To John Whorrall I am deeply indebted for his generosity and talent as shown in the artwork in this book. The late Lois Curley steadfastly steered much of this material through many obstacles and had a deep insight into the value of these "witnesses." As always, my agent Richard Baltzell has been there to advise, encourage, and solve seemingly unsolvable problems.

Various individuals at Overseas Missionary Fellowship were helpful in sending books, looking up and duplicating material, and locating people who could provide additional information. Eileen Kuhn and Henry and Mary Guinness (Geraldine Taylor's nephew and his wife, now deceased) were kind in their willingness to grant interviews. Evelyn Freeland was once again helpful in gathering material, offering advice, and in coordinating time with Ruth Bell Graham, who, along with her eldest daughter, Gigi Graham Tchividjian, gave generously of her time.

My gratitude goes also to Russ Busby of the Billy Graham Evangelistic Association for taking the time to provide a choice of pictures of Ruth Graham from his vast archives. Dr. Nancy Robbins, formerly of Dohnavur Fellowship, also gave freely of her time to answer questions about Amy Carmichael on issues not written about before but which have enhanced the accuracy of the section on Amma. To her I am grateful, as I am also thankful to Judy Peterson for her transcription of those tapes. Another new factor is the deep insight which I gleaned from reading about Dr. Vernon Grounds. In the biography *Transformed by Love* by Bruce L. Shelley, Dr. Grounds seems to me to put the last hundred years of the organized Christian church into perspective.

My usual debt of gratitude goes to my daughter Rayne Wilcox for her detailed work on footnotes and permissions, to my son-in-law Lance Wilcox for his endless hours on the computer, to my granddaughter Elizabeth Wilcox for all her little acts of kindness, and to Marilyn Pendleton for practical details too numerous to mention. Of equal value has been their enthusiasm for the importance of this volume.

In writing this book I related at times to Churchill's words, uttered when he accepted the Nobel Prize for Literature for his six volumes on the Second World War. He said: "Writing a book is an adventure. To begin with it is a toy, an amusement, and then it becomes a master, and then it becomes a tyrant. And the last phase is that, just as you are about to be reconciled to your servitude, you kill the monster."

Yet for all the hard work, the joy of compiling the material and of writing this book was still greater. Someone once said, "The worth of a thing well done is to have done it." Out of the more than 30 books that I have written, few volumes have been as uplifting to me personally. Writing of the lives and works of these saintly people has been for me like attending a spiritual retreat. I have been refreshed, lifted up, challenged and amazed at the timelessness of biblical truth. Just to have done the job has ultimately become a reward in itself.

PROLOGUE

No Scar?

Hast thou no scar?
No hidden scar on foot, or side, or hand?
I hear thee sung as mighty in the land,
I hear them hail thy bright ascendant star,
Hast thou no scar?

Hast thou no wound?
Yet I was wounded by the archers, spent,
Leaned Me against a tree to die; and rent
By ravening beasts that compassed Me, I swooned:
Hast thou no wound?

No wound? no scar?
Yet, as the Master shall the servant be,
And pierced are the feet that follow Me;
But thine are whole: can he have followed far
Who has nor wound nor scar?[1]

—AMY CARMICHAEL

ONE

Living in Our Tension-Filled World

A few years back, as I lay in a hammock overlooking the deep blue waters of Zihuatanejo Bay in Mexico, I felt I could handle anything. The hot tropical sun was at its afternoon peak, but I was shielded from it by a large tree with enormous leaves. Looking out over the water provided an experience of sheer tranquility to my being. Up and down the beach I could see singular figures at various spots, napping, reading, or resting under shelter from the sun.

My body relaxed in the afternoon heat. No deadlines pressed in on me. No telephone was available if someone had wanted to reach me. No appointments were written into my purse-sized date book. It was the closest I had come in a long time to the eradication of all pain. No pressure. No worry. No irritation. Yet when I remembered that in the morning I would have to get up early to catch a plane to Mexico City and then home, I knew with a twinge of sadness that I had not eradicated pain. All the pressures of ordinary life would be waiting when I arrived home. But I had refurbished my strength and developed a greater ability to go on.

According to some Christians, if a person is really walking with God, suffering and pain are eliminated and life is free of stress. To such people, prayer which does not receive a "yes" answer is referred to as "Unanswered Prayer." "Unanswered Prayer" usually means that the petitioner is somehow to blame.

The notion that God could say "Wait" or even "No" is inconceivable to those with such a mentality.

But realistically, pain, stress, tension, and grief are never eradicated from this earthly life. A vacation or even a special day-outing can provide temporary respite. My times in Mexico and my weekends by the ocean are good examples of this. Sometimes, too, we may experience miraculous answers to prayer. A cancer is healed; a job is salvaged; a prodigal child returns. But ultimately, suffering remains part of the condition of humankind. In the end, we will all experience physical death.

Day by day each of us is confronted by the stress and pressure of everyday life at both monumental and minimal levels. We file our tax return and discover we owe more than we have already paid out. We plan an outing, and it rains. We finish a report late at night, and our printer breaks down.

Then there are the "What Ifs." The next mammogram may indicate cancer. The next person eliminated from our place of work may be ourselves. The newest accident statistic could be a loved one. At its best, life is uncertain. Drive-by shootings and terrorist attacks; earthquakes, hurricanes, and floods; financial crunches and problems in health care—all these, added to the individualized tensions and suffering unique to each human being, illustrate that pain is a certainty.

The solutions are not always spiritual. A malfunctioning thyroid gland may create a state of depression; childhood abuse can lead to a spiraling series of events that result in a fearful adult or an abusive parent. The body, mind, and spirit are inseparably intertwined. The best solution as we deal with life's problems lies in the resources found in the combination of physical health, emotional wholeness, and above all, the indwelling Christ.

The message of the people featured in this book is that we can find meaning in the middle of suffering. We can cope with the multitude of trivial irritations that bombard our lives. We can do more than just survive.

Such a viewpoint does not imply that pain is positive or that it should be cultivated because it can contribute to growth. To the contrary, any normal person will go to great lengths to avoid pain. We are talking about *unavoidable* pain—suffering that lingers even when we try desperately to get rid of it.

In contrast to many of our misconceptions regarding our tendency to focus on happiness and the eradication of pain, Dr. Joseph Fabry of the Institute of Logotherapy stated his views simply and concisely:

> What I gained from Logotherapy is the recognition that central to man's life is the pursuit of meaning, and not the pursuit of happiness; that we only invite frustration if we expect life to be primarily pleasurable; that life imposes obligations, and the pleasure and happiness come from responding to the tasks of life.[1]

In Dr. Fabry's statement and in the writings of Dr. Viktor Frankl, who developed the ideas of Logotherapy, several concepts are clear. To live effectively requires that we deal with problems in a way that ultimately means transcending them and going beyond them, rather than eradicating them. We have not been promised a rose garden; neither have we been set down in a bed of thorns. When we are realistic, we see life as a mix of pain and pleasure.

When we view life from this vantage point, we will cease to berate ourselves for being so "unspiritual" as to suffer. Instead, we will accept God's gift of inner joy and find happiness in living lives content in a task. Meaning will be found, not lost, in suffering. For although we try by all means to avoid pain, there are times when we cannot do so. Then the best way to handle inevitable suffering is to find some meaning in it.

Only children believe that pain always goes away; and even they learn quickly that such is not the case. The insane can occasionally fool themselves into believing they have eradicated their pain, but they do so by denying reality, not by embracing it.

In this century and in this culture we look upon happiness and freedom from pain as inalienable rights, as rewards for the person who manages his or her life well. Our worship of pleasure feeds this notion. So does our distorted view of the "normal" Christian life. We easily become disillusioned with our lives. We forget what Christ told us—that in this life we will have sorrow. We quote verses referring to the joy of God without defining the word *joy*. We forget the ups and downs, the delights and despair of the psalmist David. And we often forget that even in all of David's distress of mind and anguish of soul, he was the one described in Scripture as a man after God's own heart (Acts 13:22).

In contrast to the current barrage of literature that promises fast answers, instant success, and unending happiness, earlier figures in Christian thought promised no such panaceas. What they did offer was realistic—and it worked.

As we shall see, these saints were flesh-and-blood human beings with real problems. They were sometimes wounded in their respective journeys through life. But because of the way they dealt with pain, by definition they became heroes of the faith. They were found faithful.

The eradication of pain in this life is an unrealistic expectation. We deceive ourselves and others if we deny this truth. Several years ago I was on a talk show with another guest who directed a Christian organization. At the outset this man turned to the talk-show host and stated, "I have never felt anger since the day I became a Christian."

The host turned to me and laughed. "Then we're in for an interesting show, since you just wrote a book on anger!"

The show went on, and I answered several questions about my book. The issue of our disagreement about anger did not come up again until the end of the two-hour show, when the other guest said vehemently, "You know, I get so angry at Satan!"

There was dead silence and then a roar of laughter from the talk-show host. Even the other guest had not eradicated anger. He just hoped he had and had tried to make himself believe he had succeeded. He viewed eradication, not coping, as the solution to life's problems.

As children, and even as adults, we try hard to remove unpleasant emotions from our lives. Sometimes we try so fervently that we even believe we have succeeded until we are jolted back into reality by the obvious recurrence of those emotions. But all feelings—pleasant as well as unpleasant—are a part of life. The great challenge is to use unavoidable pain for growth. It is in the *contrast* between pain and pleasure that true happiness is felt, and it is in their tension and the resulting conflict that we often grow.

In a sense, the tranquility of Zihuatanejo Bay would have been flat and lifeless had it not been experienced in contrast to the tension of everyday life. The relaxation alone would not have reenergized me. Rather, it would have lulled me into a deadly depression, leading to emptiness, not to fulfillment.

D. Martyn Lloyd-Jones (1899–1981)

*M*artyn Lloyd-Jones was a Harley Street physician who became a preacher and the handpicked successor of G. Campbell Morgan in England.

"Christianity is Christ." It is not a philosophy, indeed not even a religion. It is the good news that "God hath visited and redeemed his people" and that He has done so by sending His only begotten Son into this world to live, and die, and rise again. Our Lord Jesus Christ is "the Alpha and Omega, the First and the Last." In other words, He is the one Authority.[1]

What many are tending to do today is this. They say, "Take up Christianity. It will pay you. I am a witness to it." So a short address is given, and people are then called upon to testify. Why are people expected to want to accept Christianity? Because it works. It does this or that. It promises you happiness. It gives you peace and joy. I suggest that this is false evangelism. Our one business is to preach the Lord Jesus Christ, the final Authority. We are told to declare Him, and that men and women are to come face to face with Him. The cults can give you "results." Christian Science can tell you that if you do this and that you will sleep well at night, you will stop worrying, you will feel healthier, and you will lose your aches and pains. All the cults can do that sort of thing. We are not to do that. We are to declare Him, and to bring people face to face with Him. That was His own method.

The whole of the New Testament is clearly designed to convince us of the authority of Jesus Christ. It is clear that if He is not who He claims to be, there is no need to listen to Him. If He is, then we are bound to listen to Him and to do whatever He may tell us to do. My own happiness is not the criterion. If He allows me to go on being ill or in trouble—whatever He says, I will answer, "Yes, Lord." I will do so because He is the Lord. He is the Authority.[2]

TWO

Divine Spending Money

"*N*o place is so deep, that He is not deeper still." This concept, which forms the underlying message of the movie *The Hiding Place*, is what comes to mind when I think of Corrie ten Boom, the Dutch watchmaker's daughter who helped save Jews in Holland during the Holocaust. The words are reminiscent, too, of nineteenth-century preacher F. B. Meyer when he said, "He never puts His sheep forth without going before them.... No ascent so steep that we cannot see His form in advance; no stones so sharp that are not flecked with His blood; no fire so intense that One does not go beside us, whose form is like the Son of God; no waters so deep that Emmanuel does not go beside us."[1]

In reading the works of great men and women of God, I have been struck by their sense of balance. The writings of Corrie ten Boom and the movie *The Hiding Place* consistently emphasize the sufficiency of Christ. He is there in the rat-infested cell of the concentration camp, in the beatings, in the dying. He is Corrie's sufficiency in circumstances that go beyond normal human endurance. He is there when the suffering remains, when the pain refuses to be mitigated.

Yet in later years, when Miss ten Boom was writing and speaking of that All-Sufficient One, someone who worked closely with her told me, "Corrie ten Boom had less self-hate than anyone I knew." He continued, "She believed that God had a work for her to do, and she did it. She didn't go around questioning whether she was doing it right or not." To borrow missionary Amy Carmichael's phrase, she didn't "look back on past guidance." She trusted her Lord to guide and had confidence in her perception of that leading. She combined a deep spiritual reality with a healthy sense of positive self-worth.

Similarly, F. B. Meyer's biographer, W. G. Fullerton, stated of him, "His transparency and simplicity were his charm. He was humble, but not falsely modest: with a just estimate of his own powers he spoke again and again of some new enterprise as 'The greatest work of my life,' taking the greatness of it all for granted."[2]

Yet the self-confidence of Corrie ten Boom and of F. B. Meyer should not be mistaken for the "me-ism" of our time, which is more indicative of insecurity and self-doubt. For, in Meyer's words: "Selfishness, of every kind, in its activities, or its introspection, is a hurtful thing, and shuts out the help and love of God . . . . The soul, occupied with its own griefs, and refusing to be comforted, becomes presently a Dead Sea, full of brine and salt, over which birds do not fly, and beside which no green thing grows. And thus we miss the very lesson God would teach us. His constant war is against the self-life, and every pain He inflicts is to lessen its hold on us."[3]

But what of those who say "Why me?" to pain? What of those who insist that self-confidence demands that God instantly satisfy their desires, as though he were a cosmic Santa Claus or an extra-strength tranquilizer? For them, Meyer offers the example of a Hindu woman, who according to legend had lost her only child.

Wild with grief, she implored a prophet to give back her little one to love. He looked at her for a long while tenderly, and said, "Go, my daughter, bring me a handful of rice from a house into which Death has never entered, and I will do as thou desirest." The woman at once began her search. She went from dwelling to dwelling, and had no difficulty in obtaining what the prophet specified; but when they had granted it, she inquired, "Are you all here around the hearth—father, mother, children—none missing?" But the people invariably shook their heads with sighs and looks of sadness; for far and wide as she wandered, there was always some vacant seat by the hearth. And gradually, as she passed on, the narrator says, the waves of her grief subsided before the spectacle of sorrow everywhere, and her heart, ceasing to be occupied with its own selfish pang, flowing out in strong yearnings of sympathy with the universal suffering, tears of anguish softened into tears of pity, passion melted away in compassion, she forgot herself in the general interest, and found redemption in redeeming.[4]

A woman I counseled following the death of her husband told me of the months of illness the man had endured prior to his death. At just about the time I thought she was going to ask "Why me?" she reflected, "You know, those months were happy ones. I loved him so much. I miss him, but death is part of life. I can't expect to avoid it."

This woman did not profess a faith in Christ. But I couldn't help but contrast her to a young man whom I had seen a few weeks later. After describing the loss of a girlfriend, he almost screamed at me: "I hate her for hurting me, and God's not going to stop me from resenting Him for doing this to me. I trusted Him, and look what He did!" This young man had decided that he wanted God only as long as God did what pleased him. He had positioned *himself* as the God of his own life. The result was intensified pain.

A person who possesses a healthy self-image has a greater capacity to understand and accept the limitations of human wisdom. Such a one can grasp the desirability and, indeed, the obligation to trust God in the dark. Someone who lives in the power of that potential will not ask "Why me?"; instead he or she may inquire, "Why not me?"

God never advocates self-hatred. But He does teach us to hate sin and the sin nature as described by Paul in Romans 6. He wants us to turn away from selfishness. Moreover, God doesn't free us from the bondage of self-hatred to allow us to become enslaved by self-worship.

A number of years ago I entered a coffeehouse bookstore near the ocean. First, I picked up a book that the author had dedicated to herself. Then I nearly bumped into a large, cardboard cutout of Katharine Hepburn, standing over a stack of her books, titled Me. A number of the best-selling titles, as well as the psychology and self-help books, focused on self-worship. Topping it all was a quote from one of the bookstore's featured volumes on the Gnostic Gospels: "If you bring forth what is within you, what you bring forth will save you. If you do not bring forth what is within you, what you do not bring forth will destroy you." According to the footnote, this was written by a man named Jesus. Tellingly, this Jesus did *not* claim to be the Son of God and wrote two centuries after the death of our Lord Jesus Christ.[5]

Self-worship is not new, nor is blatant self-promotion peculiar to our day. At the time most of the heroes of Found Faithful were preaching and writing, nineteenth-century poet Walt Whitman wrote, "I celebrate myself, and sing myself," and Ralph Waldo Emerson was talking about the "spark of the divine" within each man and woman. Yet Emerson's spark and today's "me-ism" do not remotely resemble the biblical truth of "Christ in me." Nor is a healthy self-esteem anything like self-worship.

True recovery and positive self-esteem are quite different from groveling in self-hatred or glorying in blatant self-promotion. Scholar of medieval studies C. S. Lewis focused on the goal of Christ in us rather than a glorification of man, himself, without God. In *Mere Christianity* Lewis warned:

> Make no mistake. He says, "If you let Me, I will make you perfect. The moment you put yourself in My hands, that is what you are in for. Nothing less, or other, than that. You have free will, and if you choose, you can push Me away. But if you do not push Me away, understand that I am going to see this job through. Whatever suffering it may cost you in your earthly life, whatever inconceivable purification it may cost you after death, whatever it costs Me, I will never rest, nor let you rest, until you are literally perfect—until My Father can say without reservation that He is well pleased with you, as He said He was well pleased with Me. This I can do and will do. But I will not do anything less."[6]

F. B. Meyer stated it somewhat differently. "The first step towards self-reverence is to see God, to worship Him, to bow down before Him, to know that He is God alone, and then we begin to reverence the nature made in His image, which we are to hold sacred for His sake."[7]

In a way that is consistent with the sermons of that giant of nineteenth-century preachers, Charles Haddon Spurgeon, Meyer was acutely aware of the frailty of the human body and how this relates to the wholeness of the mind. A tired body can drive a person into the depths of depression and self-hatred. Said Meyer:

> The sense of failure often arises from an over-taxed nervous system, which has been strung almost to the

breaking point, and has suddenly collapsed. It was so with Elijah, when he lay beneath the juniper tree, and asked for death. But He who knows our frame knew better than to send the Angel of Death, and commissioned another to provide him with food and sleep. Often, after some great deliverance, the late Dr. Maclaren would be overwhelmed with the sense of failure. "I must not speak again on such an occasion," would be his exclamation, whilst the whole audience, as they dispersed, went away inspired and blessed. We must always allow for the depression which comes from the rebound of the over-strung bow.[8]

Furthermore, Meyer, like C. S. Lewis, gave credence to the fine but concrete difference between psychological problems and sin. People who experience emotional problems are not necessarily sinning. "We do not blame the maniac who seeks to fire a cathedral; we simply confine him; his will was impaired. But we condemn the man who clearly meant to take his brother's life, though the deed itself was frustrated; his will was murder."[9]

The basis for the free functioning of "Christ in me" is the lordship of Christ. The English poet Tennyson put it concisely: "Our wills are ours to make them Thine." Hymn writer George Matheson's lyrics are as contemporary for our time as they were in his own day:

> Make me a captive, Lord,
> And then I shall be free;
> Force me to render up my sword,
> And I shall conq'ror be.
> I sink in life's alarms
> When by myself I stand;

Imprison me within Thine arms,
And strong shall be my hand.

My heart is weak and poor
Until it master find;
It has no spring of action sure,
It varies with the wind;
It cannot freely move
Till Thou hast wrought its chain;
Enslave it with Thy matchless love,
And deathless it shall reign.

My power is faint and low
Till I have learned to serve;
It wants the needed fire to glow,
It wants the breeze to nerve;
It cannot drive the world
Until itself be driven;
Its flag can only be unfurled
When Thou shalt breathe from heaven.

My will is not my own
Till Thou hast made it Thine;
If it would reach the monarch's throne
It must its crown resign;
It only stands unbent
Amid the clashing strife,
When on Thy bosom it has leant,
And found in Thee its life.[10]

It is human nature to be in bondage to someone or something. As a counselor I see individuals who are enslaved to other people, to chemical substances, or to their own passions. I also encounter people who choose to be bond-slaves of Jesus Christ. The paradox is that only in such a choice is real freedom found.

Meyer used the image of a house to express this truth:

He stands at the door and knocks; if any will open the door He will come in. Are you willing to let Him in? Are you willing for Him to do what He likes with you and yours?—If so, He will begin to fulfill in you the good pleasure of His goodness and the work of faith with power, and you may write on the lintel of your life, "This house has passed into other hands, and will be opened under entirely new management."[11]

[Yet sometimes] instead of occupying all, our gracious Guest has been confined to one or two back rooms of our hearts; as a poor housekeeper is sometimes put in to keep a mansion, dwelling in attic or cellar; while the suites of splendid apartments are consigned to dust—sheets and cobwebs, shuttered, dismantled, and locked.[12]

You never will be happy until you let the Lord Jesus keep the house of your nature, closely scrutinizing every visitor and admitting only His friends. He must reign. He must have all or none. He must have the key of every closet, of every cupboard, and of every room. Do not try to make them fit for Him. Simply give Him the key. He will cleanse and renovate and make beautiful.[13]

Giving oneself up to the lordship of Christ doesn't mean that self-hatred is an appropriate prerequisite. On the contrary, such an act of committal has greater meaning when one surrenders to God something that has personal value. For to give away that which you hate does not involve sacrifice. It is simply an act of rational behavior resulting from desperation.

Similarly, understanding "Christ in me" as the true source of wholeness does not mean that God does not use psychological help as a means of "putting theology into shoe leather," to use a phrase often associated with J. Vernon McGee. He has ways of helping us to take biblical principles and apply them to our lives in practical ways.

Mike, a young man who had lost his job through no fault of his own, began to drink heavily. Then his wife left him, and he began to drink even more. One morning he awoke in a street gutter, covered with his own vomit, crying out for God to deliver him. The next week he wandered into a church service and sat in the last row. That night he accepted Christ, and everything began to change. As a person who had been created by God and then redeemed by Him as well, Mike experienced a newfound sense of confidence. With God's help and the support of a small local church, Mike stopped drinking. He had truly been born again. He was a new man.

Yet when Mike's wife, Sue, agreed to come with him for marriage counseling, many of his emotional scars were still evident. Because of the spiritual changes in his life, he deeply desired to treat his wife in a loving way. Yet he didn't always know how. It didn't occur to him to tell her he loved her. After all, he had married her, hadn't he? Mike's father had never told his mother that he loved her.

On a deeper level, pockets of self-doubt still haunted Mike. He hesitated to share his testimony because he was convinced that others had more impressive experiences to relate. He tended to dress shabbily because he didn't feel worth the expense of new clothes. He interpreted any small criticism as a blanket indictment of his life and personality. By the power of God, Mike had recovered. But he needed sound counseling to help make that recovery more complete. He needed to know how to apply God's Word to his everyday life.

Sara came to me for counseling because she functioned as the classic doormat who could never say no. She ran errands, baked cookies, taxied children, entertained guests, and in general did anything requested of her. To her church friends she was a saint—a woman given over to good works. And Sara liked that image.

The problem came when her health began to break down and her physician recommended counseling. Sara had fallen into the trap of thinking that no one would like her if she didn't say yes. She was committed to being nice. Through a process of learning to say no to unreasonable demands, placing boundaries on her activities, and recognizing that she had worth apart from her ability to please people, Sara began to change. Her sense of self-worth increased, and she learned to say no. Not surprisingly, her health improved too. Then came the test, spiritually.

Before counseling, Sara had felt as though she had no options. She had to say yes. Now she was able to say no and was tempted to do so whenever she didn't want to do something. She had once been enslaved to the demands of others; now she was becoming enslaved to her own desires. Sara was growing self-centered and selfish. She had recovered emotionally. Her fears and self-doubts were gone. But she still needed spiritual recovery for complete wholeness. She needed to commit her will to God so that her responses to requests would not be motivated either by fear or by selfishness, but by what God wanted to accomplish through her.

Godliness that disregards one's own emotional or physical needs can degenerate into legalism. On the other hand, psychological wholeness without godliness can breed selfishness, as well as a sense of shallowness and despair. The ultimate aim of recovery is not to do our own thing; it is to do the will of God. Recovery frees a person to make choices. But free choice brings with it the awesome obligation of responsibility. Self-hatred and spiritual rebellion lead to bondage. To be truly whole is to choose the will of God.

Some Christians deem it a sign of godliness to ignore psychological pain. Their message to others is one of condescension. "If you can't get your life together without counseling, then at least go to a Christian. But if you were really walking with God you wouldn't need this." The result is that many good people who need psychological help don't get it; or they seek help but feel guilty for doing so. Some even remove themselves from the church altogether and endure their pain away from the legalistic scrutiny of Christians who are committing what the Bible calls the greatest sin of all, that of pride.

A woman I know has been depressed for the better part of her life. She has received the best of treatment but has experienced no real cure. Yet her faith in God is tenacious. She is willing to accede to His will, even if it means remaining depressed. So far God has said, "Wait." Not "Yes, I will heal you." Not "No, you will always be depressed." Just "Wait." But as she waits and goes through her dark valley, she and her Lord are close, and my conversations with her are always a blessing to me. Far from sinning, she has chosen to find meaning in her depression and to allow it to draw her closer to God. She trusts Him in the dark, and someday she will receive an abundant reward for her faithfulness.

A deadly fire at Surrey Gardens while Spurgeon was preaching there plunged him into an illness that would affect him for the rest of his life. In his first sermon following that setback, he said, "It is not easy to tell how another ought to feel and how another ought to act. Our minds are differently made, each in its own mold, which mold is broken afterward, and there shall never be another like it."[14]

Later he stated:

> The sharpest pangs we feel are not those of the body, nor those of the estate, but those of the mind . . . . The Spirit of a man will sustain his infirmity, but a wounded spirit who can bear? You may be surrounded with all the comforts of life, and yet be in wretchedness more gloomy than death if the spirit be depressed. You may have no outward cause whatever for sorrow, and yet if the mind be dejected, the brightest sunshine will not relieve your gloom.[15]

To those who insist that there is no need for God and that recovery is a purely psychological process, I would echo the words of G. K. Chesterton: "The civilized man, like the religious man, is one who recognizes the strange and irritating fact that something exists besides himself."[16]

But for those Christians who are simply too proud to admit to psychological flaws and who discourage others from getting help by telling them that "everything you need is in the Word," there is an equally simple retort. All we need *is* in the Word, but just as the Word of God is preached and explained in sermons every Sunday in churches across this land, it is within the province of sound psychology to help make practical in everyday life the truths of biblical theology. Sound psychology and the Bible are not in conflict—not unless we leave biblical principles and distort the Scriptures or unless the psychological principles we espouse are not truly sound. For the Christian, biblical truth must always take the position of highest authority.

Biblical principles become, in the words of Meyer, the "spending money" of the Christian. But the counseling office can help us to know how to appropriate and budget that "spending money" in practical terms. The men and women whose lives are discussed in this book were deeply entrenched in their knowledge of God. But they also knew how to put their theology into shoe leather. Many of them knew how to counsel with a wisdom that extended far beyond the psychological knowledge of their own day. Above all, they themselves found a wholeness born out of the integration of good mental health and spiritual reality.

In an insightful example of practical theology, Amy Carmichael wrote:

> The one person who stands out in my memory as one incapable of ever helping others was the one who had never suffered—never even had a headache. She had beautiful children, but apparently never even suffered then. She was incapable of understanding pain in others. I have often thought of her and been thankful for pain. In a similar way, though of course different, a slip on the upward climb is sometimes the way by which we can be led into Hebrews 5:2—"Who can bear gently with the ignorant and erring, for that He Himself also is compassed with infirmity."[17]

Through our emotional and physical pain, we learn the deep lessons needed to help others.

Everyday life mixed with the divine; practical details lived out in the context of eternity; pain turned into blessing—these are God's way of putting our theology into shoe leather. Great saints through the centuries have been our example. They have become our faithful heroes of the past, who challenge us to be the sometimes wounded yet faithful heroes of the present and the future, until we all meet together with that great cloud of witnesses of Hebrews 12:1. Then "What an awakening one who has walked with Him in the twilight must have, when suddenly she awakes in His likeness and the light is shining round her—all shadowy ways forgotten."[8]

By faith we pass beyond the utmost range of sight. To act in faith—whether the action be of thought or of feeling, within our own heart or in relation to others—is to venture beyond what sight will warrant; to let go the obvious and tangible supports to which we might cling within a closely bounded field, and to commit ourselves to principles which sense cannot certify, to lines of action on which sense will not accompany us, to a sustaining power which sense has never promised.

—BISHOP PAGET

Andrew Murray (1829–1917)

*A*ndrew Murray was a Scottish preacher who spent many years in South Africa. He was known as a noted conference speaker and devotional writer. Author V. Raymond Edman describes a meeting between Murray and Amy Carmichael, who is the subject of our next chapter.

"Amy Carmichael in *Though the Mountains Shake* tells of an experience in 1895 when Andrew Murray of South Africa was in England taking part in various conventions, and because of a physical breakdown in Japan she had returned home. At one point they were both guests in the same house. 'I knew that his books were very good,' she said. 'Not that I had read one of them, but a neat row of them, dressed in sober grey, lived in my mother's room, and she and everybody said how good they were.' Amy Carmichael wondered if he was as good as his books, and found that he was even better. 'For,' said she, 'there was not only goodness, there was a delicious dry humour, dauntless courage, and the gentleness and simplicity of a dear child. And he was very loving. He never seemed to be tired of loving.'

"Then something painful happened to Mr. Murray. Miss Carmichael records that this is how he met it.

He was quiet for a while with his Lord, then he wrote these words for himself:

'First, He brought me here, it is by His will I am in this strait place: in that fact I will rest.

Next, He will keep me here in His love, and give me grace to behave as His child.

Then, He will make the trial a blessing, teaching me the lessons He intends me to learn, and working in me the grace He means to bestow.

Last, in His good time He can bring me out again—how and when He knows.

Let me say I am here,
By God's appointment,
In His keeping,
Under His training,
For His time.'

Edman then quoted from Andrew Murray's *The Secret of Adoration*:

Take time. Give God time to reveal Himself to you. Give yourself time to be silent and quiet before Him, waiting to receive, through the Spirit, the assurance of His presence with you, His power working in you. Take time to read His word as in His presence, that from it you may know what He asks of you and what He promises you. Let the Word create around you, create within you a holy atmosphere, a holy heavenly light, in which your soul will be refreshed and strengthened for the work of daily life.

Edman concluded:

Such indeed is the abiding life that draws its sustenance and strength from the Vine. By the refreshing and reviving flow of the Holy Spirit through that life there is prayer that prevails, preaching that is powerful, love that is contagious, joy that overflows, and peace that passes understanding. It is the adoration that is stillness to know God for one's self. It is the obedience that does the Saviour's bidding in the light of the Word. It is the fruitfulness that arises spontaneously from abiding in the Vine.[1]

THREE

Found Faithful

$\mathcal{I}$t was a sunny afternoon many years ago. I was fifteen. School was out for the day, and I had a long wait before my carpool left for home. But I had a new book, *Hudson Taylor's Spiritual Secret*, to help me pass the afternoon. I settled down on one of the comfortable grassy slopes that surrounded the school grounds and became lost in the story of Hudson Taylor and the China Inland Mission. The afternoon slipped away, but I was never again the same. Two truths stood out in my mind, truths that were to remain with me for the rest of my life: "Christ in me" is the key to Christian living, and God's work done in God's way will receive God's supply.

Hudson Taylor, Founder of the China Inland Mission, knew from experience that God does not eliminate need. But instead of employing cheap methods to support his work, Taylor discovered an abiding principle of the Christian life: God's work, done in God's way, will receive God's supply. This principle worked, not only for Hudson Taylor in China, but also for George Müller and his orphanages in England, and for Amy Carmichael in her work of rescuing children dedicated to the gods in South India.

From as far back as I could remember, I had heard of Hudson Taylor. At the time of my birth my Aunt Ruth was in China as a missionary under that same great mission. I had heard from childhood storybooks about Hudson Taylor, his extraordinary faith, and his remarkable missionary work in China. I had been shown pictures of my own aunt, wearing her long Chinese gown, riding on the backs of mules—and always teaching children.

Yet on this particular afternoon, as I read of the challenge of Hudson Taylor and the call to total dependence upon God to supply his work, I knew that now he had influenced my life in a new and permanent way. The old knowledge had been made new for me.

And so it has been with each of the individuals highlighted in this book. While it seems in retrospect as though none of them ever were new to me, I can remember with clarity the times when each of them first became significant to me.

Again at the age of fifteen, which was a pivotal year for me spiritually, I was introduced to the books of Amy Carmichael by one of my teachers. Amy Wilson Carmichael, founder of the Dohnavur Fellowship in India, wrote eloquently on a number of subjects, but with particular insight on the problem of suffering. She viewed life with firm realism: Suffering cannot be eliminated from life. Yet in no way did Carmichael suggest that God allows us to be tossed about by the whims of fate as we try hopelessly to escape suffering. Neither did she propose that we are to lie down helplessly in submission to its power. On the contrary, she presented practical help and realistic suggestions that can build hope and meaning into suffering.

The first book I read by Amy Carmichael was *Mimosa*. My earliest memory of the story is of Star, Mimosa's sister, the little girl in India who sought out the God who could change dispositions. That seemed sufficient proof of His power to me too. But more than that, the intellectual basis for my faith in God was strengthened by the idea that a child in the middle of India, who had no knowledge of God, could yet be sought out by Him and found.

Later, in college, I was impressed by the similarity between the experience of Star and the words of the English poet Francis Thompson in "The Hound of Heaven," where Thompson talked of God's pursuit of man and responded, "I am he whom thou seekest!"[1] This idea is repeated in John Donne's famous sonnet, an enduring favorite of mine, that begins: "Batter my heart, three-personed God...."[2] Again, the theme is that of God finding a human being.

Even at the age of fifteen, the idea that nothing matters but that which is eternal became a safety zone to me. It became an anchor for the rest of my life.

My first year of college was a year both of spiritual searching and of rebellion. Agnosticism held for me a pseudo-intellectual appeal. It was easy to see the idiocy of atheism. After all, how could anyone contemplate creation itself and absolutely deny the existence of a God? But agnosticism, with its brash "How can people really know beyond that which they can prove in a test tube?" held a certain appeal. "Perhaps," I argued to myself, "I believe the way I do just because I've been taught that way all of my life." Yet deep within I recognized that I was rebelling against the basic authority of God in my life. And I realized that I knew too much about God to feel that I could follow Him without total commitment to that authority.

During that year I read a good many books that argued against God. But one book that was life-transforming for me was *Mere Christianity* by C. S. Lewis. Lewis would become a major influence in my thinking about subjects like pain and the difference between sin and humanness—a topic not easily understood by many Protestants.

Contemporary, yet untainted by the froth of superficial religious thoughts, C. S. Lewis understood that humanness cannot be eradicated and is not intrinsically sinful. Some realities cannot be classified as black or white but are subject to varying shades of gray. Humanness is one of these. It is an inescapable reality that can and must be lived with, and can even be improved upon, but cannot be eradicated. While sin can never be excused in the name of humanness, our humanity is not sin and should not be treated as such. An understanding of this concept as discussed in the writings of C. S. Lewis will make us truly holy without our becoming legalistic and harsh.

As I moved toward my final undergraduate year in college, I began to burn out. I remember taking a graduate level class in American literature. I knew the professor well because I had been his teaching assistant. When the midterm exam came, I knew the material thoroughly but was too ill to think logically. When I went up to his desk to ask the meaning of one of the questions, he looked at me oddly as he pointed out the obvious. After I went home I realized I had taken the test with a high fever. A few days later I received my paper, a "B–." On it were written the words, "Betty, this isn't bad for the shape you were in!"

More than two years of a full course of study at the university, along with a nearly full schedule at a theological seminary, combined with teaching Sunday school, dating several nights a week, working at part-time jobs, attending Bible studies, and actively participating in Inter-Varsity Christian Fellowship, took its toll. After graduating in three-and-a-half years, with numerous extra credits, I stumbled into full-time teaching and wondered why I was so tired.

Much later I learned that these problems of fatigue had been physically based, not only from simply overdoing but also from identifiable physical conditions. But for the time being I was frightened and confused, and my first instinct was to treat the exhaustion with spiritual remedies. I memorized Romans 6 and ineffectively reckoned myself dead to exhaustion and its results.

This approach didn't work, for obvious reasons. But instead of recognizing that exhaustion didn't fit into the province of sin, I believed I must be missing some great spiritual truth. I couldn't doubt God—I knew He was real. But I certainly doubted myself and my own faith.

It was during this time that I discovered the writings of Isobel Kuhn, also a missionary in China under the China Inland Mission. Her writings did not resolve my fatigue but did to some extent quell my feelings of panic over the exhaustion. Kuhn was practical and simple in her approach, and that comforted me. I began to view my life as an arena in which my own behavior and the tests I encountered would have eternal value. In short, I began to find personal meaning in suffering.

Charles Haddon Spurgeon had been a household name already in my childhood, yet his writings only became significant to me in college. As a student I was fairly legalistic in my perspective on Christian truth. I was also both zealous and yet compassionate. Then I came across an article in *His* magazine on the subject of depression. It contained material resurrected from some old sermons of Spurgeon.

Charles Spurgeon, the "prince of preachers" in nineteenth-century England, had little hope to offer those who wished to eradicate depression. Yet because of his own periodic bouts with deep distress, he offered much good counsel on how to cope with and even draw positive benefits from the problem of depression. I have read nothing since the writings of Spurgeon that handles the subject more aptly on both a psychological and a spiritual level.

In my student days, I realized for the first time that emotions such as fear or depression, traditionally viewed as sin by many Christians, are not necessarily sinful at all. Our Lord Himself endured severe emotional pain in the Garden of Gethsemane and in His ensuing trials, including the crucifixion. The compassionate element of my personality was nurtured—a necessary growth-step if I was to become a counselor dealing with the pain and emotions of others.

F. B. Meyer and Geraldine Taylor (or Mrs. Howard Taylor, as she refers to herself in her books) are two writers who became important to me as a young adult. As a teacher I found myself trying to be patient with unruly students, attempting to love a school administrator who had been unfair with me, endeavoring to forgive a friend who had let me down. Then I discovered that F. B. Meyer, Bible expositor and preacher in nineteenth-century England, had something very important to say to me. God was not asking me to *feel* patience, love, or forgiveness. He was asking me to *act*. I was to appropriate His love and then act in love. The feelings would follow later, but they were His responsibility, not mine. I had taken another step toward freedom in Christ, once again under the tutelage of someone I would never know personally on this earth.

Geraldine Taylor, missionary to China in those early days of the China Inland Mission, had influenced me from the time I could first understand the books and stories she wrote. Yet because she rarely talked about herself in her books, I was not aware of her as a person. She simply wrote about other people, like Hudson Taylor, who were important to me.

Then as a young adult I read her biography, written by her niece, Joy Guinness. Because of my own struggle with over-extension, I related to her similar conflict. The letters from her father, along with her own comments, were of particular help to me in this area. The final vestiges of legalism, the spiritualization of fatigue, and my tendencies toward construing humanness as sin slipped away from my thought patterns.

I once had the opportunity to speak to Geraldine's nephew and his wife, Henry and Mary Guinness. They are with the Lord now, and Henry's memories when I spoke with him were those of a young schoolboy. Yet several things they said were memorable. Confirming Geraldine's life-long battle with over-extension, Mrs. Guinness related how, when Geraldine was writing a book, "Uncle Howard looked after her like everything so that she kept everything right, so that she would be able to have her quiet."[3]

According to Mr. Guinness, Geraldine was an exacting person, but also very positive. She was thoughtful and encouraging and liked to write short notes to people. She saw beauty in everything; others who may have shared in her experiences often had a different story to tell. She observed the village with the stream going through it, while others may have felt only the oppression of the heat and dust.

Consistent with this positive viewpoint, according to both Mary and Henry, Geraldine lived in the daily expectation of the Lord's return. Still she took God's work on this earth as seriously as though He would not return for a long time.

As I sought to identify the primary impression that Geraldine had made on my life, I realized that it was in the area of spiritual renewal. She had overworked, but recovered. She had suffered, and then turned that suffering into blessing. She had despaired, and then turned to God on an even deeper level.

When I asked Mr. Guinness whether anything in particular stood out in his memory regarding Geraldine, he replied that he remembered her as "just an aunt." But then he paused, recalling one sentence she had frequently repeated: "Behold, I will do a new thing."[4] The statement confirmed my own impression. To me those seven short words sum up the life of Geraldine Guinness Taylor, Hudson Taylor's daughter-in-law. I will always hold a special affection for Geraldine Taylor, until that day when I myself join the wonderful group of witnesses and spend time getting to know her better.

Thus the influences of this particular group of people has been woven into the fabric of my life since I was very small. In Hebrews 12:1 we read of those saints who have gone on before: "Wherefore seeing we also are compassed about with so great a cloud of witnesses, let us lay aside every weight, and the sin which doth so easily beset us, and let us run with patience the race that is set before us."

In writing to her children, Amy Carmichael remarked, "If this note is ever in your hands it will be because I am out of sight, with the Lord. But I shall not be forgetting you. I do not forget you now although I see you so seldom. I shall be thinking of you, loving you, praying for you, rejoicing as I see you run your race."

Another time she explained: "Surely being with Him will mean a new power to pray? It must, for to be present with the Lord must mean access in a far more vital sense than is possible now, and surely that will mean a new power to speak to Him about our beloved?"

It is the belief of this writer that the words these witnesses spoke during their lifetimes need no elaboration or explanation. Perhaps because of their influence on my own life, I can serve as a bridge between this wealth of inspiration and teaching from the past and today's world as we move into the twenty-first century. Still today these remarkable individuals are a part of that living cloud of witnesses that surrounds us.

One writer who is included in this book has influenced me as a living person rather than as a part of that great cloud of witnesses of the past. I first remember the Graham name from the summer of 1949. My parents, Uncle Blanton, my aunts Esther, Ruth, and Lydia and I went to nearby Los Angeles to a huge tent with a sawdust floor and listened to the young, upcoming evangelist, Billy Graham. The tent, the sawdust floor, and the image of a fiery young preacher stand out most vividly in my memory. After that, fairly regular donations to the crusades and the receipt of books and literature in the mail from the Billy Graham Evangelistic Association were a part of our normal family life.

Later, as a not-sure-of-myself beginning writer, it was natural for me to send a first piece, a poem, to *Decision* magazine, a publication of the association. To my surprise, it was published. I was even paid for it! When I cashed my check at Sav-On-Drug Store, the clerk laughed and said, "I thought people gave to Billy Graham instead of getting checks from him." Later on I wrote some books for the publishing arm of the Graham organization. I was privileged to interview Mrs. Graham on several occasions, and she too has made a permanent imprint on my life.

Ruth Bell Graham was born in China to Presbyterian missionary parents. From my talks with her, as well as from her writings and particularly from her poems, I have found encouragement in my day-by-day walk with God, making, as she puts it, "the least of all that goes and the most of all that comes."[5] Furthermore, because she is the only one of the people I discuss in this book with whom I have had a personal encounter, beyond the words has been the reality of the life.

It is always scary to talk to someone you have read about in books. Usually it is "better"—in the sense of *easier*—to stick with the books! To the contrary, I have never had a conversation with Ruth, nor received a note from her, that has not left me feeling blessed. In her day-by-day walk with God she has already left a legacy of her own for the twentieth and twenty-first centuries and for those who will come after her.

The eight people who are primarily featured in this book, as well as those who appear in the vignettes, have all deeply influenced me.

It is my prayer that God will take the dust of inert words on paper
and transform them by His Holy Spirit so that the lives and writings
of these people may encourage and transform each individual who
is led to read this book.

> Take this book in Thy wounded hand,
> Jesus, Lord of Calvary,
> Let it go forth at Thy command,
> Use it as it pleaseth Thee.
>
> Dust of earth, but Thy dust, Lord,
> Blade of grass in Thy Hand a sword;
> Nothing, nothing unless it be
> Purged and quickened, O Lord, by Thee.

—AMY CARMICHAEL[6]

Frances Ridley Havergal (1836–1879)

Born in England, Frances Ridley Havergal was a hymn writer, as well as the author of devotional material quoted by men like F. B. Meyer. Her most famous hymn may well be "Take My Life and Let It Be Consecrated, Lord to Thee." A poem of hers that appears in Geraldine Taylor's biography is virtually forgotten today but states beautifully the biblical view of the preciousness of life:

> *Just when Thou wilt—Thy time is best*
> *Thou shalt appoint my hour of rest,*
> *Marked by the Sun of perfect love,*
> *Shining unchangeably above.*
>
> *Just when Thou wilt—no choice for me!*
> *Life is a gift to use for Thee:*
> *Death is a hushed and glorious tryst*
> *With Thee, my King, my Savior, Christ!*[1]

Her devotional writing, while less known than her hymns, emphasizes the theme of the Lordship of Christ. In *My King* she uses the image of a house to portray the position of the believer.

> *It is when the King has really come in peace to his own home in the "contrite and humble spirit" . . . . when He has entered in to make*

His abode there—that the soul is satisfied with Him alone. It all hinges upon Jesus coming into the heart as His own house. For if there are some rooms of which we do not give up the key, some little sitting room which we would like to keep as a little mental retreat, with a view from the window, which we do not quite want to give up—some lodger whom we would rather not send away just yet—some little dark closet which we have not resolution to open and set to rights—of course the King has not yet full possession; it is not all and really His own . . . . Only throw open all the doors, "and the King of Glory shall come in," and then there will be no craving for other guests. He will fill this house with glory, and there will be no place left for gloom.[2]

F. B. Meyer

FOUR

F. B. Meyer:
Putting Faith Into Shoe Leather

*S*tanding at the gate of a prison, nineteenth-century preacher and Bible scholar F. B. Meyer watched man after man walk through the prison gates and cross the street to the closest bar. Soon afterward most of the men were back in the prison. The prison gates were like a revolving door, from the prison to the bar and back again.

The practical result in the life of Meyer was that each morning, for as long as he remained in Leicester, England, he met prisoners as they were released and invited them to a nearby coffeehouse. There in the coffeehouse this stately, scholarly man of God helped the former inmates make plans for their future and offered them concrete assistance.

On one particular occasion a man told Meyer that he could not accept help until he had fulfilled his vow to have one pint of ale on the morning of his freedom from prison. Nothing would dissuade him. Rather than walking away in disgust, but preferring that the man himself stay away from the bar, Meyer agreed to procure the ale if the ex-con would promise to stay off liquor from that time on. This left Mr. Meyer with a dilemma of considerable proportions. Keep in mind that Meyer was a well-known man by this time, easily recognizable in a public place. Said Meyer:

I was in such a position that I did not dare to send any of the men who were at that time assisting me into the public house hard by to get that pint of porter, and I knew there was no one on the premises belonging to the coffee house company that I could employ for the purpose. And so, as there was nothing else to do, I caught up the first jug that was within reach and sallied forth to the public house at the opposite corner to get this pint of porter. I felt very strange. The barmaid who served me looked at me with such amazement that I think she supposed I had suddenly lost my reason. I assured her however that it was the final pint: and explained to her that it was not for myself but for a man in whom I was deeply interested.

On arriving at my little breakfast party with the jug and glass in my hand, I poured the porter out as quietly as possible without the "head" which porter drinkers are accustomed to appreciate. He took the glass and began to drink, and I gave such an unconscious groan that, after two or three efforts, he put down the remainder and said, "This is the miserablest pint of porter I ever drank. Where's your card, sir? I may as well sign it as drink any more."[1]

The results of his work with released prisoners continued on after Meyer's death under the name of an organization. But Meyer himself had organized a window-washing and wood-cutting business; he had set up a bank where the men could save money; and he had provided a place of housing as well. Signs in Leicester read: "F. B. Meyer—Firewood Merchant" and "F. B. Meyer—Window-Washing." Yet during all of this time he remained the pastor of Melbourne Hall.

Whether it was with prisoners, orphans, or ordinary people in trouble, throughout his life Meyer was the personification of charity and no one who turned to him for help was denied. Yet the acts of charity were only vehicles by which he accomplished the greatest impact of his life—causing men and women to understand and live in the goodness of the indwelling Christ.

These acts of Christian belief put into shoe leather attracted others to Meyer and his message. His behavior validated the reality of "Christ in me." Through his good deeds, as well as in the volumes of his sermons and books, he preached one continuous and consistent sermon.

A little boy of ten was enrolled in a school in Leicester. Every day the child watched the stately-looking preacher walk away with two or three ex-cons. He saw them go together into the Welford Coffee House for "breakfast, a talk, and a fresh start in life." Related the child, now grown into a man: "I went home one day and said, 'Mother, I wish when I grow up I could be a Meyer.' She asked me what I meant, and I told her how I loved the 'one' for what he did."

"That 'one' was you, sir," the man said in later years to Meyer. "Last Christmas I visited the Leicester Gaol [jail] and recited to the fellows there . . . . I suddenly thought of the boy of ten that I was, and swiftly it came to me that I was something of a 'Meyer': the sermon has found its issue. I am—here."[2] Because of a sermon preached in shoe leather, that boy had grown to be a man who ministered to over 250,000 men in France and elsewhere. "Please receive my thanks,"[3] he said to Meyer.

Born on April 8, 1847, F. B. Meyer lived at a time of a renaissance of Christian teaching. He died at the age of eighty-two on March 28, 1929, and was a preacher in England at the same time that the popular G. Campbell Morgan and Charles Haddon Spurgeon occupied pulpits nearby. From the visits of D. L. Moody he learned the art of winning men and women to Christ. Later in his pastorate at Christ Church in London, when Meyer felt himself in danger of burning out, the great Bible expositor A. T. Pierson took his place. He was a close friend of Dr. Grattan Guinness, who was influential in missions and the father of Geraldine Guinness Taylor, Hudson Taylor's daughter-in-law. The principles upon which the China Inland Mission were founded were in agreement with the beliefs of F. B. Meyer, and so it was not surprising that Hudson Taylor and he were also very close friends.

At the tender age of five, Meyer prayed, "Put Thy Holy Spirit in me to make my heart good, like Jesus Christ was."[4] Afterward he prayed the same prayer every day. On the day before he died he was asked whether he had received any new vision of his Savior. He answered, "No, just the constant interchange between Him and me."[5] Said his biographer W. Y. Fullerton, "Between those two experiences his whole life was included . . . . Christ and he were well-known to each other."[6]

The word *interchange* sums up the thrust of Meyer's message better than any other. To him the Christ-life was just that: the constant interchange of "Christ in me," His life for my life, His life lived out from my life.

My first recollection of the influence of F. B. Meyer in my own life was when I was a young school teacher, trying desperately to live the life of a Christian in witness to my high school students. I was constantly discouraged by the failure of my efforts. Then I read something from Meyer that changed my entire outlook:

> It was first taught me by a grey-haired clergyman, in the study of the Deanery, at Southampton. Once, when tempted to feel great irritation, he told us that he looked up and claimed the patience and gentleness of Christ, and since then it had become the practice of his life to claim from Him the virtue of which he felt the deficiency

in himself. In hours of unrest, "Thy Peace, Lord." In hours
of irritation, "Thy Patience, Lord." In hours of temptation, "Thy Purity, Lord." In hours of weakness, "Thy
Strength, Lord." It was to me a message straight from the
throne. Till then I had been content with ridding myself
[of] burdens; now I began to reach forth to positive blessing.[7]

The idea of exchanging my life for the life of Christ reminded
me of the tremendous impact Hudson Taylor had made on me as
a teenager. Apparently Taylor had influenced Meyer in the same
way. Meyer described his first meeting with him.

I remember so well Hudson Taylor coming to my
church the first time I ever met him. He stepped on the
platform and opened the Bible to give an address, and
said, "Friends, I will give you the motto of my life," and he
turned to Mark 11:22: "Have faith in God." The margin
says, "Have the faith of God," but Hudson Taylor said it
meant, "Reckon on God's faith to you." He continued,
"All my life has been so fickle. Sometimes I could trust,
sometimes I could not, but when I could not trust then I
reckoned that God would be faithful." There is a text
that says, "If we believe not, yet He abideth faithful, He
cannot deny Himself." And sometimes I go to God about
a thing, and say, "My God, I really cannot trust Thee
about this, I cannot trust Thee to pull me through this
expenditure of money with my means, but I reckon on
Thy faithfulness." And when you cease to think about
your faith, and like Sarah, reckon Him faithful, your faith
comes without your knowing it, and you are strong.[8]

Quoting another man of God on the same topic of "Christ in me," Meyer further illustrated the point:

They tell me that George MacDonald, wanting to teach his children honor and truth and trust, places on the mantel-shelf of the common room in their house, money enough for the whole use of his family. If the wife wants money she goes for it, if the boys and girls want money they go for it, whatever want there is in that house is supplied from the mantel-shelf deposit. So God put in Jesus everything the soul can want, and He says, "Go and take it. It is all there for you."[9]

In a still further explanation of the credo "Christ in me," Meyer stated:

These are two great words—claim God's *fullness*, and *reckon* that whatever you can claim is yours, although no answering emotion assures you that it is. Dare to act in faith, stepping out in the assurance that you have just what you have claimed, and doing just as you would do it if you *felt* to have it.[10]

Furthermore, claimed Meyer:

If the gifts sought from the Father's hands are really such as He can bestow, there should be no need for the incessant repetition of the same requests because they would be claimed and taken from His outstretched hand. A Christian will request prayer that he may receive a certain grace of Christian character, whereas there is not the least reason in the world why he should not take as much of it as he requires, altogether apart from the inter-cession of others. We ask for health, or power, or deliver-ance, or vindication, with the accent of weary uncertainty, which proffers the same request, year after year, regardless of the voice, which is ever crying, "Whosoever will, let him take freely."[11]

In essence, the weakest man who knows God is strong to do exploits. All the might of God awaits the disposal of our faith. As a child by touching a button may set in motion a mighty steamship, making it glide like a swan into her native element, so a stripling who has learned to reckon on God may bring the whole forces of Deity to bear on men and things on the world's battlefield.[12] We must always add His resources to our own, when making our calculations.[13]

For all of his godliness, F. B. Meyer had his own flesh-and-blood struggles and irritations. When the great evangelist D. L. Moody came to England, Meyer and Moody became close friends. Yet he was less enthusiastic about Moody's singing companion, Ira Sankey, even though Moody owed a great deal of his success to Sankey's efforts. In all fairness to Meyer, solo singing in a worship service was an American invention and considered by many to be irreverent. Years later Meyer wrote, not without validity, "It is cer-tain that solo and anthem singing may become a great snare to spiritual worship unless the choir leader and organist are dis-tinctly spiritual people."[14] Still, not all of his attitude was based on conviction alone. Before a meeting in Canada he was heard to pray, "Help me to be patient while the choir sings, and let them not distract the people from the message we want them to get."[15]

At another point in Meyer's life, when Dr. G. Campbell Morgan was drawing large audiences while Meyer's devotional sermons were more sparsely attended, Meyer confided to a friend, "The only way I can conquer my feelings is to pray for him daily, which I do."[16]

Meyer's practical emphasis on the everyday problems of life arose from the fact that his own life seemed to be one of only "ordinary" greatness. In his personal life he did not experience the catastrophic events suffered by a Hudson Taylor or the ongoing depression of a Charles Spurgeon. Yet he was an extraordinary man with an extraordinary ministry. While the absence of trauma did not seem to lessen his insight into pain or his sensitivity to the suffering of those around him, it did help to make him more objectively helpful.

One afternoon in a tram-car in North London, he noticed on the opposite seat an elderly woman with a basket, evidently a charwoman returning from her day's work. She appeared to be anything but happy, and as the car emptied only he and she were left. Then, having recognized him all along, she summoned up courage to speak to him and calling him by name, she told him her story. As a widow she had been left alone in the world except for her crippled daughter who, in spite of her affliction, was a continual joy to her. Every morning, as she explained, when she came home from her work she knew her daughter was in the room where they lived, ready to greet her. She was always there, and at night in the darkness she could stretch out her hand and know she was there, too. She made tea in the morning, and left her for the day, but she knew all the time that her daughter was there to greet her with a glad face when she returned. "And now," she said sadly, "now she is dead, and I am alone, and I am miserable. I am going home, and it is scarcely home, for she is not there."

There was little time for discussion, but Meyer was "At Attention!" for his Master on the moment. "When you get home and put the key in the door," he said, "say aloud, 'Jesus, I know

You are here,' and be ready to greet Him directly when you open the door. And as you light the fire tell Him what has happened during the day; if anybody has been kind, tell Him, if anybody has been unkind, tell Him, just as you would have told your daughter. Be sure to make your cup of tea. At night stretch out your hand in the darkness and say, "Jesus, I know You are here."' Then the tram-car reached the terminus, and they parted.[17]

A few months later Meyer was on the same tram-car again. A woman greeted him. "You won't know me, Mr. Meyer," she said. "I am afraid I do not," he replied. Then she reminded him of the interview some months before. "But you are not the same woman," he said in astonishment. "Oh, yes, I am," she said. "I did as you told me. I went home and said, 'Jesus, I know You are here,' and I kept saying it, and it has made all the difference in my life, and now I feel I know Him."

For all of his practical emphasis and understanding of everyday life, F. B. Meyer was still a scholar, a brilliant thinker, and a prolific writer. His legacy to the church of more than fifty books includes two autobiographical volumes, thirteen books on great men of the Bible, and more than twenty devotional volumes. His greatest contribution is probably the large number of excellent Bible commentaries he wrote. They are not dry commentary but living words, not only explaining various biblical passages but possessing a devotional quality that never fails to bless.

If Meyer's theology was practical, it was a practicality that grew from an ability to distill the simple out of the profound. It is always easier to make a difficult truth clear to others when you first understand it in its most complex form. In both the writings and the sermons of Meyer, the truth of exchanging the life of Christ for our own life is stated simply but with biblical foundations that are sound in their truth.

While reading F. B. Meyer in preparation for writing this chapter, I discovered a book, inscribed to my maternal grandfather, Alfred Benson, from my aunts Esther and Ruth. The volume, published in 1896, is carefully marked in pencil by my grandfather, markings that highlight Meyer's depth of teaching with relationship to the indwelling Christ. Yet many of these words fit our times as much as they applied to the end of the nineteenth century.

Setting the stage for the possibility of true recovery from the bondage of addiction, memories of past grievances, and habit patterns that enslave, Meyer stated, "We reverse the Divine order. We say, *feeling, faith, fact.* God says, *fact, faith, feeling.* With Him feeling is of small account—He only asks us to be willing to accept His own Word, and to cling to it because He has spoken it, in entire disregard of what we may feel."[19]

Then, stating the theological basis for his practical theology of recovery and spiritual growth, Meyer explained:

"Master, where dwellest Thou?" they asked of old. And in reply, Jesus led them from the crowded Jordan back to the slight tabernacle of woven osiers where He temporarily lodged. But if we address the same question to Him now, He will point, not to the lofty dome of heaven, not to the splendid structure of stone or marble, but to the happy spirit that loves, trusts, and obeys Him. "Behold," saith He, "I stand at the door and knock. If any man hear my voice, and open the door, I will come in to him." "We will come," He said, including His Father with Himself, "and make our abode with him." He promised to be within each believer as a tenant in a house, as sap in the branch, as life-blood and life-energy in each member, however feeble, of the body.[20]

"It is true," continued Meyer, that

the heavens . . . with all their light and glory alone seem worthy of Him. But even there He is not more at home than He is with the humble and contrite spirit that simply trusts in Him. But there is a reason why many whose names are certainly the temple of Christ, remain ignorant of the presence of the wonderful Tenant that sojourns within. *He dwells so deep.* Below the life of the body, which is as the curtain of the tent; below the life of the soul, where thought and feeling, judgment and imagination, hope and love, go to and fro, ministering as white-stolled priests in the holy place, below the play of light and shade, resolution and will, memory and hope, the perpetual ebb and flow of the tides of self-consciousness, there, through the Holy Spirit, Christ dwells, as of old the Shechinah dwelt in the Most Holy Place, closely shrouded from the view of man.

It is comparatively seldom that we go into these deeper departments of our being. We are content to live the superficial life of sense. We eat, we drink, we sleep, we give ourselves to enjoy the lust of the flesh, the lust of the eyes, and the pride of life; we fulfill the desires of the flesh and of the mind. Or we abandon ourselves to the pursuit of knowledge and culture, of science, and art; we reason, speculate, argue; we make short excursions into the realm of morals, that sense of right and wrong which is part of the make-up of men. But we have too slight an acquaintance with the deeper and more mysterious chamber of the spirit. Now this is why the majority of believers are so insensible of their Divine and

wonderful Resident, who makes the regenerated spirit
His abode.[21]

With the sense of balance that so characterizes the ministry
of Meyer, he spoke of the indwelling work of the Holy Spirit in a
way that is soundly biblical and yet does not minimize, as some
do, the work of that One who is God the Spirit. With characteristic depth and simplicity combined, Meyer explained:

> I am not anxious here to distinguish between the fill-
> ing of the Holy Ghost and the baptism of fire. So far as I
> can understand it, they are synonymous . . . . Say not that
> this filling by the Spirit was for the first Christians and
> not for us. Certainly His gifts were part of the special
> machinery needed to impress the Gentile world; but the
> filling of the Spirit is conterminous with no one age.
> Alas! That many think that the Almighty, like some
> bankrupt builder, constructed the portico of His church
> with marble, and has finished it with common brick![22]
>
> It is of course true that the Holy Ghost is the sole
> agent in conversion, becoming the occupant of the tem-
> ple, which is presented to Him by the nature of man
> (1 Corinthians 6:19). And it is equally clear that the
> Holy Spirit as a person enters the newly regenerated
> heart. But there is a vast difference between having the
> Holy Ghost and being filled by Him. In the one case, He
> may be compared to a mighty man that cannot save, rel-
> egated to an obscure corner of the heart, whilst the large
> part of the nature is excluded from his gracious influ-
> ences. In the other, He is a welcome guest, to whom every
> part of the being is thrown open, and who pervades it
> with the freedom of the balmy air of summer, sweeping

through open windows, breathing through long corridors, and carrying into further recesses the fragrance of a thousand flowers.

There are a great many Christians who undoubtedly received the Holy Spirit at the earliest moment of faith; indeed, their faith is the result of His work; but they have never gone further, they have never yielded their whole nature to His indwelling, they have had no further experience of His pentecostal filling.[23]

There is a danger in measuring one's spiritual life by emotion. In speaking of the Spirit of God dwelling within him, Meyer cautioned: "As I had received Him without emotion, I might expect ever to retain and enlarge its measure, whether the song-birds of summer or the stillness of winter occupied my heart."[24]

Of the result of Christ living in me, by the power of the indwelling Spirit, Meyer summarized: "It is like a poor man having a millionaire friend come to live with him."[25] Yet "Christ in me" does not mean that we get everything we want, or that we never suffer. It is the opposite of the "me-ism" of our day, which depends upon the impoverished resources of *me*. To the contrary, it means that Christ is Lord. "He never leads us through a place too narrow for Him to pass as well."[26] It means that the believer is "enclosed in the invisible film of the Divine Presence, as a far-traveled letter in the envelope which protects it from hurt and soil."[27]

For those who spiritualize emotional pain, and for those who mistakenly feel that unless they are perpetually happy they are sinning, Meyer warned once again:

> *Emotion is no true test of our spiritual state*. Rightness of heart often shows itself in gladness of heart, just as bodily

health generally reveals itself in exuberant spirits. But it is not always so. In other words, absence of joy does not always prove that the heart is wrong.... Perhaps the nervous system may have been overtaxed, as Elijah's was in the wilderness, when, after the long strain of Carmel and his flight was over, he lay down upon the sand and asked to die—a request which God met, not with a rebuke, but with food and sleep. Perhaps the Lord has withdrawn the light from the landscape in order to see whether He was loved for Himself, or merely for His gifts.... Somber colors become the tried and suffering soul.[28]

Meyer, like Charles Spurgeon and missionary pioneer James Fraser, would have understood the concept of burnout, for burnout is the ever-present enemy of many who try to serve God, and far too often it is mistaken for godliness. Said Meyer, "True holiness does not consist in bare walls, and hard seats, and a dingy environment; but in all that resembles God's work in nature, which is exquisitely beautiful."

Likewise, "It is not wrong to unbend the bow in manly games, that develop the sinews and expand the lungs, or to join in the pastimes of your age and companions, so long as you can write on bat and football, on tennis racquet and piano, on oar and paddle, on skate or sleigh, the words, *Holiness to the Lord*."[29]

Consistent with his viewpoint on depression and burnout, Meyer exemplified a rare mixture of holiness and compassion. This is seen in how he dealt with the severe tests of life as well as with the trivial. A woman who often typed for Meyer misplaced two of his articles. In a note to her he wrote, "I can imagine your distress. Think no more of it and we will halve the loss. I think it was a good thing, as my second attempt was an improvement."[30]

But on a more trivial level, he once wrote about his dog:

He used to worry me very much to be fed at dinner, but he never got any food that way. But lately he has adopted something which always conquers me; he sits under the table, and puts one paw on my knee. He never barks, never leaps around, never worries me, but he sits under the table with that one paw on my knee, and that conquers me; I cannot resist the appeal. Although my wife says I must never do it, I keep putting little morsels under the table.[31]

One cannot help but feel affection for this man who was so human, while at the same time so filled with the Divine.

Meyer combined righteousness with a winsome tenderness, a quality aptly referred to as "velvet steel" by Warren W. Wiersbe, who took the term from Carl Sandberg's description of Abraham Lincoln. Nowhere is this quality more apparent than in Meyer's dealing with sin.

You may talk of chastisement or correction, for our Father deals with us as with sons; or you may speak of reaping the results of mistakes and sins dropped as seeds into life's furrows in former years, or you may have to bear the consequences of the sins and mistakes of others; but do not speak of punishment. Surely all the guilt and penalty of sin were laid on Jesus, and He put them away forever . . . . If He once began to punish us, life would be too short for the infliction of all that we deserve. Besides, how could we explain the anomalies of life, and the heavy sufferings of the saints as compared with the gay life of the ungodly? Surely, if our sufferings were penal, there would be a reversal of these lots.[32]

Meyer reminded his hearers never to waste suffering. Rather than placing blame for suffering, he saw it as having meaning and purpose. "Wait, till ten years are past," he said. "I warrant thee, that in that time thou wilt find some, perhaps ten, afflicted as thou art . . . . Thou wilt bless God that thou wert able to comfort others with the comfort wherewith thou thyself hadst been comforted of God." Then, with his ever-present sense of the practical, Meyer gently prods us to "remember to store up an accurate remembrance of the way in which God comforts thee."[33]

Meyer possessed a rare sensitivity to the inner longing and disappointment of those who have wanted to serve God in a specific ministry but found their desire thwarted. He reminded them in words reminiscent of the writings of English poet Robert Browning, or the American poet James R. Lowell, that all they aspired to be counts with God. Said Meyer, "The picture which is to gain immortality is always to be painted; the book which is to elucidate the problem of the ages is always to be written; the immortal song is always to be sung. The young man is kept at his desk in the counting-house instead of going to the pulpit; the girl becomes a withered woman, cherishing a faded flower; the king hands on to his son the building of the house."[34]

Referring to God's decision not to let David build the temple, he said:

> "The Lord said unto David my father, Whereas it was in thine heart to build a house for my name, thou didst well that it was in thine heart." David was a better man because he had given expression to the noble purpose. Its gleam left a permanent glow on his life. The rejected candidate to the missionary society stands upon a higher moral platform than those who were never touched by the glow of missionary enthusiasm. For a woman to have

loved passionately, even though the dark waters may have engulfed her love before it was consummated, leaves her ever after richer, deeper, than if she had never loved, nor been loved in return . . . . Thou didst well that it was in thine heart . . . . God will credit us with what we would have been if we might . . . . No true ideals are fruitless; somehow they help the world of men. No tears are wept, no prayers uttered, no conceptions honestly entertained in vain. . . . Somehow God makes up to us.[35]

When I was a year out of college, a friend of mine died from a lingering disease. Shortly before she passed away she stated, "I wish I could have lived longer in order to serve God more."

My Aunt Lydia didn't die young but did spend the bulk of her life in an office job when she really wanted to go to the mission field like her sister, my Aunt Ruth. She had a special burden for South America, and she even pursued a study of the Spanish language. But Aunt Lydia felt it was wrong to leave her aged mother, and so she stayed home. In later years she became the caretaker for several other family members, including my Aunt Ruth, once she had returned from China.

My young friend and my Aunt Lydia would have been encouraged by the words of Meyer. Perhaps my aunt was actually uplifted by them, since many of Meyer's books came to me from my family. Surely in the economy of heaven the aspirations of these two women have been rewarded. And certainly they have also shared in the reward of the work of those Christian workers for whom they secretly prayed.

God was real to F. B. Meyer. God's enablement, demands, comfort, priorities, and joy pervaded every area of Meyer's life. It is consistent with that reality that he recognized angels, too, as actual beings, and considered heaven a real place. Meyer conveys that reality to his reader. In one striking example, he told of a pastor who had made a passionate enemy of a man by rebuking him for his sin. The man vowed revenge.

> One night the pastor was called to visit a house that could only be reached by passing over a plank which bridged an impetuous torrent. Nothing seemed easier to his enemy than to conceal himself on the bank till the man of God was returning from the opposite end of the plank, to meet him in the middle, throw him into the deep and turbid stream, leaving it to be surmised that in the darkness he had simply lost his foothold. When, however, from his hiding-place he caught sight of the pastor's figure in the dim light, he was surprised to see that he was not alone, but accompanied by another. There were two figures advancing toward him across the narrow plank, and he did not dare attempt his murderous deed. And as they passed his hiding place, the one whom he did not know cast such a glance toward him as convinced him of the sinfulness of the act he had contemplated, and began a work in his heart which led to his conversion.
>
> After his conversion, the would-be assassin confronted the pastor and told him of his murderous intention. "It would have been your death had you not been accompanied," he said. "What do you mean?" replied the pastor. "I was absolutely alone." "Nay," said he, "there were two." Then the pastor knew that God had sent His angel.[36]

Always with Meyer there was balance, especially in dealing with a topic such as the balance between what angels may be asked to do and what only God Himself does. "He may give His angels charge concerning us when we are in danger; but He keeps our purification beneath His special superintendence . . . what a comfort it is that He surrenders this work to no other hands than His own."[37]

Not only were angels real beings to Meyer, heaven was equally real. Of that transition to heaven, death, Meyer spoke with comfort: "Obviously, in death there is no break in the soul's consciousness. The life of the spirit is altogether independent of the body in which it dwells. The signal-box may be in ruins, and yet the operator may be within—as clear in thought and quick of hand as in the day when all was new."

In a statement that should give pause to any Christian who contemplates suicide or euthanasia, Meyer expounded:

It often happens, when the body is at the point of death, that the spirit reveals itself in undiminished splendor, and flashes forth in thoughts that can never be forgotten, and words that can never die. And does not this prove, beyond doubt, that the spirit is only a lodger in the body, and when the house of its tabernacle is broken up, it is not affected, but simply passes out to find some other and more lasting home. "We know that if the earthly house of our tabernacle [this bodily frame] be dissolved, we have a house not made with hands, eternal, in the heavens" (2 Corinthians 5:1).

There is no shadow of warrant for the idea (held by some) that there is a pause in our consciousness, between death and the resurrection. "To depart," said St. Paul, "is to be with Christ, which is far better" (Philippians 1:25). But surely it could not have been far better to pass into a sort of sleep! Better to live on in this mortal life, amid the acutest sufferings, and to have the presence of Christ,

than to lose that presence during centuries of uncon-
sciousness.[38]

He concluded:

The moment of absence is the moment of presence. As
the spirit withdraws itself from the body, closing blinds
and shutters as it retires, it immediately presents itself in
the presence of the King, to go no more out forever . . .
Death is not a state, but an act, not a condition, but a passage. In this it finds its true analogy in birth, by which we
entered upon a new stage of existence . . . . A moment's
anguish; a wrench; a step; a transition; a breaking through
the thin veil which hangs between two worlds; a stepping
across the boundary line . . . . And the soul carries with it
across that boundary line its freight of thought and life, to
pursue its continuity of being and love and purpose in an
unbroken and uninterrupted course.[39]

Reminiscent of C. S. Lewis's description of heaven in the
last book of *The Chronicles of Narnia* series—a place where good
things that are enjoyable on Earth are far more enjoyable—Meyer
spoke with loving familiarity of heaven as an actual place. He
wrote to friends with a delightful attention to detail: "You dear
souls! I do love you, and we must have a thousand years in
Heaven. Let us meet at the middle gate on the Eastern aspect of
the city, and then a picnic amid the Fountain of Waters."[40]

Then, right before his death, as he had perhaps a more distinct view of that place to which he would soon be going, he
wrote to his physician and friend: "We will ask that yonder our
mansions may be together." And, "This a.m. it has been my
request to 'the Prince' that He would allow our mansions to be

simple, but situated side by side. I seem to understand that there have been so many arrivals lately that the angels have been set to make a new road, along the River Bank. I said that we should prefer this—so they are preparing two for us."[41]

Fanciful? Perhaps. But one senses in these words the reality of a life lived with Jesus Christ, not the delusions of an unbalanced mind. Words written to his church a short time later breathe sanity: "The love of God, the grace of Christ our Lord, and the anointing, quickening and empowering grace of the Holy Spirit be with you all."[42]

In reading from the fifty volumes of F. B. Meyer, I have felt uplifted by the reality and yet the practical balance from which he speaks—so much so that I, too, would like to have a mansion somewhere in the vicinity of Meyer and all of the other great heroes of this book, as well as near that great body of family and friends of mine who already live in the Celestial City. It wouldn't have to be a big mansion, but something larger than I have now— a place, perhaps, where everyone who comes to visit would fit! A riverbank appeals to me too, and perhaps a few mountains and trees.

Early in his ministry, before he sailed for his first visit to America, F. B. Meyer reassured his own church with these words: "You can do without me; you cannot do without God." Said Fullerton: "That is the great service he did for the innumerable company of which I am but one—he linked us to God."[43]

Handley C. G. Moule (1841–1920)

*F*ellow and Dean of Trinity College, Cambridge, Lord Bishop of Durham, Teacher, Bible Expositor, Bishop Moule is my favorite Bible commentator. Said Amy Carmichael:

Sometimes, when we are distressed by past failure and tormented by fear of failure in the future should we again set our faces toward Jerusalem, nothing helps so much as to give some familiar Scripture time to enter into us and become part of our being. The words "Grace for grace" have been a help to me since I read in a little old book of Bishop Moule's something that opened their meaning. (Till then I had not understood them.)

He says "for" means simply "instead."

"The image is of a perpetual succession of supply; a displacement ever going on; ceaseless changes of need and demand.

"The picture before us is as of a river. Stand on its banks, and contemplate the flow of waters. A minute passes, and another. Is it the same stream still? Yes. But is it the same water? No. The liquid mass that passed you a few seconds ago fills now another section of the channel; new water has displaced it, or if you please replaced it; water instead of water. And so hour by hour, and year by year, and century by century, the process holds; one stream, other waters, living not stagnant, because always in the great identity there is perpetual exchange. Grace takes the place of grace. Love takes the place of love, ever new, ever old, ever the same, ever fresh and young, for hour by hour, for year by year, through Christ."[1]

A letter, slipped into a book by mistake less than twenty years ago, has lately reappeared as such things kindly do sometimes. It was written from Auckland Castle soon after Mrs. Moule's death had left the Bishop very lonely, for his daughter Tesie had died a little while before, and his only other child was married. He writes of comfort "dropt like an anodyne from the hand of the Physician into my great wound. (He gives no anaesthetics, but He does give anodynes.) I bless Him who is more near and dear to me than ever, in His mercy. My beloved one is not far from me. And I bless her Lord for calling her to go upstairs, and meet Him there, and our Tesie with Him, and for trusting me to meet the solitude here, and to find Him very near in it."[2]

Amy Carmichael

FIVE

Amy Carmichael: Triumph in Suffering

On a dull Sunday morning in Belfast, a young girl walked home from a fashionable church and encountered a pathetic old woman carrying a heavy bundle. Impulsively, the girl helped her. Then, to her horror, it occurred to her that "respectable" people might see her. It was a moment of decision. In her mind flashed the words: "Gold, silver, precious stones, wood, hay, stubble. If any man's work abide..." (1 Corinthians 3:12,14). She looked around her, and everything seemed normal. "But," said Amy Carmichael later, "I knew that something had happened that had changed life's values. Nothing could ever matter again but the things that were eternal."[1]

Woven throughout her writings, "Nothing is important but that which is eternal" remained a theme Amy carried out in practical terms with regard to family relationships, friendships, or even something as weighty as illness or death. It is a principle that casts a new and vital perspective on the manner in which each of us lives our life.

In a fast-changing society with ever-fluctuating values, we may find it difficult to know what it means to live under God's approval. "God can't love me; I'm no good," sighed one lady sadly as she sat in my office and poured out her feelings of self-hatred. Another young woman refused much needed psychological help because she "can get all she needs from reading the Bible." This woman, too, suffered from a deep sense of self-hatred, and she feared that if she sought counseling God would condemn her for not trusting Him enough. It hadn't occurred to her that God might actually use the counseling to help her put biblical principles into shoe leather.

At the advice of his pastor, a young man brought his child to see me. He admitted that his real reason for coming was to talk about his extramarital affair—an affair of which the pastor had no knowledge and that, apart from the possibility of its being discovered, did not on the surface disturb the young man. When I asked him how he reconciled this sexual activity with his biblical knowledge, he replied, "I don't try to."

In the midst of such obvious confusion in a society that changes so rapidly that even Christians lose their perspective on what God wants, Amy Carmichael offers an old but continuously current point of view. Like the rest of us, she struggled to learn what God wanted of her. From that early moment in Belfast to her final years of total invalidism, she sought to be found faithful, and in the process she gave us a believable example of dealing with suffering.

After a physical breakdown while she was a missionary in Japan, she became engaged in mission work in southern India, rescuing children who had been sold to the gods as temple prostitutes. While she never actually adopted Indian citizenship, she did melt into the Indian culture, with a goal to do her work as Christ had done His on this earth.

In 1919, when she was awarded a high honor and presented with a medal from the governor of Madras, she almost refused it. "It troubles me," she said, "to have an experience so different from His who was despised and rejected—not kindly honored."[2]

To the children she raised and to those she worked with she became "Amma," the Indian word for "Mother." Even to those who never knew her but who were nurtured by her writing she was Amma. Amy seemed disrespectful and Miss Carmichael seemed too distant. Thus for the purposes of this book she will be referred to as Amma.

Amma insisted that the children be raised with the highest standards of honesty and loyalty. That the Dohnavur Fellowship of India still exists is evidence that her standards were not so high, however, as to be spiritually unrealistic. And that she could be highly practical was proven by her long journeys on hot, dusty roads to rescue a child in danger.

At the root of all her endeavors and in the midst of all her suffering was a deep desire to live under God's approval in all circumstances. Perhaps her attitude toward life can best be summarized in one of her poems, "Make Me Thy Fuel":

> *From prayer that asks that I may be*
> *Sheltered from winds that beat on Thee,*
> *From fearing when I should aspire,*
> *From faltering when I should climb higher.*
> *From silken self, O Captain, free*
> *Thy soldier who would follow Thee.*
>
> *From subtle love of softening things,*
> *From easy choices, weakenings,*
> *Not thus are spirits fortified,*
> *Not this way went the Crucified,*
> *From all that dims Thy Calvary,*
> *O Lamb of God, deliver me.*
>
> *Give me the love that leads the way,*
> *The faith that nothing can dismay,*
> *The hope no disappointments tire,*
> *The passion that will burn like fire,*

> *Let me not sink to be a clod;*
> *Make me Thy fuel, Flame of God.*[3]

The quest for assurance of God's approval becomes even more complicated when suffering is involved. Perhaps one of the toughest issues that a thinking person faces—and certainly a psychotherapist who witnesses daily the inner torture of so many—is the problem of pain. Nietzsche has quite accurately stated that he who knows the *why* to his existence can endure any *how*.

Sometimes, however, the *how* hurts so badly that the *why* is hard to remember. It is difficult for a small child with a physical disability to engage in rigorous physical therapy for eight years in order to learn to walk. The *how* seems too tedious and painful; the *why* feels remote and at times unattainable. And sometimes the *why* becomes obscured or is unknowable to finite minds. Why do people starve to death? Why do children at three years of age need psychotherapy for emotional problems so deeply ingrained that their scars will remain for life? Why, on a human level, does life seem so much more filled with pain than with pleasure, with mere survival a primary goal for many?

In her various books Amma commented on different aspects of human suffering. In so doing, she gave meaning and purpose to even the most severe difficulties of life.

Frequently, Christians who try to live in the light of eternity have severe doubts about their ability to do so. We know that we should love, but we find it difficult to love the unlovable. We fear failure and rejection, especially when we suffer and are criticized. Amma described this well when she wrote:

> Some are wonderfully created. They can go through
> a thick flight of stinging arrows and hardly feel them. It
> is as if they were clad in fine chain-armour.

Others are made differently. The arrows pierce, and most sharply if they be shot by friends. The very tone of a voice can depress such a one for a week. (It can uplift, too; for the heart that is open to hurt is also very open to love.)

The Indian [referring to the native of India] has by nature no chain-armour, and some of us can understand just what that means. But if we are to be God's knights, we must learn to go through flights of arrows, and so the teaching which was set on fashioning warriors, not weaklings, often dealt with this.[4]

Again, Amma's emphasis here is not on the eradication of suffering but on the Christian's ability to cope with it.

The principle upon which Amma operated under criticism is reflected in two of her illustrations. A mentor and co-worker,

Walker of Tinnevelly sat alone in his study reading the copy of a document addressed to the Archbishop of Canterbury. It was a petition against him and one or two other true men who had stood by him in his efforts to cut certain cankers out of this South Indian Church. It was an amazing composition, cruel and false because so ignorant.

Walker came out from his study that day looking very white, and his eyes were like dark fires. But he went straight on like a man walking through cobwebs stretched across his path. And what does it matter now? He has seen his Lord's face. *All that troubles is only for a moment. Nothing is important but that which is eternal.*[5]

In another instance Amma told of her own experience of speaking in a setting in which alcohol was forbidden to a "good Christian," and she was misrepresented in her presentation of the subject:

> One of the first meetings she was asked to take in India was for English soldiers belonging to a South Indian cantonment. It was supposed to be a Temperance meeting, but Temperance was hardly mentioned. The soldiers needed something that went much deeper. That meeting was reported in the Parish magazine. An address had been given on the benefits of alcohol. It had come as a pleasant surprise, the writer said, to hear from a missionary that alcohol was beneficial.
>
> For a minute a quite young missionary felt this rather staggering. And then suddenly the thought came, "It won't matter fifty years hence, so what does it matter now?" Nothing is important but that which is eternal.[6]

So often it was the principle of viewing life from an eternal perspective that enabled Amma to cope with suffering.

In my work as a counselor, I see many who feel hurt from unjust criticism; for the idleness and, indeed, the savagery of words can be felt as an intense form of suffering. But perhaps those who feel most acutely the sting of criticism are at times those who are in positions of power, particularly in Christian work. Such leaders are vulnerable on various levels. A leader in the Christian world may be troubled by a disturbed child. Instead of being upheld, he is often criticized by fellow Christians for bad parenting. The child does seem out of control. However, perhaps he has ADHD and needs medication. If the problem is physical, treat the physical. Suggesting such a possibility would be more helpful than carping criticism. Maybe there *is* bad parenting. Then help in finding a good parenting class could be the right thing to do. We need to be willing to *lovingly* help those who are wounded, even our leaders. In some circles emotional pain is regarded too often as the result of lack of faith. We sometimes forget that we are made up of body, mind, and spirit, all frequently inter-relating with each other.

In addition to the scrutiny they face regarding their own families, men and women earnestly helping with the problems of a congregation may find themselves suddenly accused, falsely, of sexual impropriety or other serious infractions of rules. On another level, a pastor of a church is often judged as too people-oriented rather than a good Bible teacher. Or the reverse is the complaint. Trying to make one person meet all needs is often the problem. The idea that one person can do it all is against biblical principles where each member of the Body has certain gifts. For such who are criticized unfairly, the clause "nothing matters but that which is eternal" is at times the only effective antidote.

In speaking of another form of suffering—chronic physical pain—Amma recounted this instance:

> One of our Indian Viceroys, perhaps the most dazzling figure of them all, could not stand to face an audience without support of a steel device. "I, at times, suffer terribly from my back," he wrote from out of the blaze of public life, "and one day it will finish me. But so long as one is marching, I say, let the drums beat and the flags fly." (Not many knew of that gnawing pain. Perhaps if it were remembered that often there is sackcloth under royal robes, the judgment of the world would be kinder.)

Whatever the Iron Crown may be, so long as one is marching let the drums beat and the flags fly. What does it matter that no one knows the cost of those brave words? He whose crown was of thorns knows all that is covered from casual glance of man. Where others see merely a decorous exterior, He sees a soul, sometimes a tortured soul, looking up into His eyes for courage and grace to live triumphantly a moment at a time. And if we could hear spiritual voices speak, we should hear something like this, "Thy flesh and thy heart faileth? I know, my child, I know. But I am the strength of thy heart and thy portion forever. Thou shall not be forgotten of Me."[7]

Those who are well are sometimes unable to understand and accept those who are ill. As one patient said to me, "If my friend is sick, I'm sorry; but she's going to have to forget her illness and go back to work. After all, her rent has to be paid." Or more damaging still was the comment directed at a young girl to the effect that she wore leg braces only because she didn't have enough faith.

Amma showed profound sensitivity when she wrote:

There are some for whom illness is made more difficult than it need be. Boswell shivers on the chilly boat journey from Greenwich to London, "for the night air was so cold that it made me shiver. I was more sensible of it from having sat up all the night before, recollecting and writing in my journal what I thought worthy of preservation" (of the sayings and doings of his friend Johnson). But Johnson, who "was not in the least affected by the cold, scolded me as if my shivering had been a paltry effeminacy." Another unfortunate is rebuked for a headache: "At your age, sir, I had no head-ache." There is one simple way to achieve serenity when (if ever) we meet Dr. Samuel Johnson: It is to be glad that he had never known "shivering" or "head-ache." And also to remember that he is probably like a Spanish chestnut, rather prickly outside, but inside very good.[8]

In commenting on the health of a fellow worker, an Indian nurse, Kohila, Amma reflected intuitively:

> But, God help us if we are not better than our bodies' inclinations; the spirit of man will sustain his infirmity, is a great word for the ill, if only by the grace of the Lord, the Conqueror of pain, they can lay hold upon it. And Kohila did. Her fellow-nurses say of her, "She was not an ordinary patient. She never forgot that she was a nurse, and so must be a perfect patient." From time to time also there were the trials and tests that must be if life is to be more than a painted pretence. Each one of these had a share in shaping the child of this story. We thought of everything as a preparation for service, witness-bearing and soul-winning in the Place of Healing and in the villages. But now we know that it was preparation for another Service, Elsewhere.[9]

Yet there were, and are, times when God chooses to heal. Dr. Nancy Robbins, who was a physician at Dohnavur for a number of years, including the last five years of Amma's life, described those times to me. "In the early years of her life in India, she [Amma] prayed for people and, to her surprise, they became well. This became known in the district, and people were coming to her in very large numbers for healing. And they were healed. But she realized that she was not able to follow them up and to tell them about the Lord, who had really healed them. She heard that rumors were circulating around South India about this white woman who healed people. And she felt that the Lord said to her, 'My Glory will I not give to another.' And so she stopped.

"She did sometimes pray for healing, but not as it were in a big way, you know, but rather privately. But she certainly was used in casting out demons where there was demon possession. That was something that she was very aware of."

Perhaps some of Amma's most insightful words on the subject of illness, however, come from her book *Rose From Brier*, which she dedicated "From the ill to the ill." Sensitive to a lack of understanding on the part of those who are well, she wrote from the experience of her own illness.

> One day, after weeks of nights when, in spite of all that was done to induce sleep, it refused to come, except in brief distracted snatches, the mail brought a letter which discoursed with what sounded almost like pleasure on this "enforced rest," and the silly phrase rankled like a thorn. I was far too tired to laugh it off as one can laugh off things when one is well. So this was supposed to be rest? And was the Father breaking, crushing, "forcing," by weight of sheer physical misery, a child who only longed to obey His lightest wish? This word had what I now know was an absurd power to distress. It held such an unkind, such a false conception of our Father. Till that hour, although I was puzzled, I had not had one unhappy minute. I had been given peace in acceptance. The spirit can live above the flesh, and mine, helped by the tender love of our Lord Jesus and the dearness of all around me, had done so.

But in that hour it was different, and I had no peace till I had heard deep within me soft and soothing words such as a mother uses: "Let not your heart be troubled; do I not understand? What do such words matter to me or to thee?" And I knew that the Father understood His child, and the child her Father, and all was peace again.[10]

Approval from God is sometimes most intensely enjoyed when the suffering and the abrasiveness are hidden from humans and known only to God, for the world is quick to laud those whom it can see as brave. A man with a cane or a child in leg braces is praised for bravery, and should be. But the person who suffers from depressive feelings or who is quietly assimilating the news of a terminal illness in the life of a loved one is told to "rejoice" or "cheer up." The result in the sufferer is discouragement and, at times, a feeling that not even God understands the heartache.

We Christians are too often prone to associate suffering with a righteous consequence of sin, of punishment or retribution from God. God does at times discipline His own, and sometimes there are painful consequences of sin. But often God chooses only His most valued children to entrust with the most painful of trials. Job is the most obvious biblical example of this kind of suffering. God could trust Job to believe in Him when all earthly evidence for that belief seemed to have been removed. Amma once wrote:

> Trials are not "chastisement." No earthly father goes on chastising a loving child. That is a common thought about suffering, but I am quite sure that it is a wrong thought. Paul's sufferings were not that, nor are yours. They are battle wounds. They are signs of high confidence—honors. The Father holds His children very close

to His heart when they are going through such rough places as this.

"Thy care hath preserved my spirit"—a lovely Revised Version margin which helped me a few days ago—is my word for you (Job 10:12). Think of it; all day long you are being cared for, you are in His care.[11]

In an era of "Praise the Lord" theology, the real meaning of words like *praise* and *joy* may become lost to superficiality. For it is only in deep suffering that people know the depths of all emotion, whether it be seemingly unbearable pain, or the joy that sweeps over the soul once that pain is gone. On an even more profound level, joy, accurately defined, can exist along *with* pain.

"Thunder-clouds are nothing to the Spirit of Joy. The only special reference to the joy of the Holy Spirit is bound up with the words 'much affliction,' much pressure. It is the rose under thunder-cloud again." Amma included the words of Webb-Peploe as she continued:

> "Joy is not gush; joy is not jolliness. Joy is simply perfect acquiescence in God's will, because the soul delights itself in God Himself. Christ took God as His God and Father, and that brought Him at last to say, 'I delight to do thy will,' though the cup was the cross, in such agony as no man knew. It cost Him blood. *It cost Him blood.* O take the Fatherhood of God in the blessed Son the Savior, and by the Holy Ghost rejoice, rejoice in the will of God, and in nothing else. Bow down your heads and your hearts before God, and let the will, the blessed will of God, be done."

These weighty words were spoken by Prebendary Webb-Peploe to a gathering of Christians many years ago.

In the silence that closed the hour, the speaker—some knew it—was laying, not for the first time, his Isaac on the altar of his God. It is the life lived that gives force to the words spoken. These words were not wind and froth. They sound through the years like the deep notes of a bell: "*Joy is not gush, joy is not jolliness. Joy is perfect acquiescence to the will of God.*"

This, then, is the call to the climbing soul. Expose yourself to the circumstances of His choice, for that is perfect acquiescence in the will of God. We are called to the fellowship of a gallant company, "Ye become followers of us, and of the Lord," wrote St. Paul to the men of Thessalonica. Who follows in their train?

> *Make me Thy mountaineer;*
> *I would not linger on the lower slope.*
> *Fill me afresh with hope, O God of hope,*
> *That undefeated I may climb the hill*
> *As seeing Him who is invisible,*
>
> *Whom having not seen I love.*
> *O my Redeemer, when this little while*
> *Lies far behind me and the last defile*
> *Is all alight and in that light I see*
> *My Savior and my Lord, what will it be?*[12]

In speaking of her love for others, many who knew Amma agree that her love for them was often what they most remember. And yet she always expected the best of people, and so they did a great deal better because of it. Loosely translated, Goethe once wrote that if we treat people as if they are already what they are capable of becoming we help them to become that. That, too, was Amma's way.

> "She could be forthright and she was very perceptive.
> She could put her finger on what was probably the root
> cause of the trouble and say so. But she did it so very lov-
> ingly; and it obviously hurt her so much to find fault with
> somebody else."[13]

Once when Dr. Robbins had ordered a specific dose of med-ication for Amma, the person who was to give it to her, at her own discretion gave her a smaller dose. The doctor was under-standably upset—as she put it "boiling with rage." Amma's response was to point out she would never be able to help some-one if she had anger in her heart. However, to the doctor, help-ing her had not been the issue. Treating Amma with the right dosage was the main concern. In retrospect Dr. Robbins con-cluded: "She [the person administering the medicine] was wrong, but my attitude was wrong too. And Amma, speaking of it as she did, very gently, but very, very truthfully taught me a lesson I never forgot."

Amma's love was displayed in the loving notes she often sent to various workers who found them to be just what they needed at that time. That they helped so much sometimes seemed to be somewhat of a surprise to Amma. Once when Dr. Robbins was in a temple town living with the Indian people to learn Tamil there was a huge Hindu festival that lasted for ten days. Comments Dr. Robbins: "It was simply awful. There was a tremendous oppression of evil. I evidently wrote Amma a letter when I was in the midst of this, and I must have said something about something that she had said or written that had been a great help. And she wrote back to me and mentioned this. She said 'I just didn't even a little understand such dearness. I have read and reread and read again. I can only lay it at His feet, or put it into His hands, and ask Him to read it too and say what I can't say for me and bless you and bless you and bless you.' Well, that was Amma."

One of my own personal treasures is a note in Amma's handwriting, pencilled on a slip of old paper that Dr. Robbins so kindly sent to me—one example, as she put it, of the many encouraging notes she and others received. With reference to this note, on one occasion Dr. Robbins had been left alone in charge of the hospital for too long a time for one person. When Amma found out, she wrote this note, dated May 29, 1948. "I have just heard you are left alone for five days. I had heard of a weekend and had thought it meant Sat. eve. 'till Monday morning. I shall be continually looking up for you my ... Nancy. It is far too much—But 'As thy days....'" She adds another line relating to some other workers for whom she is thankful and closes, "Amma."

Amma was a person of remarkable balance. She "had very, very high standards of obedience to what she saw as being the directions of the Lord ... tremendously high standards for herself. But she was not critical of things that were non-essential, like the minor differences of whether you stand to sing or kneel."[14]

Partly because of her balance in such issues, "Amma was tremendously respected eventually even by Hindu people because she had bothered to learn a lot about Hinduism and respected their customs. As far as possible in the hospital we respected people's customs and prejudices and religious practices. We gave every Hindu family facilities for cooking so that they didn't have to 'defile' themselves by eating food that Christians had touched. This brought people to us in large numbers because they felt that we understood, that we didn't force our ways on them. But there were things we had to draw the line at."[15]

There is a buoyancy to be found in the act of helping others, a joy in seeing the positive results of our assistance in their accomplishments. But each of us who in some way ministers to the needs of other people becomes at times drained, "weary in well doing," disappointed over disappointing results. This brings upon us the pain resulting from combined fatigue and discouragement. Referring to Demas—a biblical example of one who was led to Christ, trusted by Paul, and then turned back to his old way of life—Amma explained the pain of disappointment:

> After long prayer and toil, a soul has been led to Christ. By a thousand little signs you know that the miracle is happening for which you have waited so long. Then other influences begin to play upon that soul. Some Demas, once trusted and beloved, snatches at the chance to wound his forsaken Lord, and injects poison. The one who lately ran so well falters, looks back, goes back.
>
> Then comes a terrific temptation to regard that Demas with eyes which see only his Demas qualities. And, so imperceptibly as water oozes through an earthen vessel, power to expect his return to peace and purity begins to pass. When the next new inquirer comes there may be a fear to meet him with buoyant, loving hope.
>
> But this is fatal. Better be disappointed a thousand times—yes, and deceived—than once miss a chance to help a soul because of that faithless inhibition that grows, before we are aware of it, into suspicion and hardness. There is only one thing to be done. It is to realize that in us there is no good thing, nor faith, nor hope, nor even love; nothing human suffices here. All that we counted ours shrivels in the hot winds of disappointment. Thy servant hath not anything in the house. But the love of

God suffices for any disappointment, for any defeat. And in that love is the energy of faith and the very sap of hope.[16]

When I feel that I have nothing left to give, I find it helpful to realize that "nothing human suffices here." It is then time for me to turn to Him who will always fill an empty, surrendered vessel with Himself. Sometimes when I have nothing left to give, God is trying to tell me to slow down, to do and give less.

Speaking of the need to slow down and produce quality, Amma wrote, "We must learn, as the Tamil proverb says, to plough deep rather than wide. Only God can plough both deep and wide." Then, quoting Samuel Rutherford, "There is but a certain quantity of spiritual force in any man. Spread it over a broad surface, the stream is shallow and languid; narrow the channel and it becomes a driving force."[17]

Sometimes the person who disappoints us, however, is not only someone we have ministered to but someone who has ministered to us as well. He or she is our friend, not just an individual associated with our work, and in our tiredness and discouragement we need this person's support. Then the pain has perhaps an even greater sting.

Of this Amma said:

A beautiful quatrain is about silence where a disappointing friend is concerned; when those to whom we clung disappoint, keep the sad secret hid, cling to them still. The growing grain has husks; the water has its form; flowers have a scentless outer sheath of leaves.[18]

She continued:

Be careful also of your after-thinking as well as of your after-talking about any who have misjudged you. "The hill—man thinks upon the beauty of his hills; the farmer thinks upon his fields that have yielded him rich crops; the good think on the boons bestowed by worthy men; the base man's thoughts are fixed on the abuse he has received," is another old Tamil saying. Do not feed unloving thoughts. Remember His word, "I forgave thee all that debt."[19]

And so Amma concluded her discussion on friends with these marvelous words: "Why should we ever be bound? Of what account is anything if our King knows?"[20] Using Christ as our example is the only true comfort in times of trial.

"When Earl Jellicoe was being misunderstood by the nation he served so faithfully, a letter came from King George, whose keen sea-sense had penetrated the mist which had bemused the general public. His letter heartened the Fleet. What did anything matter now? 'Their King knew.' "[21]

"If our King knows" that is all that matters was a continuing theme in Amma's work. Therefore prayer was a vital link with her heavenly King. According to Dr. Robbins: "Any decision that affected our life or the children or our contacts on the outside were all taken to the Lord. When I traveled out to India, I traveled on a ship. There was a missionary there who had already done one term in India. And she had visited Dohnavur. She said, 'You'll find that they have wonderful prayer meetings at Dohnavur. It's not like a lot of different people bringing different requests. But it's like a lot of people all joining in one prayer.' And it really was like that. This was the way that Amma taught us to pray. We'd take a subject and people would pray short prayers about some aspect of it. Somebody else would take up another aspect. Somebody else would take up something else, until they'd really covered every contingency. And then we made a decision. And this was Amma's way . . . .

> "Nothing was decided, nothing was done that hadn't been really thoroughly prayed about. Everything was taken to the Lord. And her principle was that we all prayed together, and that God would bring us to 'one mind in our house', as she said. This so often did happen, that we prayed about some matter that was a little bit controversial. And eventually, we all knew what it was that God wanted us to do. This was very much her principle. She didn't do anything without prayer."

Furthermore, "You never went to see her without her praying with you. She'd just break off and say something to the Lord; it was a sort of continual conversation with her."[22]

While above all prayer is direct access to the throne of God, it does have a human, therapeutic aspect as well. In Hebrews 4:16 (TLB) we read, "So let us come boldly to the very throne of God and stay there to receive his mercy and to find grace to help us in our times of need." Dr. Vernon Grounds' comment on this verse reads:

> God's throne is the throne of grace . . . . Keep nothing back, verbalizing with no attempt at logic or control. It means doing exactly what a client does with a psychotherapist, letting accumulated and suppressed emotions spill out. This is the apostle's urgent invitation. Spill out all the meanness, the filth, the despair, or whatever else may have been dammed back inside. Tell it in full detail. Come *boldly* to the throne of grace.

The King who sits upon that throne is a High Priest full of love and compassion and forgiveness. The King who sits upon that throne is a Father with a mother's heart. Before that throne we need not grovel like a captured spy begging for mercy from merciless captors. Before that throne we bow in gratitude and thanksgiving.

In His omniscience He knows the fright and agony of a sparrow seized by a hawk. In His omniscience He knows the ache and pain of a bereaved mother's heart. Yet according to this text [Hebrews 4:16], He knows our feelings not by virtue of divine omniscience but by virtue, rather, of personal experience.' The omnipotent God entered human existence at Bethlehem. He became one of us!"[23]

We live in an age of loneliness symbolized by a desperate clinging to the past, of escape into alcohol and drugs, and an involvement in unlimited numbers of group activities organized not so much on the basis of common interests as from a desire to meet other people—all to avoid loneliness.

Amma found an ability to cope with loneliness as she looked at Christ's life; then she applied those principles that she had found in Him to her own life as she struggled with health problems and loneliness in India:

Years later, in an hour of need, the Everlasting Comforter came through the Septuagint version of Psalm 150:18. His soul (Joseph's) entered into iron. It was not that others put him in irons (though they did, they hurt his feet with fetters), it was that he himself acquiesced in, willingly walked into the unexplained trial of his God's dealings with him. "His soul entered, whole and entire in its resolve to obey God, into the cruel torture," is Kay's note on that great matter. But what fathomless depths it must have held for our Lord Jesus when He set His face steadfastly to go to Jerusalem, Gethsemane, Calvary, and certain it is that whatever way of pain may open before any one of us, we find as we walk in it the marks of our dear Lord's footsteps leading on. He walked alone on that road so that we need never walk alone. No star, no flower, no song was Thine, but darkness three hours long.

He was hard on Himself, but there is no hardness in His ways with us, and the dimmest pages in our story shine as we look back on them. We saw this once in parable. Some of us had gone to the coast to try to get rid of a persistent fever, and one night we bathed deliciously in a little bay between dark rocks. The night was moonless and starless, and the sea, except where it broke in ripples or waves, was as dark as sea can ever be. But when we came out of that water we were covered from head to foot in phosphorescent light, and when we sat down on the wet sand and dug our hands into it, diamonds ran between our fingers.

There are lights that watch on occasion to appear. Such are the lights of strong consolation that have come when all was dark, whether because of some black trouble like the black seas of sin, or because of threatened harm or loss to that which is so much dearer to us than ourselves. For truly the love of the Lord whose brightness is as the light, who is Himself light, passeth all things for illumination, and if I say, Surely the darkness shall cover me, even the night shall be light about me.[24]

Much has been written about trial in the Christian life. Simplistically, we assume that we suffer, recover, and go on, that the trials are gone forever. On the contrary, I often find that trials recur. Just when I have thought I was finished with illness, or the hurt of death or some other painful experience, it suddenly reappears.

In a chapter in *Gold by Moonlight*, titled "And Then the Dark Wood Again," Amma spoke of this "second wood," this repetition of trial:

> Perhaps this second wood may find the traveler startled or depressed by a recurrence of some trial which he had thought was well behind him. "I have not passed this way heretofore," he had said to himself when he entered the first dark wood. "I shall henceforth return no more that way." Nor does he, but perhaps just after a clear vision of peace from some House Beautiful he finds confronting him something very like the dark wood of earlier days. It is in fact a further reach of that wood.
>
> Here is one, perhaps an athlete, who has never been ill and never contemplated illness. He has become the vassal of Eternal Love. *Look, love, and follow*: Prince Charlie engraved this motto on his seal when he came to call the clans to suffer and die for him. The words are engraved upon the life of this soldier who has looked, loved, and followed his Prince overseas. But his first year sees him handicapped by illness. He recovers, is struck down again, he who never was ill before. This repeated illness, battle-wound though it be, so unexpected, so exhausting, can appear like a very dark wood. Battle-wounds may sound heroic, but they do not feel so.[25]

Amma continued in that same chapter:

The call to enter for the second time into any painful experience is a sign of our Lord's confidence. It offers a great opportunity. "The most powerful thing in your life is your opportunity," said Kleobulos of Lindos; it is also the most irretrievable. We must have clearness of vision and courage and a quiet mind if we are to see it, and lay hands upon it as it hurries past us on very quiet feet and disappears as utterly as the day that has gone. "As Thy servant was busy here and there" it was gone. God give us vision and courage and a quiet mind.[26]

Purpose? It lies in those words: "The call to enter for the second time into any painful experience is a sign of our Lord's confidence." To be honored as such a valued servant of our Lord is to live in the perspective of eternal values. It is to have purpose, to transcend mere coping.

Sometimes a psychotherapist sees symptoms come back that had once gone. Trauma hits again just as one is recovering from previous trauma. Such an occurrence may be interpreted by some as a sign of God's disapproval. Rather, should we not see this recurring painful experience is an indication of a further, God-given opportunity for His child to trust the Lord for the assurance and comfort He is ready to provide for traversing this second dark wood? And what is true in the psychological realm is equally true in the physical. For physical illness, too, may recur in the life of God's child.

How often each of us must be reminded that the eternal value of a situation does not lie in our feelings or in what appears upon the surface. Death is one of those experiences we Christians feel we should not face with fear or discomfort. Nevertheless, we can empathize with this expression I once heard while listening to a noted preacher: "I do not fear eternity but I do not look forward to the process of dying." Many years later I talked to him shortly before he died. His last words to me were: "Oh, Elizabeth, I cannot wait to go to be with my Lord!" His voice was full of joy and peace. The human and the divine had merged.

Ponnammal, an Indian nurse in the missionary compound where Amma worked, was dying of cancer. She expressed graphically the pain of dying, as well as the realism of God's sustenance. Said Amma of the experience:

> "Last night," [Ponnammal] said, "I had less pain than usual, and my mind was clear. When the confusion passes, and the power to think returns, then my heart rises as if released from a weight; I can pray and praise. But first I examined myself to be sure all was well with me. For many days I had felt nothing, not even comfort, all was dimness and a blank and silence; then as I told my God about it, He showed me that all through the days the joy of His salvation was within me, unchanged by any misery of pain. It was there, but I could not taste it. The darkness and the sadness of that time was caused by the medicine; it was not that I *had lost anything*. This comforted me, and I praised Him greatly and was content." For many days her mouth had had that drawn look which those who have nursed anyone through sore suffering will know too well. But as she talked, the old sweet, satisfied look returned, and all the old happy curves were there again. "Oh, is it not wonderful!" she exclaimed with a sort of vigorous joyousness. "For days and nights the waves beat hard on me, and then suddenly there is a great calm, and I lie back and rest."

Then she asked for the last few verses of 1 Corinthians 15, repeating after me the words, "Thanks be to God, which giveth us the victory." And then I read the 46th Psalm to her, and she fell asleep.[27]

This experience was not one of the eradication of pain but rather of triumph in the midst of pain because of God's provision. Ponnammal did not manage to annihilate her pain and depression but came through all of that darkness to acknowledge God's approval. She was found faithful.

One form of suffering Amma pointed out and helped to realistically resolve was the fear of failure. All of us conjure up giants in our lives—the "Might Bes," the "What Ifs." What if our child doesn't grow up to meet our hopes and expectations? What if our money doesn't last? What if our health gives way? What if I end up alone and helpless in my old age? Each of us has our own "What Ifs," and we may not relate to those of our neighbor. Amma wrote:

But we can be tormented by fear of failing before the end of a journey. We need not fear. It was George Tankervil, he who said,

Though the day be never so long,
At last it ringeth to evensong,
Who out of weakness, was made strong.

He so greatly feared lest he should flinch from martyrdom, that to test himself he had a fire kindled in the chamber where he was confined, and sitting on a form before it, he put off his shoes and hose and stretched out his foot to the flame; but when it touched his foot, "he

quickly withdrew his leg, showing how the flesh did per-
suade him one way and the Spirit another way." And yet,
a few hours later, when he came to the green place near
the west end of St. Albans Abbey where the stake was set,
he kneeled down, and when he had ended his prayer he
arose with a joyful faith. Before they put the fire to him a
certain knight went near and said softly, "Good brother,
be strong in Christ." And he answered, "I am so, I thank
God." So embracing the fire, he bathed himself in it, and
calling on the name of the Lord, was quickly out of pain.

Have we not often been like George Tankervil? We
have imagined what was coming, and perhaps tested our
constancy by some fire of our own kindling, and faith
and courage have suddenly collapsed. For grace to endure
and to conquer is never given till the moment of need,
but when that moment comes, "Savior, who does not forget thy Calvary, hast thou ever failed the soul that trusted
thee? Never, never. By the merits of thy Blood all is well,
all shall be well."[28]

Amma had her own what-ifs. She feared that at the end of
her life she would linger on to be a burden to others. Years before
her death she had written in her journal:

> Lord, teach me how to conquer pain to the uttermost
> henceforth, and grant this my earnest request. When my
> day's work is done, take me straight Home. Do not let me
> be ill and a burden or anxiety to anyone. O let me finish
> my course with joy and not with grief. Thou knowest
> there could be no joy if I knew I were tiring those whom
> I love best, or taking them from the children. Let me die
> of a battle-wound, O my Lord, not of a lingering illness.[29]

However, for years before she died, Amma was housebound and eventually bedridden. In this situation, though, she triumphed in a profound way with God, and some of her special insights in writing came during those years.

Certain rumors have existed about those last years, years of invalidism that started with a bad fall and escalated into other very real physical ailments. One rumor was that she tended toward hypochondria, which Dr. Robbins calls a "very bad misconception." Another was that she could be difficult to deal with. To the contrary, even her own doctor found it difficult at times to know when Amma needed her or was in pain. She simply did not complain.

One night when Amma was feeling particularly unwell, Dr. Robbins was called to come and see her. Until the end of Amma's life, Amma's doctor lived on the compound quite near her so she could be called if she was ill in the night. Amma was horrified that Dr. Robbins had been disturbed. The next day Amma wrote her a note telling her that when the time came, when the Lord was answering her prayer to be with Him, that she was "not to shut the door out." Life was not to be shortened but neither was the dying process to be extended. Life was to be in His timing.

Dr. Robbins adds an extra note of wisdom: "There used to be a saying when I was a student: 'Thou shalt not kill, but needs not strive efficiously to keep alive.' I at times think that that's perhaps a principle that could still be applied."

Continues Dr. Robbins: Amma "had been told early on that she'd never survive in the tropics. But she did survive for fifty years." According to Dr. Robbins, through the years she had a lot of trouble with her kidneys and had never spared herself. She had lived a very strenuous life. Then later there were the falls and broken bones. Toward the end she gradually failed—heart, kidneys, and digestive system, in addition to infections peculiar to the tropics. "Eventually she really died of old age and exhaustion. She gradually went into a coma."[30]

During those last days she kept by her side the last stanzas of an old hymn that epitomized her source of comfort:

> Green pastures are before me
> Which yet I have not seen,
> Bright skies will soon be o'er me
> Where the dark clouds have been.
>
> My hope I cannot measure,
> My path to life is free,
> My Savior has my treasure,
> And He will walk with me.[31]

In all her endeavors Christ was her motivation, her source of power, her lifetime goal. That made all the difference in her suffering.

Another myth regarding Amma has nothing to do with her illness but rather relates to her treatment of light-skinned people as compared to those with dark skin. While it is true that in South India higher caste people tend to be lighter skinned and are more highly regarded in general, to Amma it didn't matter. Newspaper advertisements would appear where someone was seeking a bride who was "fair" and "well educated." The Indian people of that day were sensitive in general about their color and avoided getting sunburned. To Amma, it didn't matter. In fact, she tried to help the less attractive, more difficult people, those who didn't have a lot going for them.[32]

Amma was very loved by the children and those she worked with. But anyone dealing with that many people would inevitably make some mistakes in judgment. Moreover, it would have been

impossible to please everyone. Perhaps there were times of com-
petition and jealousy over whom she loved most. That is the
only reason I personally can imagine as an explanation for the
criticism of favoritism. Greatness sometimes brings on competi-
tion. Those who are loved much are often disliked much as well.

Above and beyond the "gnats" of life, the petty criticisms, the
rumors, the gossip that attend any great work for God, there is
that great force of demonic attack that tries to destroy, and sometimes uses the seemingly trivial to knock us down when we are
already exhausted from the pressure of the work. In the rescue of
small children from the bondage of the Evil One, Dohnavur was
vulnerable. But we know that He that is in us is greater than he
who is without. In a note to Dr. Robbins during that early time
when she was living in a temple town learning Tamil, Amma
described the triumph over evil in a profound way: "As things
were then, so they are now. He conquered then, He conquers
now. But well I knew that awful sense of evil, of sheer, mastering,
reigning, exultant evil, just as if He'd never come into the world
and died for love of it. Just as if He'd never be king of India, or
anywhere in this sad world. Just as if creation itself was a gigan-
tic mistake, a terrible failure. But He must reign and we shall see
Him reign. And we are here to hasten the coming of His kingdom. Blessed be God for fact. Feelings go down before fact every
time. Wherefore, sirs, be of good cheer, for I believe God that it
shall be even as it was told me."[33]

It was a typically tropical day in a small coastal town in Mexico. I had come to rest, relax, and write, yet I was still terribly
tired. No book had been finished. Even my body had not
responded to the rest as quickly as I had hoped. Feeling quite discouraged but not wanting to impose that dreary feeling on my
friends, I went off by myself for a while to be alone. I looked out

at the ocean, clear and blue, and felt nothing. Coconut palms and surrounding hills were green from the recent rains, but they too could not meet my need. I was irritated with the fatigue and the gloom of going home and facing once again a full schedule with insufficient physical strength. Languidly I thumbed through the pages of one of my Amy Carmichael books. (I usually take one with me when I go on a trip.) My eyes fell on these words:

> For, lo, the winter is past, the rain is over and gone; the flowers appear on the earth; the time of the singing of birds is come ... There has been a turning of the captivity and the hard weather has passed, but there is still something stark in our landscape ... There is a fact, a memory, a possibility, that strikes up and faces us wherever we look. That knot of painful circumstances is there, that fear, that fearful thing, may be waiting in the shadows to spring upon us like a panther on a fawn.[34]

Then, in reference to a photograph full of the beauty of nature, yet including a picture of an ancient ruin in the midst of all the beauty, Amma continued:

> The picture is a figure of the true; it is full of grace and a lovely lightness, but it is the ruin that arrests the eye and gives character to the whole. Take it out, and you have merely a pretty page of scenery, and life is more than that. The charm of leaf and bud after a time of snow is not all that God has for those whom He is preparing to minister to others.[35]

My life, too, had its own "lovely lightness," but it had been the "knot of painful circumstances" that had intruded upon my thinking even in this tropical paradise. I realized afresh that "life is more than that." The pain, the fatigue, the things I would like to erase from the landscape of my life were those very things God was using in my ministry for Him. The challenge is that the ruin in my life, those painful things I would like to erase, not remain a mere ruin but be transformed by His hand into something positive.

God is in the process of bringing us to wholeness, to completeness, that we may be totally prepared for the fulfillment of His purposes in us. The process often includes fierce and fearful times. There may be ruins along the way. But we can be sure that in God's crucible we have the promise of a glorious, shining end. In Amma's words:

> One day we took the children to see a goldsmith refine gold after the ancient manner of the East. He was sitting beside his little charcoal-fire. (He shall sit as a refiner: the gold or silversmith never leaves his crucible once it is on the fire.) In that red glow lay a common curved roof-tile; another tile covered it like a lid. This was the crucible. In it was the medicine made of salt, tamarind fruit and burnt brick-dust, and embedded in it was the gold. The medicine does its appointed work on the gold, "then the fire eats it." And the goldsmith lifts the gold out with a pair of tongs, lets it cool, rubs it between his fingers, and if not satisfied puts it back again in fresh medicine. This time he blows the fire hotter than it was before, and each time he puts the gold in the crucible the heat of the fire is increased. "It could not bear it so hot at first, but it can bear it now; what would have destroyed it then helps it now." "How do you know when the gold is purified?" we asked him, and he answered, "When I can see

my face in it (the liquid and gold in the crucible) then it is pure."[36]

Thus, when our Refiner sees His own image in us, He has indeed brought us to ultimate and true wholeness! To me this was a comforting insight. The ocean uplifted once more. The fatigue even seemed to lift a bit as I rejoined my friends. In the back of my mind I could not quite forget Amma's poem, which summarized all of my feelings at that moment—and indeed, captures what this book is all about.

> *Before the winds that blow do cease,*
> *Teach me to dwell within Thy calm;*
> *Before the pain has passed in peace,*
> *Give me, my God, to sing a psalm.*
> *Let me not lose the chance to prove*
> *The fullness of enabling love,*
> *O Love of God, do this for me;*
> Maintain a constant victory.

> *Before I leave the desert land*
> *For meadows of immortal flowers,*
> *Lead me where streams at Thy command*
> *Flow by the borders of the hours,*
> *That when the thirsty come, I may*
> *Show them the fountains in the way.*
> O Love of God, do this for me:
> Maintain a constant victory.[37]

Dwight L. Moody (1837–1899)

Dwight L. Moody was born in Northfield, Massachusetts. He was a preacher and evangelist and a close friend of men like F. B. Meyer and Charles H. Spurgeon. After Spurgeon's death, in token of their closeness, his wife sent Moody a Bible of Spurgeon's, in which were inscribed the following words:

Dr. D. L. Moody, from Mrs. C. H. Spurgeon, in tender memory of the beloved one gone home to God. This Bible has been used by my precious husband, and is now given with unfeigned pleasure to one in whose hands its blessed service will be continued and extended.[1]

One of the most memorable incidents of his life occurred when Moody was attending a conference in Dublin and heard a man say: "The world has yet to see what God can do with a thoroughly consecrated man." Moody responded: "God helping me, I will be that man." Dwight L. Moody was never again quite the same.

Moody himself once penned a mini autobiography:

Some day you will read in the papers that D. L. Moody of East Northfield, is dead. Don't you believe a word of it! At that moment

I shall be more alive than I am now. I shall have gone up higher, that is all, gone out of this old clay tenement into a house that is immortal, a body that death cannot touch, that sin cannot taint, a body like unto His own glorious body. I was born of the flesh in 1837. I was born of the Spirit in 1855. That which is born of the flesh may die. That which is born of the Spirit will live forever.[2]

Charles Haddon Spurgeon

SIX

Charles Haddon Spurgeon:
Living With Depression

If I were a better Christian I wouldn't get so depressed!" is a common belief of twenty-first-century Christians who experience discouragement or deep disappointment. Such an attitude may be fostered by certain Christian literature that equates depression with a lack of faith. At times, well-intentioned friends urge those who are depressed to "claim God's promises and be happy."

"God is the only tranquilizer I need," claimed one listener when she telephoned in on a TV talk show on which I was a guest. This is by no means the first time I have heard this concept expressed. Apparently, "pray, and your problems will disappear" continues as a popular idea in certain Christian circles. Perhaps some forget that we Christians are human. Forgiven, yes, but still living within the boundaries of our humanity. We cannot be up, up, up all the time. Any view that denies this reality is neither Scriptural nor tenable. Nobody can live on a continuing emotional high, for life inevitably brings valleys as well as mountaintops.

God does not promise that our faith will free us from all discouragement and conflict, but He does promise that the peace and power of His Spirit will give us the kind of joy that enables us to weather any afflictions of the body, mind, and spirit. Amy Carmichael underscored this promise when she quoted H. W. Webb-Peploe's definition of Christian joy as that quiet, inner contentment that results from "perfect acquiescence in God's will."[1]

People in biblical times were certainly not always living on a spiritual high, nor did they attempt to use God as a giant tranquilizer to obliterate the feelings associated with their difficulties. Nor did they scoff at or condemn as unspiritual those who were hurting.

We in the twenty-first century too often consider suffering to be synonymous with defeat. If it is such, then the man who has been called "the Prince of Preachers," a man who lived with great depression and yet great joy in the Lord, must go down in the annals of history as a man of enormous failure. So too must Jesus Christ be judged for the "heaviness," the excruciating anguish of mind and spirit He suffered on the basis of His perfect submission to the will of God. To the contrary, within this total acquiescence in the will of God are to be found true joy and strength, even when that will means a Gethsemane (see Matthew 26:36–39).

We can increase our ability to recover from depression by learning from Charles Spurgeon that, though times of depression cannot necessarily be eradicated, they can be handled constructively.

"The strong are not always vigorous, the wise not always ready, the brave not always courageous, and the joyous not always happy."[2] Such words were not written today by a compromising pastor or psychologist. They were spoken in the nineteenth century by that prince of preachers, Charles Haddon Spurgeon.

In dealing with something as commonplace as money, Charles Spurgeon once wrote:

During a very serious illness, I had an unaccountable fit of anxiety about money matters. One of the brethren, after trying to comfort me, went straight home, and came back to me bringing all the stocks and shares and deeds and available funds he had, putting them down on the bed. "There, dear Pastor, I owe everything I have in the world to you, and you are quite welcome to all I possess." Of course I soon got better and returned it all to my dear friend.[3]

Such was the humanness of Spurgeon, for when it came to finances he was often plagued by this kind of anxiety, to which many of us can relate.

At the age of nineteen Spurgeon received a call to the New Park Street Chapel, one of the leading three (of the 113) Baptist churches of London. He was called because an influential Baptist deacon had said, "If you want to fill your empty pews, send for a young man I heard in Cambridge by the name of Spurgeon."[4] Called he was, and the pews filled up until lack of space became an increasing problem.

On October 19, 1856, crowds gathered in a new meeting place, which happened to be London's

"largest, most commodious and most beautiful building erected for public amusements, carnivals of wild beasts and wilder men." It accommodated ten to twelve thousand people. The news of this bold scheme ran through London like wildfire.

The crowd began gathering for the opening service, wild disorder, milling for seats; so that at evening service the hall was packed, and ten thousand more were outside." When Spurgeon saw it he was almost overwhelmed.

The service began, ran a few minutes, when suddenly a cry, "Fire! The galleries are giving away, the place is falling!" A terrible panic followed: seven were killed, many seriously injured. Spurgeon's grief over this almost unseated his reason. He was immediately hidden from the public, spent hours "in tears by day, and dreams of terror by night." A depression deepened upon him from which he never fully recovered.

But the disaster itself increased the crowds. Charles Haddon Spurgeon became a world figure overnight. On Sunday he was a local celebrity of South London, a "South of the Slot" hero; the next week he was a world figure. All London now wanted to hear him.[5]

During his lifetime of fifty-seven years Spurgeon published over 3,500 sermons in seventy-five distinct volumes. Writing was a drudgery to him; yet he authored 135 books and edited twenty-eight others; his output totaled more than 200, including albums and pamphlets. This from the man who felt that "writing is the work of a slave."[6]

The very last time Spurgeon preached in Metropolitan Tabernacle was the Lord's Day morning of June 7, 1891. He appeared a broken man, utterly weary in the Lord's work, but not of it; prematurely old, though but fifty-six, his hair white, anguish lines in his face, so enfeebled that he supported himself with his right hand on the back of a chair. His sermon subject was "The Statute of David for Sharing the Spoil," the text 1 Samuel 30:24, "As his share is that goeth down to the battle, so shall his share be that tarrieth by the baggage; they shall share alike." Throats were choked in the realization that the end was near. Yet the golden voice, gradually warmed and released by his glowing spirit, filled the Tabernacle with its mellow cadence.[7]

However, "Spurgeon, mighty as he was, could never have moved his generation as he did without the thousands who humbly upheld his hands. None knew this better than he. Once, whimsically, he told a story of a French farmer whose crops were so large that he was accused of magic. The man immediately brought forth his stalwart sons and said, 'Here is my magic!' "[8]

Spurgeon did not become great on his own. Nor was he a plastic saint. Rather, it is his combination of greatness, strength and humanness that has a refreshing appeal to the modern reader. Spurgeon was weak, yet strong; ill, yet triumphant. He endured emotional problems, but they only served to refine him into the purest of gold that bore the image of that great refiner of souls.

For Charles Haddon Spurgeon, builder of churches, preacher of preachers, can only make us stand in awe. But Charles Haddon Spurgeon, the man who suffered from terrible depression, feared financial disaster, experienced intense loneliness and spent weeks ill in bed, speaks to our present-day needs more deeply than do most of our contemporaries.

Said one of his biographers, Richard Day:

> There was one aspect of Spurgeon's life, glossed over by most of his biographers, that we must now view with utter frankness: he was frequently in the grip of terrific depression moods. This offers no difficulty whatever to any Christian who does sometimes himself walk the floor of hell, on and on, until he finds a Hand that brings him out. The sweetness of his release giveth him such radiant new love for his Redeemer, that he doth then find in his

head the tongue of the taught, enabling him to sustain with words any other that may be weary. The function of "word sustention" is the chief part of Christian ministry.[9]

Dr. J. H. Jowett, who suffered from painful neuritis, once said: "The world wants to be comforted. He [Spurgeon] knew that, and he knew wondrously well how it is done. The tongue of the taught belongs only to those who also are men of sorrows and acquainted with grief."[10]

During the days of his greatest preaching in the tabernacle, Spurgeon was often in despair, and he even thought of quitting, fearing that his illness kept him too often from the pulpit. Fortunately, the leaders of the church felt differently. They preferred Spurgeon, despite his frequent absences, to any other man, even one who could be in the pulpit every time the congregation assembled. And so Spurgeon stayed. Yet his swollen hands and tired body made him an old man while he was still young.

By means of these tragic hours Spurgeon's reliance was kept on God and not on himself. He finally came to the place where he was sure a great blessing was about to break when Depression stormed his soul: "Depression comes over me whenever the Lord is preparing a larger blessing for my ministry. It has now become to me a prophet in rough clothing. A John the Baptist, heralding the nearer coming of my Lord's richer benison."

Often enough he found that richer benison to be a deepened confidence in the sufficiency of grace.... Scarcely had he been pastor on New Park Street 12 months when Asiatic cholera swept like shellfire through the tenement section around the chapel. He gave every ounce of youthful ardor to visiting the sick and dying. But he watched his friends fall one by one, and a "little more work and weeping would have laid me low among the rest." Giant Despair had seized him. One day, returning from a funeral, ready to sink under the burden, his curiosity led him to read a paper wafered up in a shoemaker's window. In bold handwriting were these words: "Because thou hast made the Lord, which is my refuge, even the Most High, thy habitation, there shall no evil befall thee, neither shall any plague come nigh thy dwelling." He said: "The effect was immediate. I felt secure, refreshed, girt with immortality. I went on with my visitation of the dying in a calm and peaceful spirit."[11]

Many people I encounter feel that depression is a negative emotion of which they should feel ashamed and that it comes unbidden out of their own weakness. In contrast, Spurgeon took the pain of depression very seriously. At one point he declared: "The sharpest pangs we feel are not those of the body . . . but those of the mind."[12]

Furthermore, Spurgeon identified several down-to-earth causes for this unsettling emotion. Because of the painful depression that afflicted him throughout the major part of his life, he took the time to analyze its causes:

The times most favorable to fits of depression, I have experienced, may be summed up in a brief catalogue. First among them I mention the hour of great success. When at last a long-cherished desire is fulfilled, when God has been glorified greatly by our means, a great triumph achieved, then we are apt to faint . . . .

Before any great achievement, some measure of the same depression is very usual. Surveying the difficulties before us, our hearts sink within us . . . . This depression comes over me whenever the Lord is preparing a larger blessing for my ministry . . . .

In the midst of a long stretch of unbroken labor, the same affliction may be looked for. The bow cannot be always bent without fear of breaking. Repose is as needful to the mind as sleep to the body . . . .

This evil will also come upon us, we know not why, and then it is all the more difficult to drive it away. Causeless depression is not to be reasoned with . . . . If these who laugh at such melancholy did but feel the grief of it for one hour, their laughter would be sobered into compassion.[13]

Without question there can be any number of psychological, spiritual, or physical causes for emotional problems. Help in handling them is certainly found in a relationship with Jesus Christ, but the complete answer to complex emotional issues may not be spiritual at all. This realization will hopefully preclude many from feeling guilt over such problems. And recognition of this fact may prevent some from the sin of self-righteously judging others.

Charles Spurgeon lived in nineteenth-century England, during the Victorian Age, a time when the body and the mind were seen as interrelated. Problems like depression were considered to be at least partially physical in origin, and thus they were not stigmatized. Spurgeon could get up in his pulpit on Sunday mornings and declare "I am down today" and there was no negative reaction, no "spiritualized" criticism.

With the appearance of Freud and his preoccupation with sexual dysfunction as the underlying factor in emotional problems, the tolerance left. Freud and psychotherapy in general became more stigmatized. Christian thinking was affected in particular, so that until well into the sixties or seventies and beyond of the twentieth century, emotional problems, such as depression or anxiety, were not only very stigmatized but also over-spiritualized, with the result that a "confess your depression" mentality emerged.

Added to the Christian's concern was the Scopes trial in the mid 1920s. In the battle over whether or not evolution should be taught in the public schools, even though the case to teach it was defeated, William Jennings Bryan, the brilliant defender of the Bible, was made to look anti-intellectual during the cross-examination. Furthermore, because the trial was broadcast by radio the influence was profound. "The new religion in America was now 'modernism,' and 'fundamentalism' was its ardent foe. Modernism drew life from the universities and cities; fundamentalism from revivals and radio."[14]

In his description of fundamentalism theologian Dr. Vernon Grounds wrote:

> A fundamentalist ... holds tenaciously to doctrines like the plenary inspiration of the Bible, the virgin birth of Jesus Christ, His substitutionary atonement, His bodily resurrection and His literal return. And, hence, of course, we are fundamentalists theologically. But very frankly some of us do not like to be tagged fundamentalists. For fundamentalism in many quarters has degenerated into a quarrelsome bickering over incidentals: indeed, it is incidentalism rather than fundamentalism. In many quarters, moreover, fundamentalism displays an unhappy ability to forget certain fundamentals which it finds troublesome.

Take, for example, the duty of neighbor-love. That it is a fundamental of Christianity cannot successfully be disputed. Our Lord seizes upon that seemingly peripheral duty mentioned in Leviticus 19:18 and in Matthew 22:37-40, He exalts it into a life-embracing, world-girdling, age-spanning principle, a supreme fundamental. In reply to the question, "Master, which is the great commandment in the law?" He says: "Thou shalt love the Lord thy God with all thy heart, and with all thy soul, and with all thy mind. This is the first and great commandment. And the second is like unto it, Thou shalt love thy neighbor as thyself."

Neighbor love is not something trivial. It is the fruit which springs from the root of unfeigned Christian faith. Yet, strangely enough, this supreme fundamental has been grossly ignored. And perhaps that neglect explains to a large degree why fundamentalism has in many quarters degenerated into a legalistic Phariseeism: hard, frigid, ineffective, unethical and loveless.[15]

In the biography of Dr. Grounds by Bruce L. Shelley, there are two telling passages which show the development of the evangelical movement within, and as a result of, the fundamentalist movement:

Since early in the century many fundamentalist believers had turned their backs on the major denominations, justifying the move by arguing that this was a clear mandate of Holy Scripture—a strict doctrine of "separation from unbelief." These separatists loved to quote "Come out from among them, and be ye separate," and they extended this doctrine to American society generally, including schools of higher learning. But some of the children of these fundamentalists had begun to question the extremes to which their parents had gone. Their questions generated restlessness, and restlessness soon gave birth to an inspiring dream of turning America back to God.

Then came young evangelist William Franklin Graham's great Los Angeles Crusade in 1948, followed by the Boston Crusade and the Carolina Crusade. Almost overnight "Billy" Graham became a household name, and many Christians began to ask, "Isn't it time for a return to the vibrant evangelical Christianity that shaped the nation before World War I and the Scopes trial? Isn't it time to return to an evangelical Christianity marked by academic excellence and a social conscience?"

The vast majority of those from traditional fundamentalism who were now rallying in support of Billy Graham had no serious objection to the original doctrines of fundamentalism. But they felt that the movement had veered sharply from its original course and stumbled into a mire of cranky pessimism. . . .

Most of the young critics acknowledged that early fundamentalism had tried valiantly to guard revealed truth from the deadly grasp of modernistic unbelief. But as society changed, many fundamentalists failed to apply that Christian message to the social and intellectual life of twentieth-century America.[16]

Similar in thought are words written by Os Guinness a number of years ago:

On one side of the church we have the pull of a misguided liberalism which dissipates the truth and on the
other side the pull of an equally misguided conservatism
which stifles it. The one reduces theology to the Christian's "way of looking at things," makes evangelism just an
open-ended dialogue and articulates faith in a way which
previous generations would have seen as a denial of the
faith, in need of an answer itself. The other, instinctively
realizing the danger, swiftly retreats in a reflex movement
of social and theological withdrawal, but all that it does
from then on is marked by a deepening social and intellectual insecurity. One leads to an alienated theology and
the other to an alienated lifestyle.[17]

Adding the legalism of fundamentalism to the sometimes
realistic objections to Freud, his followers, and other forms of
secular psychotherapy, for the Christian the whole idea of psychotherapy became anathema. For those whose emotional problems were not solved by spiritual means, the only two available
answers were to try to deny that the problems existed or to go
against the accepted way and seek help on a purely secular level.
To do the latter, however, was to bring on ostracism from other
Christians and to hope that in some way your faith in God could
still be maintained. It was a risk and generated much guilt.

Perhaps if emotional pain had not been automatically relegated to the category of sin, just the support and the love of other
Christians would have gone far toward solving such problems as
anxiety and depression. As Spurgeon stated in a sermon: "Grief
of mind is harder to bear than pain of body."[18] That kind of understanding from a pastor or friend can be of great help in alleviat-
ing emotional pain.

In a sermon to the clergy preached on Friday morning, April 13, 1877, Spurgeon spoke eloquently about the place of love in ministry. "Love is the chief endowment for a pastor. . . . Experience testifies that we never gain a particle of power for good over our people by angry words, but we obtain an almost absolute power over them by all-enduring love; indeed, the only power which it is desirable for us to have must come in that way."

With humility he added, "I have had the high pleasure of loving some of the most objectionable people till they loved me; and some of the most bitter I have altogether won by refusing to be displeased, and by persisting in believing that they could be better. By practical kindnesses I have so won some men that I believe it would take a martyrdom to make them speak evil of me. This has also been the experience of all who have tried the sacred power of love."

Spurgeon concluded, "My brethren, learn the art of loving men to Christ. We are drawn towards those who love us; and when the most callous feel 'that man loves us,' they are drawn to you at once; and as you are nearer to the Saviour than they are, you are drawing them in the right direction. . . . Love, then, I take to be the chief endowment of the pastor. . . ."[19]

In contrast to such understanding, for some the resistance to psychological treatment has extended to forbidding the use of medication. A young woman with serious problems, who was on antidepressant medication, came to see me. She had been told earlier by a friend in her church that taking such medication was sinful. She was instructed to read her Bible more and pray. The result? Psychiatric hospitalization which might otherwise have been unnecessary.

Godly balance involves treatment on various levels. For example, people may seek psychological help as an adjunct when their need is primarily spiritual. Almost always spiritual counsel can be an aid even when the need is primarily physical or psychological. The three blend, and most of us are aware of our needs in all these areas.

One busy Saturday when I was booked solid in my counseling office I came out to my waiting room to find a very distraught man whom I had never met. When he literally begged for even a few minutes of my time I offered my lunch period. After a few minutes his immediate need was apparent. He and his family had been deeply involved in a cult, yet he was definitely a believer in Jesus Christ. In leaving the cult, he feared that he was sinning. He had spent this particular Saturday morning in Bible bookstores trying in vain to find a book that could help him. In the brief time we had we forgot psychology and went through various Bible passages. In a short time he was visibly relieved. After a few more scheduled sessions he and his wife came in and talked about how they could avoid such a situation in the future. But until the last few visits, out of under ten sessions, the focus had been biblical rather than psychological. Body, mind, spirit—none of these can be ignored.

The 1960s were a period of "letting it all hang out," self expression, and ultimately "me-ism." Unfortunately, the freedom of self expression was marred by indifference to old-fashioned concepts of faith and morality. Self worship became the fashion rather than self acceptance. The "self," the individual identity stamped into us by God Almighty, was confused with the "self," the "old sin nature," of Romans 6.

But one positive development in the sixties was that the stigmatization of problems like depression was beginning to diminish. This emboldened some even in the Christian world and many in the secular world to offer alternatives within the scope of psychotherapy—i.e., Reality Therapy and Logotherapy along with the ideas of people like Dr. Paul Tournier. Theologically, many of us began to be rather precise in calling ourselves evangelicals rather than fundamentalists. Like the original fundamentalists we too staunchly defended biblical truth. But many of us lamented the harshness and lack of love which exists in fundamentalist circles. We found such unlove incompatible with John 13:34–35: "A new commandment I give unto you, That ye love one another; as I have loved you, that ye also love one another. By this shall all men know that ye are my disciples, if ye have love one to another."

As we have come into the twenty-first century we are beginning to resemble the Victorian Age more closely in our attitudes toward emotional problems. Spurgeon once said: "What strange creatures we are! I suppose every man is a trinity, certainly every Christian man is,—spirit, soul, and body,—and we may be in three states at once, and we may not know which of the three is our real state. The whole three may be so mixed up that we become a puzzle to ourselves."[20] Now again body, mind, and spirit are seen as closely related.

The idea that we are a composite of body, mind, and spirit finds its roots in early biblical times. "The Bible says, 'A cheerful heart does good like medicine' (Proverbs 17:22), implying a relationship between the body and the mind. In Proverbs 15:30 we read, 'Pleasant sights and good reports give happiness and health.' 'Hope deferred makes the heart sick' (Proverbs 13:12). 'Reverence for God gives a man deep strength' (Proverbs 14:26)."[21]

In an interesting development of the same idea, speaking of the difference between the soul and the Spirit, Bible commentator W. E. Vine writes on Hebrews 4:12 that the word of God "divides between those emotions which belong to the realm of the soul, that part of our being which is natural and influences, or is influenced by, our fellow-men, and those of the spirit, that part of our being which, if possessed of life, is able to hold communion with God."[22]

All of this connects with the body, mind, spirit idea. And all of this denies that all emotional problems automatically have a sin connection.

Medical science reinforces this view. Genetic research relates certain emotional maladies to inheritance. And current studies suggest that biochemical changes in the brain may be connected to certain forms of depression. It is obvious that body, mind, and spirit are definitely related, both in causing symptoms and in their cure. Charles Spurgeon would, I believe, be comfortable with this as long as we always remained true to Scriptural principles. Even Freud, with whom many of us fundamentally disagree, would be less concerned than many of his followers today. Almost prophetically, Freud once wrote in his book, *An Outline of Psychoanalysis:*

> The future may teach us to exercise a direct influence, by means of particular chemical substances, upon the amounts of energy and their distribution in the apparatus of the mind. It may be that there are other undreamed-of possibilities of therapy. But for the moment we have nothing better at our disposal than the techniques of psychoanalysis, and for that reason, in spite of its limitations, it is not to be despised.

In later years Freud would elaborate:

> I am firmly convinced that one day all these disturbances we are trying to understand will be treated by means of hormones or similar substances.[23]

Therapy as practiced by the Christian therapist must not contradict biblical principles but must be careful also not to impose that thinking on a client. Some who come for therapy are not Christians but want help with a variety of problems. For these we are therapists who happen to be Christians. If the client wants to know how God fits into the picture we are free to share our faith with them.

I once saw a woman who started out our sessions by telling me how much she hated Christians. As I worked with her on some of her problems I felt very strongly that I should not try to cross into the spiritual area even when I thought it would help. With a deep sense of Godly restraint, I remained silent even though on a human level I felt guilty. One day the conversation quite logically flowed into the spiritual through a discussion about some relatives whom she disliked. This was God's timing. Then once again we focused back on the psychological nature of her problems.

A few weeks later it was Christmas. Right before the holidays she gave me a tiny framed Madonna and child picture with the words: "I just wanted you to know that I've become a Christian." It was an awesome reminder that above all the Holy Spirit is still at work as He dwells within us and we should be careful to allow Him to do His work in His timing.

Even in dealing with Christians, while we are more free to point out biblical values and truths, we have an obligation both from God and our professional ethics to care and help even when fellow Christians are going against their own faith. Our reputation for "shooting our wounded" is not a flattering one.

At the same time, as Christian therapists we must not lose sight of this truth:

"While [psychotherapy] may indeed be healing and lib-
erating, it cannot penetrate to the bottom of the frustration and failure people experience in their relations with
others if it ignores the one all-determinative interper-
sonal relationship—that between God and man. This
concept of the human predicament differs radically from
the psychotherapist's. Assume that in self-love ... man
chooses to make himself the center of things, shouldering
God aside .... Assume, consequently, a malignant relationship between the creature and his Creator .... Then
what? In this predicament a therapy far more radical than
psychotherapy is required. What man needs is something
that only God's forgiving grace can provide: the therapy
of divine love."

The major components of this therapy, according to
Dr. Grounds, are the atonement made by Jesus Christ
and the ministry of the Holy Spirit. The gospel
announces that in the miracle of the atonement "God
died *for* man and *with* man in order that he and man,
dying 'jointly to an old life,' might 'jointly rise to a "new
one."' In the Cross man beholds the consummate evidence of love. This revelation of sin-bearing love breaks
the bondage of self-love and sets man free to live according to the law of love."

In this process of redemption, this metamorphosis of
self-love, there is another "mind-staggering aspect of the
Gospel. The indwelling Spirit of God, who is the Spirit of
Jesus Christ, comes to fill the love-conquered heart with
the love of God, changing the personality more and more
into the likeness of incarnate Love.

"God, the moving Spirit of the universe, is an aggres-
sive lover who by the miracles of incarnation, atonement,

and resurrection, together with the powerful operation of the Holy Spirit, cracks through the sinner's imprisoning egocentricity and elicits love . . . . The vision of Calvary, where Love died, is brought home to the conscience with ego-penetrating power by the Holy Spirit, winning the response that produces love for God and man."[24]

As a therapist I was once confronted with an unusual situation that required the integration of spiritual and psychological help. A man and his "wife" who had recently come from another country where multiple wives were allowed sought my help in straightening out their tangled relationships. The man and his wife were new Christians with a young baby. The problem was that the man had another wife and child whom he supported and who lived in his home country. The question? Who was his wife? In this situation I referred them to a pastor who had some theological depth, while I worked with them on a more psychological level.

Many who seek our help as counselors have problems which are not related to sin. Some who call themselves "biblical counselors," for which there is now a special degree given, relegate emotional problems to "sin" and the cure to "repentance." If sin is not the cause then harm is done rather than help being given. The writings of Charles Spurgeon are one of the greatest sources of enlightenment on that issue.

Equally important to the cause of depression or any other emotional pain is its meaning, how and why it became part of our life. Is it a totally destructive, even sinful, emotion? Or is it really a God-allowed instrument of growth and effectiveness?

Frequently in his sermons and well-known expositions of the psalms, Spurgeon spent time explaining the meaning of depression. He had found assistance in handling his own depression by understanding its meaning. Here we have no phony explanation issued from the pen of the unscathed. Rather, we see the pain of one of God's greatest saints made meaningful:

> If it be inquired why the valley of the shadow of death must so often be traversed by the servants of King Jesus, the answer is not far to find. All this is promotive of the Lord's mode of working, which is summed up in these words: "Not by might nor by power, but by my Spirit, saith the Lord." Instruments shall be used, but their intrinsic weakness shall be clearly manifested: there shall be no division of the glory, no diminishing the honor due to the Great Worker . . . to hide pride from the worker is the great difficulty. Uninterrupted success and unfading joy in it would be more than our weak heads could bear. Our wine must needs be mixed with water, lest it turn our brains. My witness is, that those who are honored by their Lord in public, have usually to endure a secret chastening, or to carry a peculiar cross, lest by any means they exalt themselves, and fall into the snare of the devil . . . .
>
> By all the castings down of His servants God is glorified, for they are led to magnify Him when again He sees them on their feet, and even while prostrate in the dust their faith yields Him praise. They speak all the more sweetly of His faithfulness, and are the more firmly established in His love . . . . Glory be to God for the furnace, the hammer, and the fire. Heaven shall be all the fuller of bliss because we have been filled with anguish here and below, and earth shall be better tilled because of our training in the school of adversity.[25]

God never wastes His children's suffering. Repeatedly, I have seen persons who can bear their burdens no longer, released from the mental anguish of depression and restored to normalcy at just the "right moment" in God's timetable.

Spurgeon also affirmed this principle:

> To the tearful eye of the sufferer the Lord seemed to stand still, as if He calmly looked on, and did not sympathize with His afflicted one. Nay, more, the Lord appeared to be afar off, no longer "a very present help in trouble," but an inaccessible mountain, into which no man would be able to climb. The presence of God is the joy of His people but any suspicion of His absence is distracting beyond measure. Let us, then, remember that the Lord is nigh us. The refiner is never far from the mouth of the furnace when the gold is in that fire, and the Son of God is always walking in the midst of the flames when His holy children are cast into them. Yet He that knows the frailty of man will little wonder that when we are sharply exercised, we find it hard to bear the apparent neglect of the Lord when He forbears to work our deliverance .... It is not the trouble, but the hiding of our Father's face, which cuts us to the quick .... If we need an answer to the question, "Why hidest thou thyself?" it is to be found in the fact that there's a "needs-be," not only for trial, but for heaviness of heart under trial (1 Peter 1:6). For it is only felt affliction which can become blest affliction. If we are carried in the arms of God over every stream, where would be the trial and where the experience, which trouble is meant to teach us?[26]

This concept is antithetical to certain present-day Christian teaching, which presents depression and pain as sin and a sign of God's punishment. In contrast, sometimes God can trust only His greatest saints to suffer and yet praise Him.

Consistent with this way of thinking, Spurgeon shed further positive light on the significance of suffering for those beset by great trials:

> The Lord frequently appears to save His heaviest blows for His best-loved ones; if any one affliction be more painful than another it falls to the lot of those whom He most distinguishes in His service. The Gardener prunes His best roses with most care. [Discipline] is sent to keep successful saints humble, to make them tender towards others, and to enable them to bear the high honors which their heavenly Friend puts upon them. "But He hath not given me over unto death." This verse ... concludes with a blessed "but," which constitutes a saving clause ... There is always a merciful limit to the [disciplining] of the sons of God. Forty stripes save one were all that an Israelite might receive, and the Lord will never allow that one, that killing stroke, to fall upon his children. They are "[disciplined], but not killed."
>
> Even from our griefs we may distill consolation and gather sweet flowers from the garden in which the Lord has planted salutary rue and wormwood .... The hero, restored to health, and rescued from the dangers of battle now lifts up his own song unto the Lord, and asks all Israel, led on by the goodly fellowship of priests, to assist him in chanting a joyful Te Deum.[27]

Exchanging the word "heaviness" for "depression," Spurgeon continued his thoughts on its meaning:

> If the Christian did not sometimes suffer heaviness he would begin to grow too proud, and think too much of himself, and become too great in his own esteem. Those of us who are of elastic spirit, and who in our health are full of everything that can make life happy, are too apt to forget that all of our own springs must be in Him . . . .
>
> Another reason for this discipline is, I think, that in heaviness we often learn lessons that we never could attain elsewhere. Do you know that God has beauties for every part of the world; and He has beauties for every place of experience? There are views to be seen from the tops of the Alps that you can never see elsewhere. Ay, but there are beauties to be seen in the depths of the dell that ye could never see on the tops of the mountains; there are glories to be seen on Pisgah, wondrous sights to be beheld when by faith we stand on Tabor; but there are also beauties to be seen in our Gethsemanes, and some marvelously sweet flowers to be culled by the edge of the dens of the leopards. Men will never become great in divinity until they become great in suffering. "Ah!" said Luther, "affliction is the best book in my library," and let me add, the best leaf in the book of affliction is that blackest of all the leaves, the leaf called heaviness, when the spirit sinks within us, and we cannot endure as we could wish.
>
> And yet again; this heaviness is of essential use to a Christian, if he would do good to others. Ah! There are a great many Christian people that I was going to say I should like to see afflicted—but I will not say so much as that; I should like to see them heavy in spirit; if it were

the Lord's will that they should be bowed down greatly, I would not express a word of regret; for a little more . . . power to sympathize would be a precious boon to them, and even if it were purchased by a short journey through a burning, fiery furnace, they might not rue the day afterwards in which they had been called to pass through the flame. There are none so tender as those who have been skinned themselves. Those who have been in the chamber of affliction know how to comfort those who are there. Do not believe that any man will become a physician unless he walks the hospitals, and I am sure that no one will become a divine, or become a comforter, unless he lies in the hospital as well as walks through it and has to suffer himself. God cannot make ministers—and I speak with reverence of His Holy Name—He cannot make a Barnabas except in the fire. It is there, and there alone, that He can make His sons of consolation; He may make His sons of thunder anywhere; but His sons of consolation He must make in the fire, and there alone. Who shall speak to those whose hearts have been broken also, and whose wounds have long run with the sore of grief? "If need be," then, "ye are in heaviness through manifold temptations."[28]

How easily we equate happiness with success and well-being. Even as Christians we often deceive ourselves into believing that we are obligated to achieve perpetual happiness. We even assume, at times, that because we are Christians happiness is owed to us as some kind of earned reward. The Bible does not teach such a principle; rather it promises a deep spiritual contentment that may exist even in the depths of suffering. Charles Spurgeon knew that spiritual growth and greatness are often mixed with pain—in his case, the pain of periodic and intense depression.

> Our work, when earnestly undertaken, lays us open to attacks in the direction of depression. Who can bear the weight of souls without sinking to the dust? Passionate longings after men's conversion, if not fully satisfied (and when are they?) consume the soul with anxiety and disappointment. To see the hopeful turn aside, the godly grow cold, professors abusing their privileges, and sinners waxing more bold in sin—are not these sights enough to crush us to the earth?... How can we be otherwise than sorrowful, while men believe not our report, and the divine arm is not revealed? All mental work tends to weary and to depress, for much study is a weariness of the flesh—but ours is more than mental work—it is heart work, the labour of our inmost soul.... Such soul-travail as that of a faithful minister will bring on occasional seasons of exhaustion, when heart and flesh will fail. Moses' hands grew heavy in intercession, and Paul cried out, "Who is sufficient for these things?" Even John the Baptist is thought to have had his fainting fits, and the apostles were once amazed, and were sore afraid.[29]

Sometimes depression can be cured or even avoided. Spurgeon could be intensely practical when speaking of recovery and prevention. As he stated when recounting the causes for depression, Spurgeon cited an unnecessary form of depression arising from too much study and too little exercise. As the author of more than 200 works and the preacher of hundreds of sermons, Spurgeon experienced depression as a continuing problem: "I confess that I frequently sit hour after hour praying and waiting for a subject, and that is the main part of my study. Almost every Sunday of my life I prepare enough outlines of sermons to last me for a month."[30]

To Charles Haddon Spurgeon the most solemn place in the world was the pulpit. And he went into it week after week obviously depending upon the Holy Spirit. Such mental and spiritual intensity took its toll.

There can be little doubt that sedentary habits have a tendency to create despondency in some constitutions. Burton, in his *Anatomy of Melancholy*, has a chapter upon this cause of sadness; and quoting from one of the myriad authors whom he lays under contribution, he says:

> Students are negligent of their bodies. Other men look to their tools: a painter will wash his pencils; a smith will look to his hammer, anvil, forge; a husbandman will mend his plough-irons, and grind his hatchet if it be dull; a falconer or huntsman will have an especial care of his hawks, hounds, horses, dogs, etc.; a musician will string and unstring his lute; only scholars neglect that instrument (their brain and spirits, I mean) which they daily use.

> To sit long in one posture, poring over a book, or driving a quill, is in itself a taxing of nature; but add to this a badly ventilated chamber, a body which has long been without muscular exercise, and a heart burdened with many cares, and we have all the elements for preparing a seething cauldron of despair, especially in the dim months of fog—

> *When a blanket wraps the day,*
> *When the rotten woodland drips,*
> *And the leaf is stamped in clay.*

Let a man be naturally as blithe as a bird, he will hardly be able to bear up year after year against such a suicidal process; he will make his study a prison and his books the warders of a gaol, while nature lies outside his window calling him to health and beckoning him to joy. He who forgets the humming of the bees among the heather, the cooing of the wood pigeons in the forest, the song of birds in the woods, the rippling of rills among the rushes, and the sighing of the wind among the pines, need not wonder if his heart forgets to sing and his soul grows heavy. A day's breathing of fresh air upon the hills, or a few hours' ramble in the beechwood's umbrageous calm, would sweep the cobwebs out of the brain of scores of our toiling ministers who are now but half alive. A mouthful of sea air, or a stiff walk in the wind's face, would not give grace to the soul, but it would yield oxygen to the body, which is the next best.

> *"Heaviest the heart is in a heavy air,*
> *Ev'ry wind that rises blows away despair."*

"The ferns and rabbits, the streams and the trout, the fir trees and the squirrels, the primroses and the violets, the farmyard, the new-mown hay, and the fragrant hops—these are the best medicines for hypochondriacs, the surest tonics for the declining, the best refreshments for the weary." For lack of opportunity, or inclination, these great remedies are neglected, and the student becomes a self-immolated victim.[31]

Much of our fatigue and depression result from our refusal to avail ourselves of opportunities for small breaks and short vacations.

One weekend I escaped from the demands of patients to my favorite ocean cottage, which has no telephones. I walked on the wet sand and thought about God's timelessness as I watched the waves crash against the rocks. By Monday I was refreshed and ready to go back to work because I had taken time away. Never should we underestimate the value of even short breaks.

Ahead of his time, Spurgeon was sensitive to the needs of the body as they relate to those of the mind. He had discovered the value of rest and recreation in averting and ameliorating depression. Referring to Jesus' response to His weary disciples—"Let us go into the desert and rest awhile" (Mark 6:31)—Spurgeon commented:

> What? When the people are fainting? When they are like sheep without a shepherd? How can Jesus talk of rest? When the scribes and Pharisees, like wolves, are rending the flock, how can He take His followers on an excursion into a quiet resting place?... The Lord Jesus Christ knows better. He will not exhaust the strength of His servants prematurely and quench the light of Israel. Rest time is not waste. It is economy to gather fresh strength. Look at the mower in the summer's day, with so much to cut down ere the sun sets. He pauses in his labour—is he a sluggard? He looks for his stone, and begins to draw it up and down the scythe, with rink-a-tink, rink-a-tink. Is that idle music—is he now wasting precious moments? How much might he have mowed while he has been ringing out those notes on his scythe! But he is sharpening his tool, and he will do far more when once again he gives his strength to those sweeps which lay the grass prostrate in rows before him. Nor can the fisherman be always fishing;

he must mend his nets. So even our vacation can be one
of the duties laid upon us by the kingdom of God.[32]

In our work-oriented society, some of us are geared toward
feeling a sense of guilt regarding rest and recreation. Though we
appear to place a premium on leisure time, many of us are prone
to combining vacations with business trips, or we spend days off
worrying about business or financial problems. In light of this
tendency, Spurgeon's point is profoundly significant: A vacation
is a duty God requires of us!

As we have seen earlier, it is inaccurate to speak of depression
as a problem arising from only one source. Each of us is a composite of body, mind, and spirit, and problems in any of these areas
of our personhood can cause depression. I sometimes deal with
patients who have emotional problems arising from physical
causes. Many of these patients tend to have difficulty believing
that their emotional negativism and hopelessness can be the
result of physical malfunction.

Spurgeon was far ahead of his time in perceiving this important relationship between emotions and the body. Perhaps this
was due in part to his own chronic physical ailments, one of
which was gout, which is now known to be a painful form of
arthritis arising from an overabundance of uric acid in the system.
For this and other ailments treatment in Spurgeon's day was minimal. Pain medication was in its infancy and anti-inflammatory
drugs were non-existent. In his physical weakness and pain, he
often slumped into the depths of despair. For that reason Spurgeon understood better than most people today the relationship
between his emotions and his body.

Most of us are in some way or other unsound physically. Here and there we meet with an old man who could

not remember that ever he was laid aside for a day; but the great mass of us labour under some form or other of infirmity, either in body or mind .... As to mental maladies, is any man altogether sane? Are we not all a little off the balance? Some minds appear to have a gloomy tinge essential to their very individuality; of them it may be said, "'Melancholy marked them for her own"—fine minds withal, and ruled by noblest principles, but yet most prone to forget the silver lining, and to remember only the cloud .... These infirmities may be no detriment to a man's career of special usefulness; they may even have been imposed upon him by divine wisdom as necessary qualifications for his peculiar course of service. Some plants owe their medicinal qualities to the marsh in which they grow, others to the shades in which alone they flourish. These are precious fruits put forth by the moon as well as by the sun. Boats need ballast as well as sail; a drag on the carriage wheel is no hindrance when the road runs downhill. Pain has, probably, in some cases developed genius, hunting out the soul which otherwise might have slept like a lion in its den. Had it not been for the broken wing, some might have lost themselves in the clouds, some even of these choice doves who now bear the olive branch in their mouths and show the way to the ark. But where in body and mind there are predisposing causes to lowness of spirit it is no marvel if in dark moments the heart succumbs to them; the wonder in many cases is—and if inner lives could be written, men would see it so—how some ... keep at their work at all, and still wear a smile upon their countenances .... "Blessed are they that mourn," said the Man of Sorrows, and let none account themselves otherwise when their tears are salted with grace. "We have the treasure of the gospel in earthen vessels, and if there be a flaw in the vessel here and there, let none wonder."[33]

Many patients tell me how they have been able to help others. Sometimes the best antidote for depression is the empathic understanding another person can offer. Spurgeon through his own pain discussed compassion as an outgrowth of depression:

How low the spirits of good and brave men will sometimes sink. Under the influence of certain disorders everything will wear a somber aspect, and the heart will dive into the profoundest days of misery. It is all very very well for those who are in robust health and full of spirits to blame those whose lives are [covered over] with melancholy, but the [pain] is as real as a gaping wound, and all the more hard to bear because it lies so much in the region of the soul that to the inexperienced it appears to be a mere matter of fancy and imagination. Reader, never ridicule the nervous and hypochondriacal, their pain is real—it is not imaginary . . . . The mind can descend far lower than the body . . . flesh can bear only a certain number of wounds and no more, but the soul can bleed in ten thousand ways and die over and over again each hour. It is grievous to the good man to see the Lord whom he loves laying him in the sepulchre of desponding . . . yet if faith could but be allowed to speak she would remind the depressed saint that it is better to fall into the hand of the Lord than into the hands of men, and moreover she would tell the despondent heart that God never placed Joseph in a pit without drawing him up again to fill a throne . . . . Alas, when under deep depression the mind forgets all this and is only conscious of its unutterable misery.... It is an unspeakable consolation that our Lord Jesus knows this experience, right well, having with the exception of the sin of it, felt it all and more than all in Gethsemane when He was exceedingly sorrowful even unto death.[34]

By sharing his pain, Spurgeon was able to help others. Even in the pulpit, to a large congregation he once said, "I would go into the deeps a hundred times to cheer a downcast spirit. It is good for me to have been afflicted, that I might know how to speak a word in season to one that is weary."[35]

That such was true in Spurgeon's life was demonstrated in a letter he received after a severe down period. Here is a testimonial to Spurgeon's ability to comfort others with the same comfort by which he had been comforted. From Montreal came this rewarding letter:

> Oh, Mr. Spurgeon, that little word of yours, "I am feeling low," struck a chord which still vibrates in my spirit. It was to me like reading the Forty-second Psalm. I imagine there is nothing in your ministry to the saints that comes home more tenderly to tried and stricken souls than just what you there express, "I am feeling low." The great preacher, the author of *The Treasury of David*, this man sometimes, aye, often, "feels low" just as they do. In all their affliction he was afflicted—this is what draws hearts to Jesus; and the principle is just the same when the friends and intimates of Jesus "feel low." The fellow feeling, thus begotten, makes many wondrous kind.
>
> Your friend in Jesus,
> John Louson[36]

At another time Spurgeon stated in a sermon:

> I often feel very grateful to God that I have under-
> gone fearful depression of spirits. I know the borders of
> despair, and the horrible brink of that gulf of darkness
> into which my feet have almost gone; but hundreds of
> times I have been able to give a helpful grip to brethren
> and sisters who have come into that same condition,
> which grip I could never have given if I had not known
> their deep despondency. So I believe that the darkest and
> most dreadful experience of a child of God will help him
> to be a fisher of men if he will but follow Christ. Keep
> close to your Lord and he will make every step a blessing
> to you.[37]

Believers may find themselves vulnerable to criticism from
Christians and non-Christians alike when enduring periods of
depression. Charles Spurgeon was certainly no exception. He was
sometimes criticized for his vulnerability to this condition. But
without the compassion Spurgeon demonstrated in his own affliction, countless others suffering like him would not have been
comforted.

Rather than withering under the pressure of depression or
groveling in guilt over his supposed weakness or sin, Spurgeon
proclaimed the relationship between anguish and prayer.

Spurgeon wrote:

> When our prayers are lowly . . . by reason of our
> despondency, the Lord will bow down to them, the infi-
> nitely exalted Jehovah will have respect unto them.
> Faith, when she has the loftiest name of God on her
> tongue . . . dares to ask from Him the most tender and

condescending acts of love. Great as He is, He loves His children to be bold with Him. Our distress is a forcible reason for our being heard by the Lord God, merciful, and gracious, for misery is ever the master argument with mercy.[38]

God never fails to hear our prayers. Indeed, the God who numbers the hairs on our heads (Matthew 10:30) and preserves our tears in His bottle (Psalm 56:8) cannot fail to be concerned with our pain. But the fact that He hears our prayers does not mean that He will always give us what we want when we want it.

Again Spurgeon emphasized the importance of prayer as a weapon against depression in his famous work on the psalms. Quoting from Psalm 102:23 and 24—"He weakened my strength in the way; he shortened my days. I said, O my God, take me not away in the midst of my days"—Spurgeon commented on the psalmist's feelings and his ensuing prayer. The psalmist

> pours out his personal complaint. His sorrow had cast down his spirit, and even caused weakness in his bodily frame—and [he] was ready to lie down and die. . . . He [gave] himself to prayer. What better remedy is there for depression? Good men should not dread death, but they are not forbidden to love life; for many reasons the man who has the best hope of heaven, may nevertheless think it desirable to continue here a little longer, for the sake of his family, his work, the church of God and even the glory of God itself. [They say], do not swirl me away like Elijah in a chariot of fire, for as yet I have only seen half my days, and that a sorrowful half; give me to live till the flustering morning shall have softened into a bright afternoon of happier existence.[39]

Too often we forget that Jesus Christ is God become man and that He was subject to all the emotions that normal human beings feel. In a sermon preached at the Music Hall in Royal Surrey Gardens on November 7, 1858, Spurgeon drew upon the reality of Jesus the man, uniquely presenting depression as "being in heaviness," as our Lord was at certain times in His earthly life:

> It is a rule of the kingdom that all members must be like the head. They are to be like the head in that day when He shall appear. "We shall be like Him, for we shall see Him as He is." But we must be like the head also in His humiliation, or else we cannot be like Him in His glory. Now you will observe that our Lord and Savior Jesus Christ very often passed through much of trouble, without any heaviness. When He said, "Foxes have holes, and the birds of the air have nests, but the Son of Man hath not where to lay His head," I observe no heaviness. I do not think He sighed over that. And when athirst He sat upon the well, and said, "Give me to drink," there was no heaviness in all His thirst. I believe that through the first years of His ministry, although He might have suffered some heaviness, He usually passed over His troubles like a ship floating over the waves of the sea. But you will remember that at last the waves of swelling grief came into the vessel; at last the Savior Himself, though full of patience, was obliged to say, "My soul is exceeding sorrowful, even unto death;" and one of the evangelists tells us that the Savior "began to be very heavy." What means that, but that His spirits began to sink? There is more terrible meaning yet . . . the surface meaning of it is that all His spirits sank with Him. He had no longer His wonted

courage, and though He had strength to say, "Neverthe-less, not my will, but thine be done," still the weakness did not prevail, when He said, "If it be possible let this cup pass from me." The Savior passed through the brook, but He "drank of the brook by the way;" and we who pass through the brook of suffering must drink of it too. He had to bear the burden, not with His shoulders omnipo-tent, but with shoulders that were bending to the earth beneath a load. And you and I must not always expect a giant faith that can remove mountains. Sometimes even to us the grasshopper must be a burden, that we may in all things be like our head.[40]

In truth, the black clouds of depression never permanently left Spurgeon's life until he went to be with his Savior. Yet through all those earthly days, God was "the true source of all consolation."[41] For truly, "a dark cloud is no sign that the sun has lost his light; and dark black convictions are no arguments that God has laid aside His mercy."[42]

Referring to Psalm 102:3, "For my days are consumed like smoke," Spurgeon commented:

My grief has made life unsubstantial to me. I seem to be but a puff, a vapour which has nothing in it, and is soon dissipated. The metaphor is very admirably chosen, for, to the unhappy, life seems not merely to be frail, but to be surrounded by so much that is darkening, defiling, blinding, and depressing, that, sitting down in despair, they compare themselves to men wandering in a dense fog.

Spurgeon continued: "Now the writer's mind is turned away from his personal and relative troubles to the true source of all consolation, namely, the Lord Himself, and His gracious purposes toward His own people. 'But thou, O Lord, shalt endure forever.' I perish, but thou wilt not."[43]

In spite of, and very likely because of, the depression in Spurgeon's life, he became a spiritual giant for God. Biographer Richard Day confessed that he "was unexpectedly moved to tears in reading one of Spurgeon's travelogue lectures." Within seven lines of the end, Spurgeon suddenly concluded his remarks: "If you cannot travel, remember that our Lord Jesus Christ is more glorious than all else that you could ever see. Get a view of Christ and you have seen more than mountains and cascades and valleys and seas can ever show you. Earth may give its beauty, and stars their brightness, but all these put together can never rival Him."[44]

"Tirshatha"—as Susannah Spurgeon called her husband, using the Hebrew word for "the Reverence"—spent some of his winter months in Mentone, France, because his body could not endure the chill of London. Susannah, who herself became an invalid at the age of thirty-three, was unable to travel with him. During one of those winter separations, Spurgeon wrote this to his wife: "You are the precise form in which God would make a woman for such a man as I." Such a woman she truly was. Many times Spurgeon would come home from meetings at the great tabernacle exhausted and in the grip of depression. Then she would read to him from Baxter's *Reformed Pastor*—"he would weep at my feet, and I would weep too."[45]

Susannah herself understood the purpose of suffering. Watching a crackling oak log on the fireplace one evening, she wrote: "We are like this old log. We should give forth no melodious sounds were it not for the fire."[46]

In God's gracious plan, Susannah Spurgeon was strong enough to travel to France with her husband in the year of his death:

When he lay dying in Mentone, Susannah lingered beside him. She wept softly as he lay for hours unconscious. She smiled bravely through her tears when for short intervals he spoke with her. Out of her grief she wrote: "Perhaps of greatest price among the precious things which this little book (the *Secret Diary*) reveals, is the beloved author's personal and intense love for the Lord Jesus. He lived in His embrace, like the apostle John, his head leaned on Jesu's bosom (Jesu was his private and intimate term of endearment for his Lord). The endearing terms, used in the Diary and never discontinued, were not empty words."

When the end drew near, he whispered, "Susie." She bent close to listen, clasped his hand in hers and said, "Yes, dear Tirshatha." And he murmured—the last words before he saw Him face to face—"Oh, wifie, I have had such a blessed time with my Lord."[47]

Years before, Spurgeon had spoken of death: "The dying saint is not in a flurry; he keeps to his old pace—he walks. The last days of a Christian are the most peaceful of his whole career; many a saint has reaped more joy and knowledge when he came to die than ever he knew while he lived. When there is a shadow, there must be a light somewhere. The light of Jesus shining upon death throws a shadow across our path; let us therefore rejoice for the Light beyond!"[48]

Brother Lawrence (Nicholas Herman)

*H*e was a lay brother of the Carmelite Order. In spite of a natural aversion to work in the kitchen, Brother Lawrence quoted the poem:

"Lord of all pots and pans and things . . .
Make me a saint by getting meals
And washing up the plates!"

. . . and he could say, "The time of business does not with me differ from the time of prayer; and in the noise and clatter of my kitchen, while several persons are at the same time calling for different things, I possess God in as great tranquility as if I were upon my knees at the blessed sacrament."

Except for the kitchen, we know little of his career, only that he was born Nicholas Herman in French Lorraine, that he was lowly and unlearned in the teaching of the schools, that he served briefly as footman and soldier, and under the whips of God and conscience was driven to become a Lay brother among the barefooted Carmelites at Paris in the year 1666 and was known forever after that as "Brother Lawrence." His conversion, at eighteen, was the result of the mere sight on a midwinter day of a dry and leafless tree standing gaunt against the snow; it stirred deep thoughts within him of the change the coming spring would bring. From that moment on he grew and waxed strong in the knowledge and love and favor of God, endeavoring constantly, as he put it, "to walk as in His presence." No wilderness wanderings, no bitter winter seasons of soul or spirit, seem to have intervened between the Red Sea and the Jordan of his experience. A wholly consecrated man, he lived his life as though he were a singing pilgrim on the march, as happy in serving his fellow monks and brothers from the monastery kitchen as in serving God in the vigil of prayer and penance. He died at eighty years of age, full of love and years and honored by all who knew him, leaving a name which has been "as precious ointment poured forth."[1]

"They also serve who only stand and waite." (John Milton - 1655)

Hudson Taylor

SEVEN

Hudson Taylor:
Drawing on God's Provision

*I*t was late spring a number of years ago. The weather was beginning to warm up, and once again I began my frequent visits to the ocean. This year it was different, however. After teaching school for twelve years I had just started two new careers: building a private counseling practice and writing books relating to Christian living. The practice, however, would be my "bread and butter." Until that practice expanded I had plenty of time to go to the beach—and to think. I had given up a fixed income, paid sick leave and vacations, and general security in exchange for the unknown. Unknown, that is, except that God had led me; so the way was known at least to Him.

It was sunset as I drove home from the beach on a street overlooking the sea and shaded by large trees. Waves of doubt caused me to feel restless, and a little frantic. How would I live until I had time to build up the practice? What if I didn't make it financially? Then, with as much reality as that deepening sunset, there flashed across my mind the thoughts of a passage in Scripture:

> Ye cannot be in service unto God and unto riches. For this cause I say unto you. Be not anxious for your life what ye shall eat or what ye shall drink, or for your body

what ye shall put on. Is not the life more than food? And the body more than raiment? Observe intently the birds of the heaven, that they neither sow nor reap nor gather into barns, and yet your heavenly Father feedeth them. Are not ye much better than they?

But who from among you, being anxious can add to his stature one cubit? And about clothing why are ye anxious? Consider well the lilies of the field how they grow,—They toil not neither do they spin; and yet I say unto you not even Solomon in all his glory was arrayed like one of these!

Now if the grass of the field—which today is and tomorrow into an oven is cast—God thus adorneth how much rather you, little of faith?

Do not then be anxious saying, What shall we eat? Or what shall we drink? Or wherewithal shall we be arrayed?

For all these things the nations seek after,—For your heavenly Father knoweth that ye are needing all these things. But be seeking first the kingdom and its right-eousness—And all these things shall be added unto you" (Matthew 6:24–33, *The Emphasized Bible*).

Deep within myself, I knew that God would provide for me in an undertaking that had been instigated at His prodding. Where there had been fear there was now peace along with a sense of excitement over how and when God would work. That frame of mind does not come to me easily, so I knew that it had surely come from God.

Similarly, years ago I spent some time in a small, primitive town in Mexico. It is a place of exquisite beauty and peace. It is also remote from modern medical help and therefore not the best place to become ill. One morning I awoke with what I knew was more than a simple case of Montezuma's Revenge. I was sick and feverish. Because I am severely allergic to many medications, I wanted to avoid any local cures.

As I lay in bed that afternoon I calmly asked God to heal me—a logical request since I firmly believed that God's purposes for my life were still alive and real and that they required health. The result was a shaky but increasing return to physical well-being by the evening.

I do not believe that God unfailingly answers our prayers for healing with an answer of yes. Sometimes He says no or wait. Or He chooses to give partial help. But at a time when I was without usable medical attention God undertook to do the whole job Himself, an experience that bolstered my faith in future days. God had provided for my needs as my life was centered in His will. He had not prevented my illness, nor did He eliminate illness on future trips. But He did provide for my physical needs. He healed when that was necessary. God is not in the business of eradicating our problems, but He is definitely the One who supplies our needs in the midst of those problems.

Hudson Taylor, the man who almost single-handedly opened up the interior of China to Christianity, learned, first as a young preacher in England, a principle of God's provision: "God's work done in God's way will never lack God's supplies."[1] One might add to that "God's person, bent on doing God's will, shall have God's supply."

To Hudson Taylor a significant beginning in this life of trusting God for all practical supply came late one evening:

> After concluding my last service about ten o'clock that night, a poor man asked me to go and pray with his wife, saying that she was dying. I readily agreed, and on the way asked him why he had not sent for the priest, as

his accent told me he was an Irishman. He had done so, he said, but the priest refused to come without a payment of eighteen pence, which the man did not possess as the family was starving. Immediately it occurred to my mind that all the money I had in the world was the solitary half-crown, and that was in one coin; moreover, that while the basin of water-gruel I usually took for supper was awaiting me and there was sufficient in the house for breakfast in the morning, I certainly had nothing for dinner on the coming day.

Somehow or other there was at once a stoppage in the flow of joy in my heart. But instead of reproving myself I began to reprove the poor man, telling him that it was very wrong to have allowed matters to get into such a state as he described, and that he ought to have applied to the relieving officer. His answer was that he had done so, and was told to come at eleven o'clock the next morning, but that he feared his wife might not live through the night.

"Ah," thought I, "if only I had two shillings and a six-pence instead of this half-crown, how gladly would I give these poor people a shilling!" But to part with the half-crown was far from my thoughts. I little dreamed that the truth of the matter simply was that I could trust God plus *one-and-six-pence*, but was not prepared to trust Him only, without any money at all in my pocket.

My conductor led me into a court, down which I followed him with some degree of nervousness. I had found myself there before, and at my last visit had been roughly handled . . . . Up a miserable flight of stairs into a wretched room he led me, and oh what a sight there presented itself! Four or five children stood about, their sunken cheeks and temples telling unmistakably the story of slow starvation, and lying on a wretched pallet was a poor, exhausted mother, with a tiny infant thirty-six hours old moaning rather than crying at her side.

"Ah!" thought I, "if I had two shillings and a six-pence, instead of half-a-crown, how gladly should they have one-and-sixpence of it." But still a wretched unbelief prevented me from obeying the impulse to relieve their distress at the cost of all I possessed.

It will scarcely seem strange that I was unable to say much to comfort these poor people. I needed comfort myself. I began to tell them, however, that they must not be cast down; that though their circumstances were very distressing there was a kind and loving Father in heaven. But something within me cried, "You hypocrite! Telling these unconverted people about a kind and loving Father in heaven and not prepared yourself to trust Him without a half-a-crown."

I nearly choked. How gladly would I have compromised with conscience, if I had had a florin and sixpence! I would have given the florin thankfully and kept the rest. But I was not yet prepared to trust in God alone, without the sixpence.

To talk was impossible under these circumstances, yet strange to say, prayer was a delightful occupation in those days. Time thus spent never seemed wearisome and I knew no lack of words. I seemed to think that all I should have to do would be to kneel down and pray, and that relief would come to them and to myself together.[2]

Perhaps at this time in his life Taylor began to learn on a deep, "gut" level that God does not usually work in such a simplistic way.

He cooperates with us to work out the meeting of our needs rather than just eliminating those needs. And thus we grow and learn to trust God more.

In his process of learning this trust, Taylor continued:

"You asked me to come and pray with your wife," I said to the man; "let us pray." And I knelt down. But no sooner had I opened my lips with, "Our Father who art in heaven," than conscience said within, "Dare you mock God? Dare you kneel down and call him 'Father' with that half-crown in your pocket?"

Such a time of conflict then came upon me as I had never experienced before. How I got through that form of prayer I know not, and whether the words uttered were connected or disconnected. But I arose from my knees to great distress of mind! The poor father turned to me and said, "You see what a terrible state we are in, sir. If you can help us, for God's sake."

At that moment the word flashed into my mind, "Give to him that asketh of thee." And in the word of a King there is power.

I put my hand into my pocket and slowly drawing out the half-crown gave it to the man, telling him that it might seem a small matter for me to relieve them, seeing that I was comparatively well off, but that in parting with that coin I was giving my all; but that what I had been trying to tell them was indeed true. God really was a Father and might be trusted. And how the joy came back in full tide to my heart! I could say anything and feel it then, and the hindrance to blessing was gone—gone, I trust, forever.

Not only was the poor woman's life saved, but my life, as I fully realized, had been saved too. It might have been a wreck ... had not grace at that time conquered and the striving of God's Spirit been obeyed.

I well remember that night as I went home to my lodgings how my heart was as light as my pocket. The dark, deserted streets resounded with a hymn of praise that I could not restrain. When I took my basin of gruel before retiring, I would not have exchanged it for a prince's feast. Reminding the Lord as I knelt at my bedside of His own Word, "He that giveth to the poor lendeth to the Lord," I asked Him not to let my loan be a long one, or I should have no dinner the next day. And with peace within and peace without, I spent a happy, restful night.

Next morning my plate of porridge remained for breakfast, and before it was finished the postman's knock was heard at the door. I was not in the habit of receiving letters on Monday, as my parents and most of my friends refrained from posting on Saturday, so that I was somewhat surprised when the landlady came in holding a letter or packet in her wet hand covered by her apron. I looked at the letter, but could not make out the handwriting. It was either a strange hand or a feigned one, and the postmark was blurred. Where it came from I could not tell. On opening the envelope I found nothing written within, but inside a sheet of blank paper was folded a pair of kid gloves from which, as I opened them in astonishment, half-a-sovereign fell to the ground.[3]

God's work done in God's way had received God's supply. Need had not been eradicated, for there will always be great need on this earth. The particular and immediate need had been supplied, which is a basic principle of God's work.

In all fairness it should be added that Taylor lived in an economy different from ours. Additionally, we must glean from great lives principles of living rather than strict dogma. For it is dangerous to attempt to become a carbon copy of anyone else.

To illustrate, I know an elderly lady who gave all she possessed to a radio broadcast under the duress of questioning her loyalty to God unless she so gave. A few months later she was living in misery with the grudging help of some relatives.

Each one of us must consider his or her finances in the light of God's will for our individual lives—each with its own needs.

There is another principle of truth to be gleaned, however, from Taylor's experience with the coin. As he himself expressed it, "If we are faithful to God in little things, we shall gain experience and strength that will be helpful to us in the more serious trials of life." More than that, God's training is unique for each of us. Taylor's "more serious trials of life," later on in China, forced him to the extremity of faith. The losses of his wife, children, and missionary co-workers were all to weigh heavily upon this man. At such times he would pace his study for hours, calming himself as he softly sang:

> "Jesus, I am resting, resting,
> In the joy of what Thou art;
> I am finding out the greatness
> Of Thy loving heart."

Truly, "the life that was to be exceptionally fruitful had to be rooted and grounded in God in no ordinary way."[4]

It was in experiences such as that of the coin that Hudson Taylor learned what George Müller had also learned: *God's work can be done expansively and with quality, and we can expect God's supply.* The needs would never go away. They would remain a daily constant. But they would unfailingly be met in God's way and in God's time.

In Taylor's founding of the China Inland Mission, one of the great foreign missions of all time, Taylor brought together deeply dedicated Christians who gave and were given to. They gave up this world's goods. Yet years later, when his daughter-in-law and biographer, Geraldine Taylor, was in need of rest in the middle of her writing, she was sent to a lovely ocean resort for six months—with household help! And she should have been.

Individual saints must consider their finances in the light of God's will for their individual lives and in light of their unique needs. Sometimes God asks for a financial plunge of faith. If this seems to be the case for you, then take it! Sometimes He asks for hardcore, common sense. Then use it! An older person lovingly cared for by five adult children may be more generous financially than one who has no living relative. Hudson Taylor in his youth could more reasonably give away his last coin than he could have later in life had he been facing open-heart surgery for his child or the poverty of his parents. For it is a biblical principle that one should care for those of his or her own household first. Even apart from direct Christian teaching, this principle is considered valid in most people's thinking.

In commenting upon the absolute degradation and ruin of the Ik, a tribe in Uganda, and applying his conclusions to the Western world, anthropologist Colin Turnbull said: "The rot is in all of us, for how many of us would be willing to divide our riches among our own family, let alone the poor or needy, beyond, of course, what we can easily afford—for if we were willing, why have we not done it?"[5] Should those in the Body of Christ have such low standards?

On this principle Müller built orphanages that excelled all others in England at that time. For Müller believed that if God's work was to be done, it was to be done well. Reports of Müller's success greatly influenced the lives of both Hudson Taylor in China and Amy Carmichael in Dohnavur, in her work with children rescued from the temples of South India. Taylor, Müller, and Carmichael held several of the same basic principles—with Müller as a major influence on the other two. The three shared the unshakeable conviction that God's work done in God's way would receive God's supply.

All three also believed a second principle: that one can move people by prayer alone, with no pledges signed or financial pleas expressed. And, certainly not least, they each believed that if they were in the employment of a King, the work could afford to have quality. Müller's success based on these principles was dramatic and influences the work of God throughout the world yet today.

Unlike so many of the orphanages of his time Müller's orphanages were set up attractively and with neatness and order. Each child had their own "pigeon hole" in which to store their toys. Each was given attractive toys, well-kept clothing, and more than one pair of shoes. There were work-rooms where instruction in sewing and mending was given to the girls. There were play-rooms with ample toys. And all around the buildings were well-kept grounds and attractive flower gardens.

One of the best, what we call today, treatment centers for children that I have ever visited was headed by a man who read Müller's biography once a year. The pattern given by God to Müller and Taylor and Carmichael was indeed passed down and continues.

God's work, done in God's way, receives God's supply!

There is an incident that highlights the remarkable, God-given relationship between Taylor and Müller. A servant had made off with Mr. Taylor's belongings, and proof was given. Wrote Geraldine Taylor:

> For the recovery of the property it would not have been difficult to institute legal proceedings, and Mr. Taylor was strongly urged to secure the punishment of the thief; but the more he thought about it the more he shrank from anything of the sort. Yoh-hsi was one whose salvation he had earnestly sought, and to hand him over to cruel, rapacious underlings who would only be too glad to throw him into prison that he might be squeezed of the last farthing would not have been in keeping, he felt, with the spirit of the gospel. Finally concluding that his soul was worth more than the forty pounds worth of things he had stolen, Mr. Taylor decided to pursue a very different course.

> "So I have sent him a plain, faithful letter," he wrote in the middle of August, "to the effect that we know his guilt, and what its consequences might be to himself; that at first I had considered handing over the matter to the Ya-men, but remembering Christ's command to return good for evil I had not done so, and did not wish to injure a hair of his head.

> "I told him that he was the real loser; not I; that I freely forgave him, and besought him more earnestly than ever to flee from the wrath to come. I also added that though it was not likely he would give up such of my possessions as were serviceable to a Chinese, there were among them foreign books and papers that could be of no

use to him but were valuable to me, and that those at least he ought to send back.

"If only his conscience might be moved and his soul saved, how infinitely more important that would be than the recovery of all I have lost. Do pray for him."

In course of time, and far away from England, this letter came into hands for which it had never been intended. Mr. George Müller from Bristol, founder of the well-known Orphan Homes, read it with thankfulness to the Lord Himself. His sympathies were drawn out to the young missionary who had acted in what he felt to be a Christ-like spirit, and from that time Hudson Taylor had an interest in his prayers.

But more than this. As soon as the incident became known to him, he sent straight out to China a sum sufficient to cover Mr. Taylor's loss, continuing thereafter to take practical share in his work, until in a time of special need he was used of God as the principal channel of support to the China Inland Mission. And all this grew out of one little act, as it might seem, of loyalty to the Master at some personal cost. Only there are no little acts when it is a question of faithfulness to God. And it was just his simple adherence, in every detail, to scriptural principles that gradually inspired confidence in Hudson Taylor and his methods, and won for the Mission the support of spiritually minded people in many lands.[7]

This incident reflects the principles upon which both Taylor and Müller stood, their respect for each other and, for the purposes of this book, the character of the man Hudson Taylor.

Hudson Taylor not only emphasized God's ability to meet the needs of His work; he was also deeply committed to the principle that God's work was to be done with quality. While that quality would at times be more costly, the needs would be met because they were sanctioned by God. Faith was the focus. Not faith abstractly without an object, but faith that God could be trusted with great tasks. For certainly one who serves a King should expect a King's supply as long as he operates under a King's command. Our King often chooses to supply us daily, momentarily, rather than to supply our needs in a long-range fashion. For the daily need is what keeps our focus of direction and faith upon Him and His orders.

God had given Hudson Taylor superb training for his life of balance in obtaining God's supply. For as the son of James Taylor, he had before him the perfect pattern for learning both financial wisdom and godly trust.

Taylor was born to James and Amelia Taylor on May 21, 1832. He lived during the years of Charles Haddon Spurgeon, and shared ideals with Amy Carmichael and George Müller. When he was tempted to take a more comfortable mode of travel at a higher cost—a most reasonable and justifiable option—he cited a financial principle with which all of these people would have agreed: "Well, it is the Lord's money, you know; we had better be very careful about it."[8] Interestingly enough, to balance out the abandon with which Hudson Taylor gave money and trusted God financially, he was no fanatic. His father's upbringing was deeply entrenched in him and is epitomized in the statement James Taylor once made regarding a bill: "If I let it stand over a week," he said, "I defraud my creditor of interest, if only a fractional sum."[9]

James Taylor was a businessman. Yet he never sued for a bill. And at times he returned in whole or in part sums that his customers could not afford. Still he was a man of so much business skill that his fellow townsmen who recognized his financial skill appointed him manager of their Building Society for a term of twenty-two years. It was in such an atmosphere of balance, integrity and faith that Hudson Taylor was born and grew up.

Perhaps it was because he learned firsthand such balance that he could afford to appear unbalanced to the world, even to the Christian world. That, too, was faith. While in China, in such matters as dress his faith and sincerity were put to the acid test.

> Chinese dress and a home somewhere in the country—the thought was becoming familiar. But it was an expedient almost unheard of in those days. Sometimes on inland journeys, a missionary would wear the native costume as a precautionary measure. But it was invariably discarded on the traveler's return, and he would have been careless of public opinion indeed who would have ventured to wear it always, and in the Settlement.
>
> But it was nothing less than this that the young missionary was meditating, driven to it by his longing to identify himself with the people and by the force of outward circumstances. If he could not find quarters in Shanghai he must go to the interior, and why add to his difficulties and hinder the work he most desired to accomplish by emphasizing the fact that he was a foreigner?[10]

Again Taylor succeeded in establishing an intricate balance in his life. Chinese dress was a key to his success in China. He became part of the people in a more meaningful way, not only because by this sign they could observe his sincerity, but because Chinese dress helped him blend into the culture rather than stand out. By his compromise in dress Taylor was better enabled to meet and engage the Chinese people.

Compromise has come to be a dirty word in the Christian world, although it was never intended to be that. The word has become abused in our culture. Enthusiastic do-gooders dabble with drugs in order to reach drug addicts, or in general prostitute their principles to fit in with those they wish to help. Taylor would not have compromised his principles—nor should we. But he knew the true meaning of compromise. While in China, he compromised on issues that had no moral overtones in order to win the souls of people. He took the chance of offending his own colleagues rather than those among whom he lived and worked.

Yes, it was growing clearer. For him, probably, the right thing was a closer identification with the people; Chinese dress at all times and the externals of Chinese life, including chopsticks and native cookery. How much it would simplify traveling in the interior! Already he had purchased an outfit of native clothing. If, after all the prayer there had been about it, he really could not get accommodation in Shanghai, it must be that the Lord had other purposes.

Thursday night came. It was useless to seek premises any longer, so Hudson Taylor went down to engage the junk that was to take them to Hang-chow Bay with their belongings. His Chinese dress was ready for the following morning when he expected to begin a pilgrim life indeed. And this, apparently, was the point to which it had been necessary to lead him. He had followed faithfully. It was enough. And now on these new lines could be given the answer to weeks and months of prayer.[11]

Later he took the step he had been prayerfully considering—called in a barber, and had himself so transformed in appearance that his own mother could hardly

have known him. To put on Chinese dress without shav-
ing the head is comparatively a simply matter, but Hudson
Taylor went [to] all lengths, leaving only enough of the
fair, curly hair to grow into the *queue* of the Chinaman. He
had prepared a dye, moreover, with which he darkened his
remaining hair, to match the long, black braid that at first
must do duty for his own. Then in the morning he put on
as best he might the loose, unaccustomed garments, and
appeared for the first time in the gown and satin shoes of
a "Teacher," or man of the scholarly class.[12]

As the work went on by faith, Taylor received what he
needed, not always what he wanted or *when* it was desirable. A
note dated January 27, 1874, found in the margin of his Bible,
reflects the proportion of his vision and the urgency of his need:

> Asked God for fifty or a hundred additional native
> evangelists and as many missionaries as may be needed to
> open up the four *Fu's* and forty-eight *Hsien* cities still
> unoccupied in Chekiang, also for men to break into the
> nine unoccupied provinces. Asked in the name of Jesus.
>
> I thank thee, Lord Jesus, for the promise whereon
> thou hast given me to rest. Give me all needed strength
> of body, wisdom of mind, grace of soul to do this thy so
> great work.
>
> Yet, strange to say, the immediate sequel was not
> added strength, but a serious illness. Week after week he
> lay in helpless suffering, only able to hold on in faith to
> the heavenly vision. Funds had been so low for months
> that he had scarcely known how to distribute the little
> that came in, and there was nothing at all in hand for
> extension work. But, "We are going on to the interior," he

had written to the secretaries in London. "I do hope to see some of the destitute provinces evangelized before long. I long for it by day and pray for it by night. *Can He care less?*"[13]

Faith again was required to clarify its focus. The work was God's, Taylor was God's—and God would not fail. Taylor continued:

Never had advance seemed more impossible. But in the Bible before him was the record of that transaction of his soul with God, and in his heart was the conviction that, even for inland China, God's time had almost come. And then as he lay there slowly recovering, a letter was put into his hands which had been two months on its way from England. It was from an unknown correspondent.

"My dear Sir (the somewhat trembling hand had written), I bless God—in two months I hope to place at the disposal of your Council, for further extension of the China Inland Mission work, eight hundred pounds. (Then equal to about four thousand dollars, gold). Please remember for *fresh* provinces . . . .

"I think your receipt-form beautiful: 'The Lord our Banner'; 'The Lord will provide.' If faith is put forth and praise sent up, I am sure that Jehovah of Hosts will honour it."

Eight hundred pounds for 'fresh provinces!' Hardly could the convalescent believe he read aright. The very secrets of his heart seemed to look back at him from that sheet of foreign note paper. Even before the prayer [had been] recorded in his Bible, that letter had been sent off; and now, just when most needed, it had reached him with its wonderful confirmation. Then God's time had surely come![14]

And all that was true of the mission was true of God's vision for Hudson Taylor, the man. For God cares about His work, but He is not some mechanistic Taskmaster who is disinterested in people as individuals. Let's not forget that we are an extremely important possession of God and that His care is never removed from us.

Said Taylor in a letter to his sister:

The sweetest part, if one may speak of one part being sweeter than another, is the *rest* which full identification with Christ brings. I am no longer anxious about anything, as I realize this; for He, I know is able to carry out *His will*, and His will is mine. It makes no matter where He places me, or how. That is rather for Him to consider than for me; for in the easiest positions He must give me His grace, and in the most difficult His grace is sufficient. It little matters to my servant whether I sent him to buy a few cash worth of things, or the most expensive articles. In either case, he looks to me for the money, and brings me his purchases. So, if God place me in great perplexity, must He not give me much guidance; in position of great difficulty, much grace; in circumstances of great pressure and trial, much strength? No fear that His resources will be unequal to the emergency! And His resources are mine, for He is mine, and is with me and dwells in me. All this springs from the believer's oneness with Christ. And since Christ has thus dwelt in my heart by faith, how happy I have been! I wish I could tell you, instead of writing about it.[15]

On a deeper, more personal level, after sending home to England two small sons and a daughter for health reasons, Mrs. Taylor gave birth to another son. One week later the baby died as a result of Mrs. Taylor's attack of cholera. At the age of thirty-three, slightly over a week later, Mrs. Taylor died too. It seemed that all earthly comfort had been snatched from Taylor, for within two months his youngest child hung between life and death and had to be sent to friends in another province.

In a letter to Miss Blatchley, the guardian of the other three children, Mr. Taylor's feelings are poignantly reflected: "You will love them all the more," he wrote, "now that they can never again know a mother's care. God will help you to bear with them, and to try to correct them by lovingly pointing out the right way rather than by too frequent reproof—'Don't do this or that.' This I feel is where I most failed with them; and now, there is only you to make up for my deficiencies."[16]

During this time Taylor himself was almost destroyed physically. He suffered from a badly "deranged liver," that brought on sleeplessness and painful depression. Said Geraldine Taylor: "He had to learn more than ever before of the close and often humbling connection between the one and the other (mind and body)." Lung problems and newly enforced bachelorhood did not help his condition. Yet the work went on. And Taylor went on.

Taylor's attitude toward life was epitomized in a brief incident that occurred a few years later.

Despite absence from home and loved ones, and the limitations of ill health which he was feeling keenly, Mr. Taylor was enabled so to cast his burdens on the Lord that, as he wrote to Mr. Hill in February (1877), he "could not but rejoice seven days a week." Whenever work permitted, he was in the habit of turning to a little harmonium for refreshment, playing and singing many a favorite hymn, but always coming back to:

> *"Jesus, I am resting, resting,*
> *In the joy of what Thou art:*
> *I am finding out the greatness*
> *Of Thy loving heart."*

Some around him could hardly understand this joy and rest, especially when fellow-workers were in danger. A budget of letters arriving on one occasion, as Mr. Nicoll relates, brought news of serious rioting in two different stations. Standing at his desk to read them, Mr. Taylor mentioned what was happening and that immediate help was necessary. Feeling that he might wish to be alone, the younger man was about to withdraw, when, to his surprise, someone began to whistle. It was the soft refrain of the same well-loved hymn: "Jesus, I am resting, resting in the joy of what Thou art . . . ."

Turning back, Mr. Nicoll could not help exclaiming, "How can you whistle, when our friends are in such danger?"

"Would you have me anxious and troubled?" was the long-remembered answer. "That would not help them, and would certainly incapacitate me for my work. I have just to roll the burden on the Lord."[17]

Taylor was not tranquilized into oblivion by his spiritual support. His pain was not obliterated by God. But he was enabled to go on by the very presence of God Himself. He survived. He was not destroyed. He knew the secret of true recovery.

Day and night that was his secret, "just to roll the burden on the Lord." Frequently those who were wakeful in the little house at Chin-kiang might hear, at two or three o'clock in the morning, the soft refrain of Mr. Taylor's favorite hymn. He had learned that, for him, only one life was possible—just that blessed life of resting and rejoicing in the Lord under all circumstances, while He dealt with the difficulties inward and outward, great and small.[18]

Of such was the fiber of Hudson Taylor, the China Inland Mission and all those connected with it. In every aspect of life there was God's provision.

After his death a handwritten meditation was found. It was dated 1874, when Taylor was forty-two. In the words of A. J. Broomhall: "He opened a window on his soul."[19] It portrays a view opposite of the "me-ism" of our times. It offers a challenge few Christians have ever heard.

If God has called you to be really like Jesus in all your spirit, He will draw you into a life of crucifixion and humility, and put on you such demands of obedience that *He will not allow you to follow other Christians*; and in many ways He will seem to let other good people do things that He will not let you do. Other Christians and ministers who seem very religious and useful may push themselves, pull wires and work schemes to carry out their schemes; but you cannot do it; and if you attempt it, you will meet with such failure and rebuke from the Lord as to make you sorely penitent. Others may brag on themselves, on their work, on their success, on their writings, but the Holy Spirit will not allow you to do any such things, and if you begin it, He will lead you into some deep mortification that will make you despise yourself and all your good works.

Others may be allowed to succeed in making money, but it is likely God will keep you poor, because He wants you to have something far better than gold, and that is a helpless dependence on Him, that He may have the privilege (the right) of supplying your needs day by day out of an unseen treasury. The Lord will let others be honoured and put forward, and keep you hidden away in obscurity, because He wants some choice fragrant fruit for His coming glory which can only be produced in the shade. He will let others do a work for Him and get the credit for it, but He will let you work and toil on without knowing how much you are doing, and then to make your work still more precious, He will let others get the credit for the work you have done, and this will make your reward ten times greater when Jesus comes.

The Holy Spirit will put a strict watch over you, with a jealous love, and will rebuke you for little words and feelings or for wasting your time, over which other Christians never seem distressed. So make up your mind that God is an infinite Sovereign, and has a right to do as He pleases with His own, and He may not explain to you a thousand things which may puzzle your reason in his dealings with you. He will take you at your word and if you absolutely sell yourself to be His slave, He will wrap you up in a jealous love and let other people say and do many things which he will not let you say or do.

Settle it for ever that you are to deal directly with the Holy Spirit, and that He is to have the privilege of tying your tongue, or chaining your hand, or closing your eyes, in ways that He does not deal with others. Now when you are so possessed with the Living God, that you are in your secret heart pleased and delighted over the peculiar, personal, private, jealous guardianship of the Holy Spirit over your life, you will have found the vestibule of Heaven.

It is important to keep such words in perspective. We cannot always anticipate the mind of God. Missionaries with great talent have been called of God to go to China, only to die within a few months time, seemingly wasted. On the other hand, all of us know of evil people who have prospered and grown rich. In biblical times Job, a man whom God could trust enough to allow Satan to take everything he had except his life, was blessed in the last part of his life with unprecedented prosperity and material goods.

If deprivation and material loss are for you the result of following hard after God, so be it. But let us be sure that our suffering is unavoidable, that it is truly from the hand of God and not self-inflicted. Only then will that suffering and deprivation be of value to God. For "The Lord maketh poor, and maketh rich" (1 Samuel 2:7). And "Shall not the Judge of all the earth do right?" (Genesis 18:25).

My favorite picture in my family photograph album is of my Aunt Ruth dressed in a padded Chinese gown, holding a lamb in one arm and a baby in the other.

I met Aunt Ruth when I was three, at a train station in Chicago, when she first returned from her work in the far north of China with the China Inland Mission. I remember as a child remembers: chopsticks; tiny Chinese shoes from before the days when foot-binding was abandoned; strange foods that nonetheless tasted good; brass bowls with Chinese dragons; a Bible with strange Chinese writing. She taught me how to hold a Chinese brush and grind Chinese ink. She taught me to count in Chinese. Above all, she taught me to love the Chinese people.

I remember lots of doctors and tests and bottles of food supplements that she took constantly to build herself up. I know now that she suffered from malnutrition and needed much medical help.

I remember names like D. E. Hoste, Howard Taylor and, most of all, Hudson Taylor. I remember the China Inland Mission and the endless photographs and slides. These were household names to me then. Now I know they were not common at all—not even in my life. They became a major formative influence for me, affecting all of my ideals and aspirations. Years later I discovered on my own—or perhaps I had just forgotten—the hymn

> *Jesus! I am resting, resting,*
> *In the joy of what Thou art,*
> *I am finding out the greatness*
> *Of Thy loving heart.*
>
> *Thou hast bid me gaze upon Thee;*
> *And Thy beauty fills my soul,*
> *For, by Thy transforming power,*
> *Thou hast made me whole.*

Hudson Taylor's favorite hymn. Then my aunt's. Now mine.

I may never know how much Hudson Taylor and his belief in God's provision have influenced me. Maybe he too was part of that great cloud of witnesses on that warm, sunny day as I was coming home from the beach. For it was then that I knew God's provision would be enough for God's work through me.

H. A. Ironside (1876–1951)

H. A. Ironside was at one time the pastor of Chicago's Moody Memorial Church and a prolific writer and Bible commentator. His earlier roots in the Plymouth Brethren show in the following piece on the Lord's Table, the Holy Sacrament of Communion.

The Lord's Supper, if given the place our Savior intended it to have, will constantly preach to the world, and will say more than any words of ours can say: "As often as ye eat this bread, and drink this cup, ye do preach the Lord's death till He come."

You may have known the Lord Jesus Christ for years, but I wonder whether this ordinance is precious to you. I am afraid to some it is just a legal thing, a feeling that one ought to come and take the Lord's Supper because He has commanded it. Let me suggest that it is not so much a command as a request. When our Savior says, "This do in remembrance of Me," He does not mean, "You must do this," but rather, "I would like to have you do this." It is as though a loved one were dying and before slipping away should call the children around the bed and handing each one of them a photograph would say, "Here are pictures of myself; I am going to leave you, you won't see me again for a little while, but I would like each of you to take one of these pictures. I wish you would cherish it and from time to time take it out and look at it, and as you do, remember me." Would it be a task to do that in response to the request of a loving mother or a precious father or possibly a darling child? Surely not. If you loved that one, you would be delighted again and again to take down that picture and as you looked at it, you would say, "There is the one who loved me and is now gone from me, but I call my dear one afresh to mind." That is the place the Lord's Supper has in the Church of God. There is nothing legal about it; you do not have to participate in the Lord's Supper if you do not want to. You can go to Heaven by trusting the Savior even if you have never once partaken of the cup that speaks of His suffering and death, but if your heart is filled with love for Him, you will be glad from time to time to gather with His people to remember Him.[1]

Geraldine Taylor

EIGHT

Geraldine Taylor: Divine Renewal

*I*t was Christmas Eve, the eve of Geraldine Guinness's own birthday, in this, her first year in China. Significantly, it was also her first year away from home and parents. She had arrived in Honan province by houseboat, traveling up the Han River in the company of Hudson Taylor's son and daughter-in-law, Mr. and Mrs. Herbert Taylor, and their little son, Howard. A few days later they reached the town where they were to serve, a place where no white woman had been seen before.

As she traveled from place to place that first year, ministering to the sick and sharing the gospel, Geraldine experienced frustrating language barriers and cultural conflicts over the status and behavior of women. She lived among those enslaved to opium and encountered "terrible revelations . . . horrible ways of sinning . . . her soul had been scorched as she thought of innocent little lives cruelly sinned against. These were things she could never tell."[1]

But one incident remained more agonizingly haunting than any other. A little granddaughter was given to Hudson Taylor, the daughter of his eldest son, Herbert. A trained nurse had been there for the delivery, and the child was healthy and strong. Mrs. Herbert Taylor, however, was not well and required special nursing. Along with the care required for the baby and for little Howard, Geraldine, already tired and in need of medical treatment for her eyes, stepped in to do her share.

Then the baby became ill with dysentery. Geraldine prepared a dose of medicine, which was administered by the nurse. But Geraldine had picked up the wrong bottle. Soon afterward the baby died. The people among whom they lived did not value the death of a baby girl, so there could be no funeral. The grief-stricken father quietly buried his little daughter in Honan, in the middle of the night.

Devastated, Geraldine wrote to Hudson Taylor, who was in England at the time. She hoped that as a physician Dr. Taylor could assure her that the baby may have died from the disease, not the medication. With characteristic wisdom, Taylor gave the letter to his son, Howard, also a doctor and very much in love with Geraldine. Otherwise the incident was kept private. The comfort Howard offered to Geraldine became precious to her and helped lead toward their marriage some five years later. Said biographer and niece Joy Guinness: "The enemy had overreached himself, and God had overruled."[2]

"God had overruled." This was divine renewal. *Baker's Evangelical Dictionary of Theology* refers to *renewal* as the "reinvigorating effect of Christian committal on conduct."[3] Ephesians 4:23 reads, "And being renewed in the spirit of your mind . . ." (Darby). H. C. G. Moule, in commenting on this verse, stated, "As regenerated members of Christ, you have exchanged doom for peace and moral bondage for spiritual freedom." The *Expositor's Greek Testament* emphasizes that the verb here is passive. We do not renew ourselves; we are renewed by the Spirit of God. Renewal, therefore, is something God does in us.

In her book *Weather of the Heart*, Gigi Graham Tchividjian quotes her mother, Ruth Bell Graham: "Make the least of all that goes, and the most of all that comes." Ruth explains that this was how she handled all the "good-byes" that occurred as a result of Billy Graham's ministry. It is what we mean by "going on." It also summarizes the principles of renewal as practiced by Geraldine Taylor. A poem by Ruth Graham further expresses the thought:

> *We live a time*
> *secure,*
> *beloved and loving,*
> *sure*
> *it cannot last*
> *for long,*
> *then—*
> *the goodbyes come*
> *again—again*
> *like a small death,*
> *the closing of a door*
> *One learns to live*
> *with pain.*
> *One looks ahead,*
> *not back—*
> *never back,*
> *only before.*
> *And joy will come again—*
> *warm and secure,*
> *if only for the now,*
> *laughing*
> *we endure.*[9]

Geraldine endured more than her share of pain in her experiences with children. Because of her parents' intense involvement in missions, by the time Geraldine was a teenager she had literally raised her younger brother and two sisters. One day her father took his little son with him when he went away to speak. Within a week the two small girls, Phoebe and Agnes, contracted diphtheria and died. Geraldine and her mother became ill with a milder form of the same disease and survived. Geraldine was just sixteen. According to her biographer, "She never attempted to be young again."[4]

Later, the pain of those losses and the death of the Taylor baby would be aggravated by Geraldine's own miscarriages. Perhaps due to the rigors of her life in China, she was never able to bear her own children.

Then, when Geraldine was in her mid-forties, her sister Lucy died, leaving two small boys in Geraldine's care. "I want you to have Auntie Geraldine for your Mamma,"[5] Lucy wrote to the boys. And Mother she became in reality for the rest of their lives. But after six years, when the boys' father remarried, it was appropriate for them to return to him. Once again, Geraldine experienced a sense of wrenching loss.

Through all these painful experiences Geraldine learned what it meant to be renewed. Her recovery was not born of self-effort nor was it stamped with bitterness. She resisted the urge to self-ishly think of herself first so that she would not be wounded in the future. Instead, her renewal grew into a divine tenderness and understanding. Thirty years after her own miscarriages, Geraldine wrote to a couple who had just buried their stillborn baby.

He called you to be a father, a mother; He gave you a precious little daughter. This can never be done back upon. You *are* parents; the little one is yours forever. He is keeping her for you, far more perfectly and safely than you could have kept her. And He will give her back to you when Jesus comes. Your lives are permanently enriched by all this and your usefulness for the work. The Lord has wanted this—it is part of the fruit, "more fruit" that He has planned for your lives. How much richer and deeper now is the love with which He can love through you, the sympathy into which He can bring you with His own heart and the hearts of others.... How dearly He must love you to have trusted you with this sorrow, and to have put Himself to the grief of giving you pain. For the little life He has taken, though only to restore, may He give you many, many precious lives in His eternal kingdom.[6]

Out of the deep pain had come the truest form of recovery and renewal: selflessness and abandonment to the will of God. In some paradoxical fashion Geraldine's love had become gentle at the same time it dared to make demands. Hers was not a softening love. It was a love that held one to the highest standard. It strengthened rather than weakened. It expected the best of others. In the words of Amy Carmichael:

> *O Father, help us lest our poor love refuse*
> *For our beloved the life that they would choose,*
> *And in our fear of loss for them, or pain,*
> *Forget eternal gain.*[7]

"Why me?" was not part of the vocabulary of Geraldine Taylor. True recovery and renewal were woven throughout the fabric of her earthly life. No matter what happened she went on, and in her life story as well as in her many writings one senses the deep settled joy of the Lord. Some twelve years before her death she herself spoke of the meaning of renewal. In a journal entry dated July 16, 1937, she wrote of the meaning of renewal:

> Taking into account all the facts of the case,
> "Renewal—day by day." 2 Cor. 4:16.
> Yes, the outward man is perishing.

Yes, the heart would faint.

Waking later this morning (6:30) after hours of sleeplessness last night, I should have been discouraged—but
the Lord Himself made haste to comfort. And oh, what
wealth opens up from His Word through this truth
applied by His Spirit.

Uplifting, transforming, overwhelming in grace and
glory: Divine renewal.
"Transformed by the renewing of your mind!" Rom.
12:2.
"We faint not ... though." 4:16.
"While we look not at ... but at ... " 4:18.
"Strength renewed . . . to walk and not faint."
Is. 40:31.
"Always to pray ... not to faint.'" Luke 18:1.[8]

Mary Geraldine Guinness was born to Fanny and Grattan
Guinness in Waterloo, near Liverpool, on Christmas Day in the
year 1862. Grattan Guinness was the son of a soldier who had died
when his young son was only fourteen. Grattan went to sea at sev-
enteen and sought adventure. After his conversion he developed a
deep sense of the spiritual needs of others and became a preacher.
Some years later he offered his services to Hudson Taylor. Since
Guinness was already thirty and his wife thirty-five, which Taylor
felt would hinder the couple in developing fluency in the Chinese
language, Taylor advised against the mission field but suggested
they support missions from the home side. This the Guinness family did for the rest of their lives. All of their children eventually
went to foreign mission fields, while the parents stayed home, supported missions, and trained young missionaries.

At the time of Geraldine's birth her father had gone through a period of ill health and discouragement. Grattan Guinness was a preacher who had come into fellowship with the Plymouth Brethren, a group flourishing in England at the time. The "Brethren," noted for their deep biblical teaching, commitment to worship, and lack of ecclesiastical organization, influenced Guinness to proclaim more than just the simple gospel. As a result he was criticized, and his popularity diminished. The hard work and criticism took their toll.

Geraldine's mother, Fanny, had come from a tragic background. Her father had killed himself after losing his wife and their only son. Fanny Fitzgerald and her three sisters were taken in by Quakers. After her conversion, Fanny joined the Brethren. Later, broken in health and depleted financially, the second man whom Fanny called "Father" committed suicide. Fanny learned that only God remained.

Fanny Fitzgerald and Grattan Guinness met while he was on a vacation in Norway. Fanny was there as a paid companion for an elderly lady. Their meeting was casual; Fanny simply met Guinness after hearing him speak. Yet within three months they were married, the result of a proposal Guinness sent by mail. Immediately they sailed for America, where Fanny also took part in the public meetings.

Unlike her mother, Geraldine and Howard waited seven years before marrying. According to Howard, it all started when both families were in England. Howard, age eleven, was sent to the Guinness home to deliver a letter from his father, Hudson Taylor. Another eleven-year-old, this one a girl with braids, answered the door. Geraldine didn't really notice Howard, but Howard never forgot Geraldine. It was the start of a relationship that would help shape Christian missions and influence Christian thinking.

Geraldine knew how to go on. She knew the deepest meaning of the word *renewal*. And it would seem that all through her life she was tested on this point. Her tragic experiences of losing children are but one example. Yet out of those losses came a unique ability to comfort mothers who had lost children and a gentle, nurturing manner with children who were not hers by birth.

There were other painful areas in their marriage, sacrifices that were made by choice for the good of furthering God's work. Late in life, in 1927, she and Howard were allowed to come to the United States and to live in a little cottage above the sea for six short months. Geraldine wrote from Casa Mia in La Jolla, California: "I have never had the opportunity of doing anything in the way of cooking before we came to La Jolla, but I am very much interested in it, and Howard appreciates my efforts!"[10]

In reading some of her correspondence from that time one realizes how much she would have enjoyed her own home, a place to go back to. A missionary from China wrote aptly: "Home still means an inn . . . I might almost say any inn, we are so accustomed to traveling."[11] Yet Geraldine's attitude was that of a cup half full, not empty. How nice that she could have this cottage for six months, not how terrible that it was her first real home.

In her personal life as well as in public Geraldine knew how to turn difficulty into blessing. She knew how to recover and go on. She did not manage to eradicate suffering, but she did use it for good. Once married, Dr. and Mrs. Howard Taylor were the perfect balance for each other. What started out as a sometimes frustrating in and out seven years of seeking God's will became a life-preserving relationship for Geraldine. In a 1934 letter written by Howard, he said of Geraldine's tendency to overextend: "Did I ever tell you of a time when my efforts to shield her from overwork were unwelcome? Seeing she was grieved I asked her:

'Darling, where would you have been by now if I hadn't been taking care of you?' 'In my grave long ago,' she replied."
    Continued her biographer: "It was Howard who saw to it that
she took daily exercise, that she went to bed early, and had sufficient and regular nourishment. She was not allowed to decide
these things for herself. There were occasions when with gleeful
pleasure she played truant."[12]
    Burnout was a condition Geraldine Taylor fought all of her life.

    Any vital personality tends to become the pivot of a
    multitude of other lives. Geraldine's was no exception. The
    common experiences of every day create contacts which
    draw upon the inner resources. It is impossible to record
    these things, they are too many and too small, yet they fill
    the greater part of our days . . . a human life is limited and
    there is always the danger of attempting too much.[13]

Early in her life, after the deaths of her young sisters and in
the middle of arduous efforts to win those around her to a commitment to Jesus Christ, Geraldine "burned out" and became ill.
Treatment in London did not help, and she was sent out of the
city for six weeks of complete rest. During that time she received
a life-transforming letter from her father. She wrote on the envelope: "Father—to go with me wherever I go."[14] She kept the letter with her all of her life; and only at the end did she consent to
the publication of so intimate a piece of correspondence. She now
felt that "the need of many is so great of just the reassurance that
came to me through my Father's letter."[15]
    Wisely, Dr. Guinness started the letter by offering her hope:

    I do tenderly feel for you in your present, and I trust
    passing, deeply trying mental exercise. I know what it

means and am not in the least surprised that you should have to pass through it. I have been through it and myriads more of the Lord's servants. "No strange thing" has happened to you, my child, in this "fiery trial," for such it truly is, though mental and not physical . . . . The deepest joys are not born in Paradise, but in Gethsemane! Fear not, my child![16]

Then he went on to explain the causes of her burnout.

The cause is easy to trace. You love, and you sorrow. It is always thus . . . . You are laid aside, weary, for God is not going to work a miracle to support your body, or to make you an exception to the law of nature, that work wearies body and mind, brain and nerve . . . . You have in your work been brought face to face with sorrow, want, pain, death, bereavement, miseries of many kinds. You see the world full of them. The problem presses upon your thoughts; it is too much for the weary nerves and heart seen then and thus. For how do you see it? You see it disconnected from the two elements which alone can explain it, in any degree: first, the element of sin, of moral evil; and second, the element of redemption, of moral good, triumphing over moral and physical evil.[17]

Yet her father kept in mind that Geraldine was feeding, counseling, and teaching the girls of poor families:

God does not build crowded cities; He made a paradise, and says to man, "Take possession of it." Man does otherwise, and then dares to blame God for it, and for the pain he suffers for his wrongdoing. What does God do in

His wondrous grace? He comes down into that wilderness, which man has made such, to dwell with the poor outcast, to be homeless there ("hath not where to lay His head"), to *die* there upon a cross that He may save these lost ones, and change that wilderness into a better paradise.[18]

Only then did Grattan Guinness discuss the cure. He reminded her:

When you pitied and loved those poor wanderers and told of redeeming grace, you felt what God is, for He is Love. Dwell then in love, as He is love. Love Him; love all.... Then also, my child, cultivate humility.... Do not imagine that you can judge the Judge of all the earth and all the universe—not even in little things, much less great. "What I do thou knowest not now, but thou shalt know hereafter." And what was it He did? He laid aside His glory to wash His disciples' feet!

Lie low, quiet the heart. He is better than we are.... Turn, then, away from the patch of darkness close beside you to the blue breadth of azure stainlessness above.... Now one word more: Don't think too much about these great themes. You are not well; the body is weak and nerves tired. Change the theme. Give the brain a rest, give it sleep, give it fresh subjects. Read about other things, about natural history, and whatever interests and pleases you. Go out; let the sweet influences of Nature refresh your tired physical frame, and mental nature too. Let sunshine and breeze, singing of birds, flowers and springtime do their work. Let friendship do its work; talk with others, enter into their concerns. Forget yourself, for-get these themes, and the mind shall gain energy and the body health, while the heart rests in Him who rests in His own for evermore.[19]

How different from much of current Christian thinking and behavior regarding burnout! There are those who first warn against overdoing and then urge a pace of ministry guaranteed to create burnout. "You should cut back," they say, "and get some rest." Yet these same people are often the first to make a demand of some sort. The busiest people in a church are the ones most likely to be asked to do more. When burnout occurs, others are amazed that this one who has worked so hard could actually break down, become depressed and, as Elijah of old, even seek to die. The overworked laborer is condemned for his or her sin or weakness and advised to "confess" the depression.

When Geraldine decided to publish her father's letter at the end of her life, someone remarked, "Perhaps it will mean more than all the others." That was a remarkable statement in view of the wealth of writing produced by the woman who had become the biographer of the China Inland Mission. Yet it is a comment revealing sensitive insight into the crying needs of Christians living at a time of tremendous change and world tension. As we have moved forward into the twenty-first century we too need the compassion and wisdom of this letter—its potential for divine renewal—more than ever.

The comment that this letter would be so valuable when shared with others illustrates most strikingly how vulnerable very godly people can become to the pressures of a work for God, especially when that pressure comes from those whom we respect. To put its meaning into more current terminology, the letter talks in part about boundaries. To declare a boundary simply means that we must each establish our own limits and then declare those limits for *ourselves*, not for someone else. We don't change others to fit our boundaries. We just declare our own. With such a declaration any anger at others for pressuring us into what we feel is too much leaves, and we usually feel a sense of peace.

Marie was a young woman with three children under ten. At her church there was a potluck dinner served every Sunday morning after the service. Like some of the other women of the church Marie usually brought some food—a pie, a casserole, or some other homemade item. However, almost every Saturday night she would be called to "fill in" for someone else who was now unable to bring what they had committed to. This meant bringing two things. Sometimes Marie had a sick child or she herself was exhausted from an overloaded schedule. Yet she always said yes. Angry and tired, she finally sought professional help.

Marie learned some things about herself that had been obvious to her friends. Marie was committed to nice. Sometimes she said yes just because she couldn't say no, not because she thought it was the will of God. Like many other people, Marie also felt that the need constitutes a call. If there is a need, then God must be leading us to fulfill that need. And so they burn out for lack of discernment or because of unwarranted guilt. And so, also, their anger builds. Declaring boundaries, on the other hand, diminishes anger.

Declaring boundaries does not mean that we become selfish or simply think of our own needs. In contrast, boundaries should be declared under the direction of the indwelling Holy Spirit in order to avoid unnecessary burnout. Burning out for God may sound noble but in truth it handicaps us in the fulfillment of God's work through us. Crises, war, spiritual attack, and other such emergencies can provide exceptions. But the normal Christian life should be lived within boundaries of balanced living.

Later in her life, when Geraldine was once again pushing herself beyond her resources, she began to evidence symptoms of burnout. Her book on the Chinese preacher Pastor Hsi had met with widespread acceptance. But the intense effort she put into that book, coupled with her extensive speaking schedule, had taken their toll.

Once again there came a letter from her father—a letter steeped in personal experience:

> How well I understand that nervous breaking down from which you have suffered. Let it be a warning. There is a limit you should not attempt to pass in exhausting labors. It is not easy to fix it, but experience shows pretty clearly where it is. I have been beyond it at times, when all the foundations of life seemed gone. I cannot express what that means, and hope you will never know. Most people have no conception how thin the foundations are which keep them above the abyss, where the interests of life exist no more. I tell you this, for you need to be warned. Learn to say "No" to invitations or calls to labour which destroy the power to labour and the possibility of service. I do think Howard, as your husband—and doctor—should say "No" for you, and forbid suicidal toils absolutely, firmly, finally. Tell him that with my sincere love.[20]

Howard Taylor did his job well for forty years. It was one of his major contributions to the relationship. At the age of seventy-five Geraldine began work on her last biography after a life of steady writing, speaking, and caring for others.

Sometimes people with a strong sense of focus fight a lifelong battle against overdoing, over-extension, and high-wire living. For that reason, and because of her own ongoing battle against burnout, Geraldine wrote with unusual insight about burnout, and renewal from that burnout, as she told of the lives of some of the greatest missionaries this world has known.

D. E. Hoste, General Director of the China Inland Mission after Hudson Taylor, from 1900 to 1935, was high-strung by nature and prone to exhaustion. "'In weariness often' is something you must know about, dear Mrs. Taylor," he once wrote.[21] With that weariness came a tendency toward depression. Similarly, at another time he wrote to her: "I am feeling a good deal tired at times .... I often wonder how I manage to keep on."[22]

Once, when talking to Geraldine about the book she had just written on Hudson Taylor, he permitted a glimpse into his inner feelings: "The pressure!" he said. "It goes on from stage to stage, pressed beyond measure, every true work of God. It changes with every period of your life. The most killing years of my life were 1904, 1905, 1906—terrible! The pressure of the work. I was half-killed. One has been able to make arrangements since then. There is less strain of work now, but other things develop. He eases you at one end, brings you into new things at the other ..."

Geraldine added:

"The pressure." It does not speak of an easy life, or one that was free from care. At one time the floods of a personal anxiety and grief threatened to engulf him to such an extent that he seriously contemplated resigning from his position. "Pressed beyond measure—cast down but not forsaken"; such phrases present no pictures of those who walk straight through every trial or difficulty as though they did not exist! Neither are they applicable to those who walk under cloudless skies with the happy confidence of treading an assured pathway.[23]

One time, during a period of fatigue, Hoste wrote to Hudson Taylor, asking for his prayer because he was distressed that in his own prayers "wandering thoughts come in, and then in confessing them, often more wandering thoughts come in."[24]

In a wonderful example of balance, not willing to make the situation worse by spiritualizing physical exhaustion, Taylor wrote, "I do not think that wandering in thought at all necessarily indicates a loss of spiritual life, but it does show a loss of nerve-tone and calls for . . . use of such measures as will generally give vigor to the health." Geraldine commented, "The man who was indeed father of the Mission had suffered himself from the attacks of Satan upon a mind that had become faint and wearied."[25]

Both Hoste and his wife, Gertrude Broomhall Hoste, suffered from somewhat fragile health; and so the General Director knew the frustration of a willing mind and spirit hampered by a weakened body. The practical result in Hoste was a heightened sensitivity to the feelings and needs of others.

For example, Hoste viewed prayer as work—intense, hard work! He was human enough to realize this. He would never have urged a fellow worker to take some time off to relax at the same time he told them to engage in intercessory prayer. Wrote "one," who was probably Geraldine herself, since in her biographies she studiously avoided a direct reference to herself:

> Intercessory prayer was a tremendous physical exercise to him—a wrestling with "the powers of darkness." One morning, a few days before he would recognize that he was really ill, during our time of intercession, he simply wrestled in prayer, and cried to the Lord in agony to deliver poor China from the awful power of demons and principalities and powers, and he quite broke and burst into tears—the only time I ever saw him weep.[26]

Far away from the main mission station in Shanghai, James Fraser was doing a highly strategic and difficult work among the Lisu. By both temperament and life situation, he, too, was a perfect candidate for burnout. At a time when Fraser felt that it was imperative for him to remain where he was, Mr. Hoste issued an order for him to go to a place where the mission felt he was more greatly needed. Appeals were made and turned down. Fraser felt confused over the apparent discrepancy between his own perception of the will of God and that of the general director.

Fraser reacted physically, as well as with depression. Then a telegram came from Hoste, showing him to be a man who was strong enough to admit the possibility of a way other than his own. "If you feel distinctly led to stay on for Lisu work, I would not press your going to Sapushan."[27] Respecting the leading of his superior, but at the same time recognizing that he himself understood the needs of the work with the Lisu, Fraser once again sought God's will—and stayed, with Hoste's blessing.

The Fraser incident struck me on a personal level. From 1919 to 1935 my Aunt Ruth was a missionary in China, part of that time under the China Inland Mission. She, like Fraser, worked in a fairly remote area. Like Fraser, too, there came the day when the mission directed her to move on to a different area, despite the fact that she felt a call to stay where she was.

In a 1934 letter, written from Kansu to her mother and sisters in Chicago, Aunt Ruth wrote:

> This morning Mr. Warren saw me again about my leaving the Mission. He was very nice and sympathetic and he is doing all he can to keep me from leaving . . . . I told him that if I am given the freedom to obey the Lord's will, I will stay in the CIM, of course. They say that is

what they want to do... and I know that at Shanghai (Mission Headquarters) they are anxious for us to fully obey the Lord's will; but they do not always see or know what takes place in the interior.

Apparently my aunt felt by 1935 that she must leave the mission, but then had reason to hope that things could still be worked out. In late 1935 she wrote to my mother: "Letters from Shanghai have been so different lately, such a different tone, that I feel there is now some hope that I may be able to remain in the C.I.M.... They still say I have not left and I've left it to them." Anticipating a meeting with the mission heads in Shanghai, where she had been requested to come, she was delayed because of potential danger in the travel involved. She wrote, "Do please pray about my visit to Shanghai."

The letters I have found stop there, but I recall her being home about six years later, when I was about three or four. I remember a mission for the Chinese that she opened in Los Angeles after China's doors were closed to foreign missionaries in 1949. And I recall seeing her off at the harbor when she went as a missionary to Taiwan. Always she remembered and loved China and the Chinese people.

By approximately 1936, my aunt had become independent of the China Inland Mission. I remember hearing, in later years, of my family's sadness over this and of their increased concern for her safety. But this time there was no backing down on the part of the mission.

God continued to use the China Inland Mission, and He continued to use my aunt. Recently I found a little book, published in 1898, titled *Christ Our Example* by Caroline Fry. Scrawled on the front inside cover are the words

Miss Ruth Benson
with the assurance of prayer
and remembrance of us both.
D. E. Hoste

March, 1936
"Let us consider one another to provoke
unto love and good works."

By the time my aunt left the CIM, Mr. Hoste had stepped down as general director. Apparently he did not make the final decision relative to my aunt, since that would have occurred after 1935. But his sense of responsibility toward her, and his tender understanding of her situation, are clear in this inscription.

It takes a person finely tuned to the will of God to express kindness in the midst of disagreement. Even though he could be very firm, his personal suffering and life-long battle with burnout refined D. E. Hoste into a gentle servant of God. He was continually being renewed.

In her biography of James Fraser, Geraldine showed other aspects of Hoste's continuous battle against burnout. It is noteworthy that burnout was often accompanied by some psychological symptoms that were not viewed by any of these saints as sin or something to be confessed. Furthermore, burnout was consistently viewed by them as something to be avoided rather than as an indication of weakness or sin. "It's better to burn out rather than rust out" was not a slogan that had much appeal for these people. They were not into that kind of ego satisfaction. They did not want to be martyrs, although any one of them would have been the first to be willing, had that been the call of God for them. Many of their predecessors, along with missionaries from other missions and national Christians, had been burned with flames, cut into pieces, beheaded, or tortured by other unspeakable methods during the early days of the mission.

James Fraser opened up a ministry to the Lisu, who lived high in the mountains of inland China where the Burma Road comes through. He was young and strong, but he was also alone and engaged in pioneering areas where the gospel had never before been preached. He ventured into areas where out and out demonism flourished. Fraser was attacking Satan's stronghold. Understandably, physical, spiritual, and emotional reactions set in. In Fraser's words, "He would be a missionary simpleton who expected plain sailing in *any* work of God."[28] Understanding the truth of Satan as a conquered foe was of primary importance to him and others like him.

Great men of God sometimes suffer from depression *because* they are in the center of the will of God, not because they have strayed from it. In his early years of struggle with the language, along with his loneliness and incredible physical expenditure, Fraser grappled with feelings of hopelessness that were caused or aggravated by spiritual warfare. Said Geraldine, "It was not lack of interest in his surroundings that led to the depression of spirit that now began to assail him. He did not know at first what to make of it."[29] He questioned whether the root cause could be the food, the loneliness, or the drizzling mist descending over the mountains. But as the days and weeks wore on, he realized that there were influences of another kind to be reckoned with.

> For strange uncertainty began to shadow his inward life. All he had believed and rejoiced in became unreal, and even his prayers seemed to mock him as the answers faded into nothingness .... In his solitude, depression such as he had never known before closed down upon him .... Deeply were the foundations shaken in those

days and nights of conflict, until Fraser realized that behind it all were "powers of darkness," seeking to overwhelm him. He had dared to invade Satan's kingdom, undisputed for ages.[30]

In a conversation with Geraldine, Fraser explained:

I am an engineer and believe in things working. I want to see them work. I have found that much of the spiritual teaching one hears does not seem to work. My apprehension at any rate of other aspects of truth had broken down. The passive side of leaving everything to the Lord Jesus as our life, while blessedly true, was not all that was needed just then. Definite resistance on the ground of The Cross was what brought me light. For I found it worked . . . . People will tell you, after a helpful meeting perhaps, that such and such a truth is the secret of victory. No: we need different truth at different times. "Look to the Lord," some will say. "Resist the devil" is also Scripture (James 4:7). And I found it worked![31]

"Different truth at different times." How much we need that biblical principle as we deal with the principalities and powers of the twenty-first century.

Listlessness and depression were common foes. But in her portrayal of Fraser, Geraldine expounded much about that sometimes confusing tangle of spiritual, physical, and psychological causes for depression. Fraser explained his own approach: "I have had many such experiences [failure] before, but have made the mistake of giving way to depression instead of calmly investigating the cause of things. This time however, the thief is not going to escape."[32]

After one such experience

> Fraser came to see that it was due to physical as well
> as spiritual causes. He had confined himself too much to
> his room—the only place in which he could count on pri-
> vacy—and had neglected exercise and the mental bal-
> ance of good hard study. Loneliness and the pressure of
> surrounding darkness had driven him to his knees too
> exclusively. The laws of nature are also the law of God;
> and he had to learn that ignorance or forgetfulness of
> either the one or the other does not save us from the
> penalty of breaking them.... "I now think," he wrote
> quite simply, "that a long, healthy walk was indicated, or
> wholesome Lisu study, rather than the 'knee-drill' I prac-
> ticed with such signal failure."[33]

One of Geraldine Taylor's most successful books in terms of
popular appeal was on Pastor Hsi, the Chinese scholar and opium
addict who became a leader in the Chinese church. In her portrayal
of the life of this pastor, she touched on the possible exception to
the usual laws of nature and God that exist in the area of burnout.

Sometimes one must simply go on, even when rational
thought demands pause. During the last nine months of World
War II a Swedish diplomat named Raoul Wallenberg, along with
a Swedish career diplomat Per Anger and a handful of others,
saved 100,000 Jewish lives in Budapest. The Jews of Europe had
been scattered and systematically exterminated. This was the one
major group remaining. There was no time to wait, and there
were few people to whom to delegate work. This situation was an
exception to the usual precautionary rule against burnout.

For the Christian, it is vital that any exception be based on
the distinct, personal call of God, not just the desire of some

Christian leader or one's own ego. Each of us who tends toward overextension can be deluded into thinking that our own situation qualifies as this exception. Our self-talk tends to go something like this: "My work is unique, special, and immediate in its demands." "There is no one else to do it." And least defensible of all reasons, "I can't say no."

We have trouble separating the good from the important, the better from the better still, or even from the best. Most of us are not choosing between good and evil when we burn out. To the contrary, what we are doing seems so important that we assume that, just this time, God will grant the extra strength to see us through. Then when He doesn't—because he does allow the laws of nature to take their course—we question His power, we say He didn't answer our prayer, or we feel weak, or allow ourselves to become bitter. All this because we tried to walk on water on the basis of our own strength and volition and found that, consistent with the laws of nature, we sank.

When the call to overextension is really from God—and that situation will be rare indeed—I believe that it is normally short-term and for a specific purpose. Sometimes God will, for that time only, contradict the laws of nature, imbue us with extra strength, and surround us with a special protection. It is conceivable that at other times the same servants will suffer the natural fallout from burnout, but that this very suffering will build great treasure in eternal reward. God doesn't always make it easy to obey.

Burnout, if it is allowed to develop, should never be taken lightly, as though we believe that God will make it easy because it is His call. God enables us to perform His task, but He doesn't promise that there will be no pain or sacrifice. When He does request sacrifice, our willingness to offer it up pleases Him deeply. That in itself is reward. Easy Christianity is neither biblical nor realistic. A "Christianity" promising freedom from pain, rather than enablement through suffering, doesn't work and is in fact simply a delusion. Sadly, like Job in the Old Testament, the sufferer is too often cast out by his fellows as a failure, rather than viewed as one who has triumphed through his or her faith.

Pastor Hsi lived a life that was, at times, an exception to the general prohibition against burnout. In view of the future of the Chinese church under communist rule, active Chinese Christians were vital to the survival and growth of that church. Pastor Hsi was an unusual Chinese leader who did much during his life to build that church. His was no ordinary life. Hoste himself became Hsi's intimate friend and said of him, "The more one saw of him, the more one felt that Christ had taken possession of his life—the real Christ, the living Christ."[34]

Regarding over-extension, Geraldine wrote:

> One remarkable feature of his [Pastor Hsi's] life, during those busy years, was the energy and endurance he manifested under long-continued strain, both mental and physical. "I always felt," said Mr. Hoste, who was with him constantly, "that Hsi had a bodily strength not his own. He was a man whom God specially sustained for the work He had given him to do. I have known him to walk thirty miles at a stretch, in case of need; quite a remarkable feat for a man of his age and training, and after fasting entirely for two days, he was able to baptize by immersion as many as fifty men at one time."[35]
>
> "He was not infrequently warned of danger by a curious, sudden failure of physical strength. 'I often know,' Hsi would say, 'when special trial or temptation is at hand. I become so weak in body, that it is necessary to stop whatever I am doing, and cry to [the] Lord . . . . It was not faintness exactly; but overpowering weakness, with a

sense of great apprehension.... Rest and food did not relieve it. But prayer always did.'"[36]

Curiously, when Pastor Hsi died "there was no disease or suffering; it was just the gradual withdrawal of life, before the vital powers failed."

"The Lord is taking away my strength," he said. "It must be because my work is done."[37]

Pastor Hsi dealt with open demon worship, opium addiction, and the attacks of unseen spiritual forces that raged against the sovereignty of God in the lives of these people. The time was short before all outside influences beckoning the Chinese people toward the gospel of Jesus Christ would be shut off by the evil of communism. God endowed a surrendered human vessel with special resources, through which He poured Himself out to a people who had been so long without the gospel. Pastor Hsi's life was an exception to the normal rules of burnout. But often no truth is really complete without some consideration of the exceptions.

Whether by a wise, God-directed conservation of strength, or by the direct intervention of God, in renewal and going on, Geraldine Guinness Taylor lived a life of balance in spite of her tendency to burn out. In her personal life, in her work with the Chinese people, and in her task as biographer for the China Inland Mission, she knew the secret of divine renewal. Much of her ability to go on was drawn from a deep, balanced leading from God, but the true source of her power goes back to a day early in her missionary life.

Referring to some special meetings she had attended in Shanghai, Geraldine wrote of herself in the third person:

> Four years in China had taught her something of the joy and blessing to be found in deeper fellowship with the Master, but something also of the deadening influences of

heathenism, the powers of evil within as well as around her, the blank despair of seeking to help others when her own soul was out of living touch with Christ . . . Praying in anguish no one suspected for light and help, it was the last Sunday before Christmas when a word was spoken that, under God, brought deliverance and made all things new. After the evangelistic service in the C.I.M., Hall, an entire stranger—a Christian seaman—came up to her and said earnestly: "Are you filled with the Holy Ghost?"

Filled with the Holy Ghost? She remembered no more of the conversation, but the question burned deeper and deeper into her heart. . . . She knew that the Holy Spirit must be in her life in a certain sense, for "if any man have not the Spirit of Christ, he is none of His." And yet, just as certainly, she knew that she was not "filled with the Spirit," and was experiencing little of his power.[38]

Her immediate reaction was fear of being misled or of mistaking emotion for reality. Yet as she studied the book of Acts, she realized that it was filled with reports of deeds performed in the power of the Holy Spirit. According to her, "It was indeed the Holy Spirit she needed."

She recognized that the Spirit was a Person, to be welcomed by faith into the heart. "All the rest that can be told is that she took the step, though with fear and trembling—scarce knowing what it meant—and trusted the Holy Spirit to come in and possess her fully . . . . Feeling nothing, realizing nothing, she just took God at His word."[39]

For many months Geraldine had been troubled by her lack of power in leading people to Christ. She now prayed specifically each day for the following week for some conversions. Twenty people came to know Christ. That was how the Holy Spirit was leading her in prayer, and the request was honored.

The encouragement to Hudson Taylor was great, especially when he visited a young missionary who lay dying and had been filled with fear. When he entered her room to try to console her, he found the fear gone and the room filled with a sense of peace and triumph.

"She told me about the Holy Spirit," whispered the one who had so dreaded the dark valley, "and it was just what I needed.'"

Said Geraldine, "In answer to prayer, the blessing spread."[40] The members of the mission sought the filling of the Spirit, and through divine renewal came divine power. In Hudson Taylor, as well as in the lives and work of others, the testing at times increased, but each experience became "a special opportunity for God to work and for faith to triumph."

In the middle of a period of severe financial need, Hudson Taylor turned to his wife and stated, "Now you will watch. You will watch and see what God will do." And, according to Geraldine, there was "even a touch of joyous confidence about the words."[41]

Renewal had found its source. *Recovery*—a word so bandied about in our time—is the opposite of "me-ism" when it is defined in its truest form. Recovery is actually to be found in "Christ-in-me," by the power of the Holy Spirit, at times administered by the counsel and comfort of other human beings, by changed circumstances and through appropriate medical treatment. True recovery is greater, however, than any human cure, which at best puts the pieces back together as they were. True recovery goes further: it is divine renewal.

Arthur T. Pierson (1837–1911)

*B*orn in New York, Arthur T. Pierson became a Presbyterian minister in 1860. He was a Bible speaker, a leader at the famous Keswick Convention, and the author of many books. Pierson wrote:

Our Father who seeks to perfect His saints in holiness knows the value of the refiner's fire. It is with the most precious metals that the assayer takes most pains, and subjects them to hot fires, because only such fires melt the metal, and only molten metal releases its alloy, or takes perfectly its new form in the mould. The old refiner never left his crucible, but sat down by it, lest there should be one excessive degree of heat to mar the metal, and so soon as, skimming from the surface the last of the dross, he saw his own face reflected, he put out the fire.

How beautifully are we told that the Redeemer "shall sit as a Refiner and purifier of silver" (Mal. iii:3). Being determined to perfect His saints, He puts His precious Metal into His crucible. But He sits by it, and watches it. Love is His thermometer, and marks the exact degree of heat; not one instant's unnecessary pang will He permit; and as soon as the dross is released so that He sees Himself reflected the trial ceases.[1]

A. T. Pierson possessed a rare insight of great spiritual depth, which issued forth in simple, practical application.

He that receiveth a prophet in the name of a prophet, shall receive a prophet's reward; and he that receiveth a righteous man in the name of a righteous man, shall receive a righteous man's reward. And whosoever shall give to drink unto one of these little ones a cup of cold water only in the name of a disciple, verily, I say unto you, he shall in no wise lose his reward . . . .

Perhaps you cannot give the cup, but you can give the water that is in it, which costs nothing but the dipping. If you give so much as the water which the cup will hold, to a thirsty soul in the capacity of a disciple, you will find it written in the book of God's remembrance that, on a certain day, you gave to a certain disciple a cup of cold water![2]

Isobel Kuhn

NINE

Isobel Kuhn: A Platform of Testing

*I*t was a hot, humid summer day in Chicago. A young student working as a waitress to put herself through Moody Bible Institute was pouring coffee from a huge, hot tureen. Suddenly the room began to spin, and Isobel Miller knew that she was going to faint.

Visions of hot coffee pouring down on her as she fell flashed through her mind. With a last burst of consciousness, she cried out: "Lord, help me to get the tureen turned off first!"

"Instantly a most wonderful thing happened," she was to write in later years.

> I felt the Lord Himself come and stand behind my left shoulder. He put His right hand on my right shoulder and a tingle shot through me from head to foot. Healed completely, I calmly turned off the tureen and stood for half a second in deep, unspeakable worship and communion with Him. Then He was gone, and I turned to my tray. Not only had the nausea and faintness left, but a wonderful exhilaration thrilled through me. I seemed to fly rather than walk; I was lifted above all my circumstances until it seemed I was an onlooker at my own body in its ill-fitting uniform serving the tables. That exhilaration and physical refurbishment lasted for days.[1]

She had asked for physical healing, and God had said yes. She had been tested and then healed.

Nineteen years later, in the war years of 1944, Isobel Miller Kuhn was headed home from missionary work in China on a troop ship. The ship's route and date of arrival were top secret, and the men and women on board were separated. Apart from the two hours each day when she was allowed to see her husband, John, Isobel was left alone, sick with fatigue, and solely in charge of their active fifteen-month-old son, Danny.

The trip lasted for thirty-six days. A ship's officer had sternly reminded the passengers that this was not a passenger ship. For that reason, there was no deck that was safe for babies. Many of the decks had no railings, and there were large holes into which a child could easily fall. Perhaps worst of all, the officer warned, "If your child falls overboard, the ship will not stop to pick it up."[2]

Standing in line for food, some two weeks into the journey, Isobel began to feel as though she were going to faint. The feelings of nineteen years earlier were present once again. Once again she cried out to God to help her in her physical need. But this time God said wait. The testing did not immediately pass.

Enablement was provided, however. A lady standing nearby offered her help, not just then but for the remainder of the trip. Danny was safe, and the pressure on Isobel eased. She was not healed, but a person was given to be her "door of escape" (1 Corinthians 10:13, Way's Translation). "God used a natural means to deliver me, that is all," she concluded.

The condition that Isobel described as "taut nerves" was not removed until months later, when she could finally rest and relax for a prolonged period of time. In her words, "He allowed [my nerves] to stretch and stretch and stretch—but not to snap."[3] Then the time came when He said, "Enough,"[4] and the testing ended.

A number of years elapsed. Isobel was in her fifties when she entered into the greatest test yet in the area of physical illness. There came a day when God said no to her requests for healing. It was "the platform of a dread disease."[5] This time the platform became a "springboard for Heaven."[6]

First there was a private word from God. A couple of relatively minor accidents had occurred, each with its own inner warning of impending illness. Isobel's impression was not specific in terms of the final outcome, but the sense of becoming ill and needing to return home to the United States was pressing. To Isobel there was a positive side to this: she would be able to spend time with her two children. The idea of death had not yet entered her thoughts.

She was aware of the danger of emotions entering into such an inner leading. In her words: "The only safe way . . . is to distrust it until its source is manifest. When it is clear that it is given of God then we may humbly extract from it all the comfort we need."[7]

Most of us who have known the Lord for a period of time understand what it is to have a private word from Him. In 1973 my father had a stroke that left him unconscious and unlikely to recover. Yet I had a private dread of having him placed in a convalescent home and/or getting a phone call in the middle of the night, telling me that he had died. I slept nervously, alternating between hope and despair regarding the final outcome. Then the dreaded day came when the hospital announced that they could do no more. We were to decide which convalescent home we wanted to place him in.

That night before I went to bed I stood in front of the long, full mirror in the hallway of my parents' home, brushing my hair and praying aloud to God. "Do we really have to make this decision?" I implored. But as I drifted off to sleep I realized that, for the first time during his six-week illness, my fear of a telephone call in the middle of the night was lifted. At 5 a.m. the telephone did ring. Deep inside I knew what it was, but I was strangely calm. My father had gone to be with his Lord, and I was okay.

Seven years later my mother lay in another hospital room, badly injured from an automobile accident. She was expected to live. It was mid-afternoon on Wednesday, August 13, 1980. I received a call from a producer at NBC, asking me to appear on a talk show on Monday evening. I hesitated. With a flash I thought, "I can't do that. That might be the day of my mother's funeral." Then, collecting myself, I corrected myself, "How ridiculous. Your imagination is running away with you." I accepted the invitation and tried to push away all thought of death and funerals. But somewhere deep inside I wondered.

Eight hours later the phone rang. "You mother is not doing well," a physician informed me. I hurried to get dressed. Within minutes the phone rang again. "Your mother is not doing well," the same voice announced. Confirmed in what I had believed to be the truth at the time of his first call, I asked, "Are you trying to tell me that she's already died?" "Yes," he replied simply. "We didn't expect this to happen." In the middle of my grief, once again I was somehow prepared, not really taken by surprise. Furthermore, no matter how hard I tried to make other arrangements, the only day available for her funeral was Monday.

In both instances, a "private word" from the Lord had not been something for me to act on. These instances were nothing like fortune-telling, which is condemned by God. Rather, they were both examples of that quiet, inner preparation from God Himself, buffering for me the sharp edges of the pain. And they became the early beginning of inner healing and ultimate recovery. For in both cases I had received assurance that I would be okay, even when that ultimate fear from my childhood, the death of my parents, became reality.

Isobel quoted Amy Carmichael regarding this "private word":

> Before we reach the place where such waters must be crossed, there is almost always a private word spoken by the Beloved to the lover. That is the word which will be most assaulted . . . . The enemy will fasten upon it, twist it about, belittle it, obscure it, try to undermine our confidence in its integrity, and to wreck our tranquility by making us afraid, but this will put him to flight: "I believe God that it shall be even as it was told me."[8]

For Isobel, after the private word came the earthly reality: a diagnosis of cancer. First had come a sense that she would merely come home for a while. Then came the knowledge of the nearness of death, that "I am getting ready to move."[9] Death became for her the final platform of testing. Isobel wrote, "For the Christian, death is not the dissolution of life but the consummation . . . . Or as Amy Carmichael words it, 'The days of our bloom and our power are just about to begin.'"

> *Gone, they tell me, is youth;*
> *Gone is the strength of my life.*
> *Nothing remains but decline,*
> *Nothing but age and decay.*
>
> *Not so, I'm God's little child,*
> *Only beginning to live.*
> *Coming the days of my prime,*
> *Coming the strength of my life,*
> *Coming the vision of God,*
> *Coming my bloom and my power!*[10]

Isobel Kuhn thought of all of life's difficulties as platforms upon which God shows Himself. For Isobel, as for most of us, one of these platforms was that of physical and emotional stress and illness. As Hudson Taylor put it, "Difficulties afford a platform upon which He can show Himself."[11] The verse to which Isobel clung when she was thinking about such platforms was: "For I think that God hath set forth us . . . last . . . for we are made a spectacle unto the world (1 Cor. 4:9)."[12]

She explained:

> The Word says that we will be a theatron to men and angels. Some of our most painful platforms may have no human witness. In that case we should remember the significant words, *and angels*. I'm sure that the suffering of the saints, while its purpose is to teach us more of Himself, to develop and enrich us, also bears fruit in other lives.[13]

In a preface to Kuhn's book *Green Leaf in Drought-Time*, J. Oswald Sanders explains the concept of "platform," using the word *testing*. "God does not waste suffering," asserted Sanders, "nor does He discipline out of caprice. If He plows, it is because He purposes a crop . . . life apparently is meant to be a series of tests in the school of God. The tests He sends or permits are in reality His vote of confidence, for He undertakes not to allow us to suffer any testing beyond our powers of endurance."[14]

Born in 1901, Isobel entered the field of teaching before becoming a missionary and writer. After leaving education, she became a missionary to China under the China Inland Mission and married John Kuhn. Isobel wrote a number of books on the couple's joint missionary work and on the mission in general.

Much of her writing is highly devotional, as well as biographical and autobiographical.

For years John and Isobel served as missionaries to the Lisu in China, continuing the work of James Fraser, who had died, and developing their own work. After the communist takeover of China, the CIM changed its name to Overseas Missionary Fellowship. The Kuhns then served under its auspices in Thailand until Isobel's death in 1957.

Before I became a family counselor and a writer, I, like Isobel Kuhn, was a teacher. To me, therefore, and obviously to her, it makes sense that a discussion of any individual Christian life could be effectively expressed in the testings that comprise that life as well as in the principles upon which it is built.

The word *testing* has many connotations. We test products, like lawn mowers and chairs, to make certain they function well and endure. We test drugs and foods for their safety and purity. We test gold for its value and gems for their authenticity. Testing is a major factor that ensures quality in the commercial realm.

This is true in the human realm as well. We test children in school. We each have to pass a test in order to operate a motor vehicle or to obtain a certain license or credential to do a job. We test people for physical illnesses or mental disorders. We judge quality by tests. We use tests to demonstrate excellence and uncover problems.

In God's school testing goes one step further. By testing, by using various platforms in which to manifest Himself, God develops us and makes us exactly what He wants us to be, in order for us to fulfill our role on this earth, as well as to prepare us for our role in heaven.

Just as problems relating to physical health and healing were platforms of testing throughout Isobel's Kuhn's life, the correct valuation of things was another area that was tested. At the outset of her missionary career, the general director of the CIM, D. E. Hoste, announced, "Miss Miller, if I had a beautiful bedspread, I would throw it in the river." Recalls Isobel, "I was startled. Did he have X-ray eyes? I did have a beautiful quilt in my boxes, a wedding gift from a girl friend. But how did Mr. Hoste know that? And if he did, why should he object?"[15]

Later on she understood his remarks. Following her marriage to John, just after she had fixed up their little home as attractively as possible, they had guests from the church where they ministered. The visitors admired the pretty things. But then, to Isobel's horror, an elderly woman

> blew her nose with her fingers, and—wiped the stuff off on my beautiful traveling rug! In another minute a young mother laughingly held her baby son out over my new rattan rug. She carried him to the door, but as she went she carefully held him out over the rug so that a wet streak ran down the center of my cherished floor covering. Since their own floors were of earth my visitor had no idea that she was doing anything offensive to me.[16]

Outwardly Isobel remained courteous, but after the guests had left,

> I returned to my deflated sitting room and stood looking at it—that disgusting gob on my traveling rug and the discolored streak across my pretty new mat. Hot resentment rose in my heart, and then there followed my first battle over things.
>
> Suddenly I understood what Mr. Hoste had meant: "Miss Miller, if I had a beautiful bedspread, I would throw it into the river." He did not mean that he did not like

beautiful things. He meant that if possessions would in any way interfere with our hospitality, it would be better to consign them to the river. In other words, if your finery hinders your testimony, throw it out. In our Lord's own words, if thine hand offend thee, cut it off; He was not against our possessing hands, but against our using them to hold on to sinful or hindering things.

So I faced my choice. In our first home—what was to come first? An attractive sitting room just for ourselves? Or a room suited to share with the local Chinese? . . . . Mentally I offered that pretty rattan furniture to the Lord to be wrecked by the country peasants if they chose.[17]

After Isobel had been in China for a number of years, she and her husband came home to the United States. In her words:

We were invited to a house, a house beautifully decorated and furnished with all that modern art and household conveniences can offer. The two who owned it had no children. They both worked all day and could use their house only at nights and on holidays. As we were shown through its perfectly ordered, spotlessly clean rooms, where two human lives were being spent just in order to maintain these things, a desolating sense of barrenness swept over me. What a terrible waste! Two lives spent for just this . . . . I felt what an aching tragedy those two barren human lives were—all their God-given sympathies, energizing love, and passion spent on things. Physical hardship and spiritual luxury; physical comfort and spiritual death. Oh, that we would waken to the real values of life.[18]

On another furlough at home, Isobel related a similar incident:

> I met a lady who said to me, "I have no interest in anything but my house and my garden. My house and my garden are my life." I thought how pitifully poor she had confessed herself to be; even though hers was a large expensive house and mine a mere shanty on the wild mountain side . . . . And my heart cried out, "What a waste! For her to spend that human life and sympathies on a wooden house and a dirt garden when God's spiritual house is calling out for living stones and His garden has Seedlings of Eternal Destiny that need to be trained!" But America is full of human beings (church-goers, many of them) who live just for things. When that lady dies, she must leave behind her house and her garden—everything that spells life to her by her own confession . . . . What are you living for—what is your life?[19]

In the twenty-first century we human beings seem to be more *thing*-conscious than ever. More than ever before we are prone to judge success by the criteria of money, fame, power, and possessions. Character, kindness, and sacrifice are not popular as goals. The rot is in us all. Sometimes I feel defeated and defensive because I don't have the big home and the expensive car. To be honest, all I really need in a car is safety and durability. A bigger place to live is becoming important to me for some good, practical reasons, but I can live—and accomplish God's will—without it.

Not long ago a friend shared a thought with me that has remained in my mind. We were talking about *things*. He cited Bishop Fulton Sheen, who stated that, in the area of clothing, the quality, type, and quantity that any one individual possesses should be appropriate to the vocation or occupation of that person. The statement made sense. After all, a big-game hunter in Africa would not need the impeccable dress clothes of a conductor of the New York Philharmonic Orchestra.

The danger is that even we Christians tend to judge our work for God by how splashy it appears, by how prosperous we look. Material possessions become status symbols. Yet we, above all others, recognize that we are only a heartbeat away from heaven, where all that will count is how much we have built in the gold, silver, and precious stones of heaven—not the wood, hay, and stubble of Earth. Only that which is eternal really matters. In Isobel's Kuhn's words, "Lisuland is a place of physical hardship and spiritual luxury, but if you have ever tasted that luxury, all else will be tame ever after."[20]

There is another category of testing that goes beyond the testing of things. That is the determination of how much we are willing to suffer for His sake. Such testing was another platform in the life and ministry of Isobel.

One Christmas night, high up in those mountainous precipices of Lisuland, Isobel was asked to give the message to the little group that had gathered. She took as her theme, "When they had opened their treasures, they presented unto Him gifts; gold and frankincense, and myrrh."

> Gold represents our wealth, the possession we may offer to our King. Frankincense is a type of our worship. But the myrrh? That bitter thing? Surely that can have only one meaning—the things we are willing to suffer for His sake. We were all bringing our gold to Him, making our freewill offerings. Some were also bringing a bit of frankincense. But was anyone bringing Him myrrh?

As I put the question, one face in the audience stood out sharply, a lean brown face with understanding eyes that burned with hot tears. He was one who had been beaten by the feudal lord because he had become a Christian, beaten so mercilessly that he could not walk for three days. Yes, in that faraway rim of the earth, among those poor and ragged tribes people in their barren mountains, there were offerings of myrrh that Christmas time.

"Lord, I bring Thee my myrrh." That was the silent heart-cry that had taken the hurt and fear out of our journey to Lisuland. I had seldom before been able to offer Him that gift, and I have never forgotten the joy of it.[21]

In making application of the concept of offering myrrh to those of us who live in this country, Isobel asked, "Isn't the coldness in our churches today due to the fact that we offer Christ only our gold? We have for a long time ceased to offer Him myrrh."[22]

Then, putting the idea into shoe leather,

Most myrrh is undramatic. There are those who would be willing to be beaten for Christ's sake or willing to climb over landslides, but yet would be quite unwilling to spend half an hour daily in prayer for His cause and His kingdom. It is myrrh when you say quietly to a pressing friend, "No, I cannot go tonight—there is something I must do," and then spend that time in intercession . . . . The cost of myrrh is monotony and obscurity . . . . "Lord, I bring Thee my myrrh."[23]

The bringing of myrrh is another testing ground, another platform of exhibit for the world to see and for the encouragement of angels.

All of us have our special platforms for testing. Relationships with parents, spouses, children; marriage; choice of a life work; daily organization of our lives; hospitality; financial loss or gain; rejection—these and many more can become situations of testing, platforms for glory or doom. The life of Isobel Kuhn reads like the story of a pilgrim, a modern *Pilgrim's Progress*.

In Hebrews 11:13 we are called "pilgrims on the earth," "sojourners among aliens." Weymouth adds, "For men who acknowledge this make it manifest that they are seeking elsewhere a country of their own." This world is truly not our home, but a testing ground of importance for all eternity. We are continually being tested and shaped in the school of God.

Testing in the school of God rests upon living in the truth of biblical principles that God has shown in His Word and through the lives of His saints. One of the strengths of Isobel's writing lies in her ability to present concise principles for godly living that God made real to her. Those principles that stand out in any individual life may vary according to personality, as well as to our calling.

In discussing scriptural principles, Isobel often uses imagery, particularly as it relates to gemstones. Using a quote from G. Campbell Morgan, she explains, "What a strange bringing together of contradictions! 'Stones of fire.' A stone is the last embodiment of principle—hard and cold. Fire is the essence of passion—warm and energizing. Put the two together, and we have stones—principle, fire—passion; principle shot through with passion, passion held by principle."[24] In God's Kingdom we are, indeed, living stones made up of two key components: passion and principle.

Again using a quote about gemstones to illustrate a different slant on the same idea:

> Do you know that lovely fact about the opal? That in the first place, it is made only of desert, dust, sand, and silica, and owes its beauty and preciousness to a defect. It is a stone with a broken heart. It is full of minute fissures which admit air, and the air refracts the light. Hence its lovely hues and that sweet lamp of fire that ever burns at its heart, for the breath of the Lord God is in it.
>
> You are only conscious of the cracks and desert dust, but so He makes His precious opal. We must be broken in ourselves before we can give back the lovely hues of His light, and the lamp in the temple can burn in us and never go out.[25]

Passion held by principle involves perfect balance; not the coldness of straight principle, nor the uncontrolled emotion of absolute passion. When our feelings, our passions—even our godly passions—become the overwhelming force in our lives, we need to apply principle. When principle leaves us cold, unfeeling, and even legalistic, we need to infuse that principle with passion. Following are a few of the basic principles that appear in the writings of Isobel Kuhn.

Again quoting G. Campbell Morgan, Isobel offers a scriptural principle that is simple but widespread in its application: "The whole difference between faith and fear is that of the difference of putting our 'buts' before or after God. God commands, but there are difficulties. That is paralysis. There are difficulties, but God commands. That is power. So," continues Kuhn, "we shook off our paralysis and deliberately placed the *but* before God."[26]

Someone has said, "Satan rushes men. God leads them." Dr.
F. B. Meyer addressed that subject with these potent words:

> Never act in panic, nor allow man to dictate to thee;
> calm thyself and be still; force thyself into the quiet of thy
> closet until the pulse beats normally and the scare has
> ceased to disturb. When thou art most eager to act is the
> time when thou wilt make the most pitiable mistakes.
> Do not say in thine heart what thou wilt or wilt not do,
> but wait upon God until He makes known His way. So
> long as that way is hidden, it is clear that there is no need
> of action, and that He accounts Himself responsible for
> all the results of keeping thee where thou art.[27]

Offering a further principle regarding guidance, Isobel speaks
of a time when

> He had given me no Bible verse on which to lean. I
> had asked for one but none came. It would have been so
> comfortable to have a Bible verse to stand upon ....
> [But] God expects His children to grow. I believe it was
> D. E. Hoste who said that the older he grew the harder it
> seemed to get guidance from the Lord. I believe he meant
> that guidance becomes less simple. God expects us to
> exercise spiritual discernment, and He guides by a certain
> pressure on the spirit, by a still small voice, by something
> so delicately intangible that unless you are carefully tuned
> in to His Spirit, so to speak, you can miss it widely. It
> requires a close and experienced walk with the Lord, so in
> one sense, He has a hold on us that might not be if He
> always supplied us with a Bible verse every time we asked
> for one!

When it is only a still small voice which is our guide, it is easy for Satan to throw us into confusion by causing us to question if we heard aright. It is a good plan not to go back on past guidance.[28]

When Isobel returned to the United States due to her cancer, a whole new platform of testing began—and the need to control her emotions. In her book *In the Arena* she cited 2 Corinthians 10:5: "... casting down imaginations ... and bringing into captivity every thought to the obedience of Christ."

Commenting on that verse, she wrote:

> I found that imagination could give me a bad time. If I coughed, for instance, I immediately had lung cancer (although X-rays showed the chest to be clear)! If I had a toothache, then I was getting cancer of the mouth! And so on. Every tickle or twinge was instantly interpreted as related to my grim enemy. But if I asserted my right to a sound mind (2 Timothy 1:17), these fears left me and the twinges never developed into anything further. "For God hath not given us the spirit of fear, but of power and of love and of a sound mind." A sound mind is our gift from God, this verse says, but we need to claim it. The American Standard Version translates the word as *discipline*. And the one includes the other, for a sound mind is necessarily a disciplined one.[29]

Discipline is a principle of Christian living. For me personally, this verse and others like it always seemed impossible to put into action until I began to view the "what ifs" as "tapes," that, when they play out of control, can throw any of us into panic. We all carry around with us a library of tapes: "what ifs" of the future;

"why nots" of the past; and memories of events, both bad and good. These tapes are not like emotions of grief and guilt, which are feelings that need to be expressed. Unlike emotions, tapes turn into obsessive analyses and repetitive replays, usually of a negative nature.

Sometimes a tape can be positive, for example a memory of a loved one now revisited in the imagination. Chocolate chip cookies play a positive tape for me of coming home from school on a rainy day to the aroma of cookies baking in the oven. But the tapes that torment us are the ones filled with regret over what was and fear of what will be.

To deliberately remove such a tape from my mental tape recorder and refocus by playing a new, positive tape is my way of exercising mental discipline with regard to my nagging "what ifs?" It is one way to put this biblical principle into shoe leather. "Cut" and "refocus" are two words that describe a way to deal with painful tapes. The old tapes are never eradicated, but they can be cut or turned off. "Refocus" is the key to success. The new focus must be specific and concrete if it is to work. Otherwise the old tape will keep popping back. Work on a project, make plans for a birthday party, absorb yourself in someone else's problem, go for a walk, or try a new recipe. Eventually the tape will slip back into your library of old tapes and you will go on. This is a vitally important principle, for if one problem more than most troubles people who come to me for counseling, it is that of negative tapes.

It is a principle of living the Christian life that God is in control. When Arthur and Wilda Mathews were imprisoned by the communists in China, Arthur asserted, "We have His promise, we are not the prey of the terrible. We are the prisoners of the Lord Jesus Christ—just lent to evil men to show forth the abundance of His power! Our days are on deposit with Him; let Him hand them out to use as He will."[30]

In her own troubles, Isobel found great comfort in

> the gathering of the edelweiss of God. I owe this thought to Miss Carmichael. In her book *Gold by Moonlight*, she has a whole chapter on it. Edelweiss grows on barren mountain heights, and its soft beauty is a cheery surprise to the toiling climber. So Miss Carmichael likens it to the little things of joy which can always be found in any painful experience, if we only gather them as we go along. Sound health and a normal life I cannot have while on this platform (cancer); therefore I accept the fact and do not fret about it. But this very trial has brought me unexpected joys and these I dwell on and delight in them as His kind tokens of remembrance.[31]

In discussing her fear of leaving loved ones behind when she died, Isobel concludes that the same loving God who gave her constant small tokens of His love would not forget those she loved either. Then, quoting Amy Carmichael:

> *For my beloved I will not fear. Love knows to do*
> *For him, for her, from year to year, as hitherto,*
> *Whom my heart cherishes are dear*
> *To Thy heart too.*[32]

Isobel concluded, "It may not be long before He comes for all His own—then what a foolish waste fretting about it would have been."[33]

Once again speaking of small comforts, Isobel quotes words from Oswald Chambers that were a comfort to Wilda Mathews during her imprisonment in China: "The things that make God dear to us are not as much His great big blessings as the tiny things; because they show His amazing intimacy with us; He knows every detail of our individual lives."[34] For Wilda, the "tiny thing" was the ability to give a little birthday party for her child, in spite of their confinement.

Before Isobel Kuhn ever went to China, she attended a Bible conference where she heard James Fraser speak. At the time she had no idea of the effect that unknown man would have on her life or on that of her husband, John, whom she was yet to meet. Still, words he spoke on that occasion remained imprinted on her mind forever.

> One lecture was on the spiritual battle in the heavenlies. How he roughed it, and labored, and had given them (the Lisu tribes) a written language—and still there were so few converts and such as did come were not stable. Then he wrote his mother in England to gather in the neighbors and pray. It was only after this prayer group began to function in earnest that "the break" came in the Lisu tribe. At that time he on the field had been led to resist in Christ's name the devil and his host who were holding this tribe enchained.

"As I sat listening," wrote Isobel, "I saw plainly that it was true the Lisu church was born in prayer travail, and I decided that I must also employ this weapon of 'all-prayer.' It is so obviously effective and is attainable to any of us. I received a life-pattern at that moment for which I have ever been grateful."[35]

On a different occasion she learned another lesson in prayer from Fraser. In the midst of frustrations, "those that are from the Devil we must refuse in Christ's name. Mr. Fraser taught us to pray, 'If it is from the Devil I refuse it and all his works in Christ's name.'"[36] A parallel to these words may be found in the writings of John Bunyan: "If it be of God, let me not despise it; if it be of the Devil, let me not embrace it."[37]

Isobel relates an instance at the same Bible conference when she heard Fraser speak on prayer and was afterward able to talk privately to him about her own call to China. She never forgot that time, sitting alone with him on a rocky shore by the ocean.

"Missionary life can be very lonely," he said quietly, and then he proceeded to unfold some of his own early sufferings. I believe now that he did it deliberately to sift me. If I were truly called of God, I would not be discouraged by plain talk about the cost. If I were not called by God, but just had romantic notions about a foreign land, the sooner my gossamer dream wafted away the better. But he little knew the unveiling of his own life that he was giving unconsciously. In fact, as he reminisced he seemed to forget for a while that I was present. His blue-grey eyes brooding out over the sunny, sparkling ocean, he seemed almost to be talking to himself. In the quiet of contemplation, as now, his eyes seemed to reveal an understanding of all the sorrows and loneliness that a human heart can know. Acquainted with grief, they were sad eyes; knowing the victory possible, they were steadfast and patient.

I told him of Mother's viewpoint and her opposition to my call. He answered with the slow drawl which was his when thinking out a question—for none could talk faster than he on occasion. "I have sensed that Satan is opposing you and working through your mother and your brother. We are taught 'whom resist' when it comes to obstacles produced by the devil. I think that should be your stand. In prayer resist the devil, always remembering to be kind to those who are unconsciously his tools at the moment (2 Timothy 2:24). I have a prayer-formula which I use on such occasions. It is this: 'If this obstacle be from thee, Lord, I accept it; but if it be from Satan, I refuse him and all his works in the name of Calvary.' I have found that this formula works." I was to use it throughout my life and never found it to fail when prayed with the honest intention of obeying all that it implied.[38]

Then with a prophetic note he warned her that even after she got to Bible school, Satan might try to stop her. "I wonder if you will ever get to China," he mused thoughtfully. "You are very young, and you have great obstacles to face." He warned her that if she ever got a telegram urging her to go home immediately because of the illness of her mother she should not immediately leave.[39] Instead she should consult with someone who was unprejudiced and yet godly enough to advise her.

Because of that warning from Fraser, when his prophetic word came true and the telegram arrived regarding her father's illness, not her mother's, she was prepared. It turned out that Isobel could stay in school, and her father went on to live for nearly twenty years longer. Because of the godly insight and counsel of James Fraser, Satan's attempt to end the lifework of Isobel Kuhn was defeated. She did, indeed, get to China, and in her short life she left behind a legacy of writing and ministry.

In speaking of Christ's love, Isobel used the words of F. B. Meyer: "You would like to love with a strong, undying flame—but perhaps you fail to distinguish between love and the emotion of love. They are not the same. We may love without being directly conscious of love . . . they love who obey."[40]

When speaking of the unlovable and the need for actual physical contact in dealing with them, she quoted Hudson Taylor:

There is a mighty power in contact . . . . They are not clean, and sometimes we are tempted to draw our skirts together, but I believe there is no blessing when that is the case . . . . There is much power in drawing near to this people, and there is a wonderful power in touching people. A poor woman in Cheng-tu when she heard of Mrs. Riley's death said, "What a loss to us! She used to take hold of my hand, and comfort me so . . . ." If you put your hand on the shoulder of a man there is power in it . . . there is something in contact: it is a real power we may use for God.[41]

In his book *Life in Christ*, John Stott gives a remarkable example of the kind of love that touches the "untouchable."

What is Mother Teresa's secret? On a board in the parlor of the Mother House in Calcutta are inscribed her own words: "Let each sister see Jesus Christ in the person of the poor; the more repugnant the work or the person, the greater also must be her faith, love and cheerful devotion in ministering to our Lord in this distressing disguise." Desmond Doig describes his first memory of her in Nimal Hriday, her home for dying destitutes in Kalighat, under the shadow of the Temple of Kali. She was kneeling beside a dying man whom she had just admitted. "Stripped of his rags, he was one appalling wound alive with maggots." What did Mother Teresa do? She fell on her knees beside him. Then with quiet efficiency she began to clean him as she talked to him caressingly in Bengali. A young Indian called Christo Das joined her, and then took over. When he had finished he said: "When I cleanse the wounds of the poor, I am cleansing the wounds of Christ." He had learned this from Mother Teresa, for she has written: "I see Christ in every person I touch, because He has said 'I was hungry, I was thirsty, I was naked, I was sick, I was suffering, I was home-less . . . .'" It is as simple as that. Every time I give a piece of bread, I give it to Him."[42]

Isobel gives valuable help to those who feel forgotten by God or wonder why He has not answered their prayer in the way that they might wish. Once again, she quoted from Wilda Mathews during her imprisonment:

> Another great help was on Hebrews 11:39. [Someone has put it in a free paraphrase.] "They were trusted to trust without receiving what others received. They were trusted not to be offended." How I pray that I may not be offended in the least bit! He could have gotten us home in time. There is much He could have done and yet He hasn't. Oh, may my heart truly be able to say "not my will but Thine be done."

> *Teach us in the silence of the Unexplained.*
> *To see Love's dearest, Love's most secret sign;*
> *Like the White Stone, a precious thing unstained,*
> *And as at Bethany, the glory Thine.*

In the words of Arthur Mathews: "'The silence of eternity, INTERPRETED BY LOVE . . . .' We trust your love has been able to find the right interpretations . . . ."[43]

It is a principle of God that He is no man's debtor. He can never make a mistake. To rest in the unexplained is perhaps one of the highest tests this earth can offer.

Once more against the backdrop of the imprisonment of the Mathews' family, Isobel quoted, this time from Andrew Murray. In doing so, she gives us a concise principle for dealing with discouragement: " 'In commerce, in study, in war it is so often said: there is no safety but in advance . . . . To stand still is to go back. To cease effort is to lose ground. To slacken the pace, before the goal is reached, is to lose the race.' "[44]

Arthur added a note of additional wisdom: "The yoke is light only as it is *taken*, and not as it is suffered."[45]

In a day of "easy" Christianity, when becoming a Christian is viewed by some as simply a passport to heaven or a way to become "successful" on this earth, the challenge and demands of Christianity remain the same as they have always been. There is nothing on this earth to compare with the joy of belonging to the King of kings. But the price tag of such belonging is still the cross. And the obligation of those so purchased is still total committal to the lordship of Christ. We are not saved by works, but the reality of our faith is made evident by our works. The words of Samuel Rutherford, quoted in Carolyn Canfield's biography of Isobel Kuhn, remain as true today as when they were written:

> "Ye will not get leave to steal quickly to Heaven, in Christ's company, without a conflict and a cross."[46]

But oh, what a joy it will be when after the conflict and the cross there will be the crown and the "Well done, thou good and faithful servant." In the words of Amy Carmichael, whom Isobel Kuhn loved so much, words that have come true for Isobel: "What an awakening one who has walked with Him in the twilight must have, when suddenly she awakes in His likeness and the light is shining around her—all shadowy ways forgotten."[47]

George MacDonald (1824–1905)

A devout Scotsman, author George MacDonald was a minister who gained renown for his writings, especially through his magnificent treatment of myth in his many novels. C. S. Lewis wrote of him: "I never concealed the fact that I regarded him as my master; indeed I fancy I have never written a book in which I did not quote from him."[1]

A sampling of George MacDonald's insights appears here:

Of children: *"To require of a child only what he can understand the reason of, is simply to help to make himself his own God—that is a devil."*[2]

Of the home: *"It is not house, and fire, and plenty of servants, and all the things that money can procure, that make a home—not father or mother or friends—but one's heart which will not be weary of helping, will not be offended with the petulance of sickness, nor the ministrations needful to weakness. This 'entire affection hating nicer hands' will make a home of a cave in a rock, or a gipsy's tent." David Elginbrod, Book III, XXI.*[3]

— *The World of George MacDonald*

Of suffering: "There are tenderhearted people who would never have force used nor pain suffered, who talk as if kindness could do everything. Yet were it not for suffering, millions of human beings would never develop an atom of affection. It is folly to conclude that a thing ought not to be done because it hurts. There are powers to be born, creations to be perfected, sinners to be redeemed, all through the ministry of pain, that could be born, perfected, and redeemed in no other way."

—*The Highlander's Last Song.*[4]

. . . The little child that's happy to the core,
Will leave his mother's lap, run down the stair,
Play with the servants—is his mother annoyed?

I would not have it so. Weary and worn,
Why not to thee run straight, and be at rest?
Motherward, with toy new, or garment torn,
The child that late forsook her changeless breast,
Runs to home's heart, the heaven that's heavenliest:
In joy or sorrow, feebleness or might,
Peace or commotion, be thou, Father, my delight.[5]

C. S. Lewis

TEN

C. S. Lewis:
Dealing with Imperfection

*I*f I were to say what I really thought about pain, I should be forced to make statements of such apparent fortitude that they would become ridiculous if anyone knew who made them."[1] So wrote C. S. Lewis—scholar, teacher, professor of Medieval and Renaissance English at Cambridge University—with an honesty about his inner feelings that could only characterize a person strong enough to face his own imperfection.

Many theologians and philosophers look to the profound utterances of ancient thinkers for their inspiration. Lewis could find depth of expression in the simplicity of a child's story. He discovered one contemporary example of the awesomeness of God in a children's story, *The Wind in the Willows.* Lewis cited the scene in which Rat and Mole approach Pan:

> "Rat," he found breath to whisper, shaking. "Are you afraid?" "Afraid?" murmured the Rat, his eyes shining with unutterable love, "Afraid? Of Him? O, never, never. And yet—and yet—O Mole, I am afraid."[2]

And so was the man Lewis: intellectual, but human; fearful, yet honest; questioning, yet believing—like all of us, human and

imperfect. Yet Lewis could accept imperfection as neither virtu-
ous nor sinful, but as simple human frailty. While volumes have
been written on C. S. Lewis the intellectual, the strain of humanness that exists throughout his writing, and especially in his letters, has been neglected.

For Christians and non-Christians alike the concept of
humanness is a major roadblock for many who want to get psychological help. For some emotional pain spells out weakness.
"Am I weak if I need counseling?" is the often-repeated question.
Many other misconceptions persist regarding those who seek professional counseling. The least accurate and most unsophisticated
misconception is that people consult a psychological counselor
only when they are insane. The idiocy of that statement is self-
evident. More subtle is the notion in the mind of some Christians
that people need only to confess their sins, and then their problems will vanish. The underlying idea is that sin is at the root of
all emotional problems. Unfortunately, many Christian writers
also reflect this erroneous concept.

To the contrary, many people who consult me with emotional problems have difficulties that cannot accurately be labeled
as sinful. Anxiety, depression, sexual dysfunction, and other
symptoms a counselor confronts certainly reflect human imperfections, but they are hardly sins. The sin label not only makes the
problem harder to bear because of the added dimension of guilt,
but it also frequently hinders people from getting the help they
need. For, in a sense, seeking psychological help becomes an
admission of guilt.

We are all imperfect. And when any imperfection becomes
overwhelming, we may need professional help. We do not need
self-righteous theological putdowns or unsolicited declarations of
our sinfulness and inadequacy. "Be ye perfect," is a valid scriptural

principle, but it is a call to holiness, wholeness and completeness. It is not a denial of humanity's inevitable imperfections.

> You would like to know how I behave when I am experiencing pain, not writing books about it? You need not guess, for I will tell you; I am a great coward. But what is that to the purpose? When I think of pain—of anxiety that gnaws like fire and loneliness that spreads out like a desert, and the heartbreaking routine of monotonous misery, or again of dull aches that blacken our whole landscape or sudden nauseating pains that knock a man's heart out at one blow, of pains that seem already intolerable and then are suddenly increased, of infuriating scorpion-stinging pains that startle into maniacal movement a man who seemed half dead with his previous tortures—it "quite o'ercrows my spirit." If I knew any way of escape I would crawl through sewers to find it. But what is the good of telling you about my feelings? You know them already; they are the same as yours. I am not arguing that pain is not painful. Pain hurts. That is what the word means. I am only trying to show that the old Christian doctrine of being made "perfect through suffering" is not incredible. To prove it palatable is beyond my design.[3]

Again, this time in relationship to anaesthetics, Lewis described the same fears:

> My reason is perfectly convinced by good evidence that anaesthetics do not smother me and that properly trained surgeons do not start operating until I am unconscious. But that does not alter the fact that when they have me down on the table and clap their horrible mask

over my face, a mere childish panic begins inside me. I start thinking I am going to choke, and I am afraid they will start cutting me up before I am properly under. In other words, I lose my faith in anaesthetics.[4]

How many times do we fear pain before that pain occurs? I dreaded the phone call from the hospital announcing my father's death for weeks. Yet when the call finally came, I didn't crumble, become hysterical, or do any of the things my imagination had conjured up. I absorbed the shock for a time, cooked breakfast for my mother and sister, and then helped with funeral arrangements. Our anticipated fear of physical and emotional pain supercedes its reality. But we are human, and so we fear pain.

In response to the idea that a good God will not inflict pain, Lewis replied, "What do people mean when they say, 'I am not afraid of God because I know He is good?' Have they never even been to a dentist?"[5]

At the height of his life-pain, his anguish over the death of Joy, his wife of three years, Lewis wrote not only of the agony he was experiencing, but also of his doubt that he would ever totally recover:

Getting over it so soon? But the words are ambiguous. To say the patient is getting over it after an operation for appendicitis is one thing; after he's had his leg off it is quite another. After that operation either the wounded stump heals or the man dies. If it heals, the fierce, continuous pain will stop. Presently he'll get back his strength and be able to stump about on his wooden leg. He has "got over it." But he will probably have recurrent pains in the stump all his life, and perhaps pretty bad ones; and he will always be a one-legged man. There will be hardly any moment when he forgets it. Bathing, dressing, sitting down and getting up again, even lying in bed, will all be different. His whole way of life will be changed. All sorts of pleasures and activities that he once took for granted will have to be simply written off. Duties too. At present I am learning to get about on crutches. Perhaps I shall presently be given a wooden leg. But I shall never be a biped again.[6]

Those who experience severe psychological pain often feel that things will never be normal again. Such a reaction is common and normal. A depressed woman who consulted me after seeing several other therapists kept saying, "I have a hard time coming here because I keep feeling that nothing can help." Lewis would have understood.

In a profoundly sympathetic view of the potential despair in everyone else and the anguish deep within himself over Joy's death, Lewis exclaimed, "They say an unhappy man wants distractions—something to take him out of himself. Only as a dog-tired man wants an extra blanket on a cold night; he'd rather lie there shivering than get up and find one. It's easy to see why the lonely become untidy; finally, dirty and disgusting."[7]

And thus, as Lewis was realistic about himself, he was equally aware of the frailties of his fellow humans. His description in *Mere Christianity* of the questionable "niceness" of Christians says it well:

We must, therefore, not be surprised if we find among the Christians some people who are still nasty. There is even, when you come to think it over, a reason why nasty people might be expected to turn to Christ in greater numbers than nice ones. That was what people objected to about Christ during his life on earth; He seemed to attract "such awful people." That is what people still object to, and always will.

Do you not see why? Christ said, "Blessed are the poor" and, "How hard it is for the rich to enter the Kingdom," and no doubt He primarily meant the economically rich and economically poor. But do not His words also apply to another kind of riches and poverty? One of the dangers of having a lot of money is that you may be quite satisfied with the kinds of happiness money can give and so fail to realize your need for God. If everything seems to come simply by signing checks, you may forget that you are at every moment totally dependent on God. Now quite plainly, natural gifts carry with them a similar danger. If you have sound nerves and intelligence and health and popularity and a good upbringing, you are likely to be quite satisfied with your character as it is. "Why drag God into it?" you may ask. A certain level of good conduct comes fairly easily to you. You are not one of those wretched creatures who are always being tripped up by sex, or dipsomania, or nervousness, or bad temper. Everyone says you are a nice chap and (between ourselves) you agree with them. You are quite likely to believe that all this niceness is your own doing; and you may easily not feel the need for any better kind of goodness. Often people who have all these natural kinds of goodness cannot be brought to recognize their need for Christ at all until, one day, the natural goodness lets them down and their self-satisfaction is shattered. In other words, it is hard for those who are "rich" in this sense to enter the Kingdom.

It is very difficult for the nasty people—the little, low, timid, warped, thin-blooded, lonely people, or the passionate, sensual, unbalanced people. If they make any attempt at goodness at all, they learn, in double quick time, that they need help. It is Christ or nothing for them. It is taking up the cross and following—or else despair. They are the lost sheep; He came specially to find them. They are (in one very real and terrible sense) the "poor": He blessed them. They are the "awful set" He goes about with—and of course the Pharisees say still, as they said from the first, "If there were anything in Christianity those people would not be Christians."

There is either a warning or an encouragement here for every one of us. If you are a nice person—if virtue comes easily to you—beware! Much is expected from those to whom much is given. If you mistake for your own merits what are really God's gifts to you through nature, and if you are contented with simply being nice, you are still a rebel; and all those gifts will only make your fall more terrible, your corruption more complicated, your bad example more disastrous. The Devil was an archangel once; his natural gifts were as far above yours as yours are above those of a chimpanzee.

But if you are a poor creature—poisoned by a wretched upbringing in some house full of vulgar jealousies and senseless quarrels—saddled, by no choice of your own, with some loathsome sexual perversion—nagged day in and day out by an inferiority complex that makes you snap at your best friends—do not despair. He knows all about it. You are one of the poor whom He blessed. He knows what a wretched machine you are trying to drive. Keep on. Do what you can. One day (perhaps in another world, but perhaps far sooner than that) He will fling it on the scrap-heap and give you a new one. And then you may astonish us all—not least yourself: for you have learned your driving in a hard school. (Some of the last will be first and some of the first will be last.)

"Niceness"—wholesome, integrated personality—is an excellent thing. We must try by every medical, educational, economic, and political means in our power to produce a world where all have plenty to eat. But we must not suppose that even if we succeeded in making everyone nice we should have saved their souls. A world of nice people, content in their own niceness, looking no further, turned away from God, would be just as desperately in need of salvation as a miserable world—and might even be more difficult to save.[8]

Most of us recognize that Christians are not always "nice." But we find this hard to admit. We even realize that *we* are not always nice, and that is even harder for us to accept.

A Christian businessman confided to me that if he were in the habit of looking closely at himself or other Christians for evidence of God, he might have become discouraged and never known God. But because he focuses his attention on God, his relationship with his Maker is vigorous and authentic.

The concept of human frailty must never become an excuse for sin. Gossip, pride, sexual perversion, cheating, hatred—such behaviors are not frailties but sins and, as such, roadblocks that separate the non-Christian from God. Lewis would be among the first to agree with this. Although he was not accepting of sin, he was ever mindful of his own humanness.

A man of contrasts, C. S. Lewis was without a doubt one of the great intellectuals of the twentieth century. Yet in his letters he often wrote about simple things—his cats, his seemingly end-less illnesses, and his homespun remedies for them. He shocked *Time* magazine by stating that he enjoyed monotony. He admit-ted his deep fear of poverty; yet after his death it became known that he had consistently been giving away two-thirds of his income. He hated solitude; and perhaps partly because of that dis-taste he endured the presence of an increasingly irascible house-keeper, Mrs. Moore, for years until her death. He preferred the discomfort of an incompatible housemate to that of solitude.

He found comfort in established routines, such as his after-dinner glass of port and his evenings spent with fellow author J. R. R. Tolkien, during which the two read one another's manu-scripts. Yet he could be spontaneous, as in his travels with Joy just months before her death.

Lewis's awareness of his fundamental aloneness in this world came early, when as a child he learned of his mother's death. This experience was the beginning of his conscious confronta-tion, while still a child, with his impending adulthood. In his words: "... many pleasures, many stabs of joy; but no more of the old security. It was a sea and islands now; the great continent had sunk like Atlantis."[9]

Lewis never became comfortable with his aloneness. Thus his fears, his closeness to his brother, his tolerance of Mrs. Moore and, finally, his ecstasy over his marriage and subsequent deep sense of loss over the death of his wife are all understandable.

It is this combination of greatness and humanness in Lewis that so encourages those of us who at times denigrate ourselves for the very fact of being human.

Lewis had a deep respect for so called "ordinary people." In speaking of the average man he commented:

It seems that there is a general rule in the moral universe which may be formulated "The higher, the more in danger." The "average sensual man" who is sometimes unfaithful to his wife, sometimes tipsy, always a little selfish, now and then (within the law) a trifle sharp in his deals, is certainly, by ordinary standards, a "lower" type than the man whose soul is filled with some great Cause, to which he will subordinate his appetites, his fortune, and even his safety. But it is out of the second man that something really fiendish can be made; an Inquisitor, a Member of the Committee of Public Safety. It is great men, potential saints, not little men, who become merciless fanatics. Those who are readiest to die for a cause may easily become those who are readiest to kill for it.[10]

Placing each person's value in proper perspective, as dependent upon God for real value, Lewis further explained:

Starting with the doctrine that every individuality is of infinite value, we picture God as a kind of employment committee whose business it is to find suitable careers for souls, square holes for square pegs. In fact, however, the value of the individual does not lie in himself. He is capable of receiving value. He receives it by union with Christ. There is no question of finding for him a place in the living temple which will do justice to his inherent value and give scope to his natural idiosyncrasy. The place was there first. The man was created for it. He will not be himself till he is there. We shall be true and everlasting and really divine persons only in Heaven, just as we are, even now, coloured bodies only in the light.[11]

It was not that Lewis either glorified or denigrated the status of a human being. He simply saw the imperfection in all levels of humankind. He realized that a person's true potential for good lies only in his or her relationship with God.

As an extension of that thought, Lewis believed that each of us is indeed our brother's keeper. As he put it, "There are no ordinary people." We are special to God and to each other in that each of us has been endowed with sacred spiritual potential. Thus, said Lewis,

> the load, or weight, or burden of my neighbor's glory should be laid daily on my back, a load so heavy that only humility can carry it, and the backs of the proud will be broken. It is a serious thing to live in a society of possible gods and goddesses, to remember that the dullest and most uninteresting person you talk to may one day be a creature, which if you saw it now, you would be strongly tempted to worship, or else a horror and corruption such as you now meet, if at all, only in a nightmare. All day long we are, in some degree, helping each other to one or other of these destinations. It is in the light of these overwhelming possibilities, it is with the awe and the circumspection proper to them, that we should conduct all our dealings with one another, all friendships, all loves, all play, all politics. There are no ordinary people. You have never talked to a mere mortal. Nations, cultures, arts, civilizations—these are mortal, and their life is to ours as the life of a gnat. But it is immortals whom we joke with, work with, marry, snub, and exploit—immortal horrors or everlasting splendours. This does not mean that we are to be perpetually solemn. We must play. But our merriment must be of that kind (and it is, in fact, the merriest kind)

which exists between people who have, from the outset, taken each other seriously—no flippancy, no superiority, no presumption. And our charity must be a real and costly love, with deep feeling for the sins in spite of which we love the sinner—no mere tolerance or indulgence which parodies love as flippancy parodies merriment. Next to the Blessed Sacrament itself, your neighbor is the holiest object presented to your sense. If he is your Christian neighbor he is holy in almost the same way, for in him also Christ *vere laitat*—the glorifier and the gloried, Glory Himself, is truly hidden.[12]

Were we to translate this viewpoint into actions in each of our lives, there would be less need for psychotherapists. This is not because therapy or counseling are sinful, but because loving my neighbor with all his or her imperfections, and receiving that love in return, would be a good insurance policy against many of the problems that cause people to seek professional help.

Imperfection can be deceptive, however. In spiritual matters, our perception sometimes seems inadequate when compared to all that we perceive in the natural realm because we are so accustomed to the natural. In our humanness we confuse reality with fiction, perfection with imperfection. Lewis offered an apt example:

When I was a boy, gramophone records were not nearly so good as they are now. In the old recording of an orchestral piece you could hardly hear the separate instruments at all, but only a single undifferentiated sound. That was the sort of music I grew up on. And when, at a somewhat later age, I began to hear real orchestras, I was actually disappointed with them, just because you didn't get that single sound. What one got in a concert room seemed to me to lack the unity I had grown to expect, to be not an orchestra but merely a number of individual musicians on the same platform. In fact, I felt it "wasn't the Real Thing." This is an even better example than the former one. For a gramophone record is precisely a substitute, and an orchestra the reality. But owing to my musical miseducation the reality appeared to be a substitute and the substitute a reality.

Lewis explained the philosophy behind his metaphor of the gramophone:

> Things do look so very much as if our whole faith were a substitute for the real well-being we have failed to achieve on earth. It seems so very likely that our rejection of the World is only the disappointed fox's attempt to convince himself that unattainable grapes are sour. After all, we do not usually think much about the next world till our hopes in this have been pretty well flattened out— and when they are revived we not infrequently abandon our religion. And does not all that talk of celestial love come chiefly from monks and nuns, starved celibates consoling themselves with a compensatory hallucination? And the worship of the Christ child—does it not also come to us from centuries of lonely old maids? There is no good ignoring these disquieting thoughts. Let us admit from the outset that the psychologists have a good prima facie case. The theory that our religion is a substitute has a great deal of plausibility.

Faced with this, the first thing I do is to try to find out what I know about substitutes, and the realities for which they are substituted, in general. And I find that I don't know as much as I thought I did. Until I considered the matter I had a sort of impression that one could recognize the difference by mere inspection if one was really honest—that the substitute would somehow betray itself by the mere taste, would ring false. And this impression was in fact, one of the sources from which the doubts I mentioned were drawing their strength. What made it seem so likely that religion was a substitute was not any general philosophical argument about the existence of God, but rather the experienced fact that for the most of us at most times the spiritual life tasted so thin, or insipid, compared with the natural. And I thought that was just what a substitute might be expected to taste like. But after reflection, I discovered that this was not only not an obvious truth but was even contradicted by some of my own experience.[13]

Years ago when psychiatrist Viktor E. Frankl was still living, I vividly experienced this perception of blurring—the real with the unreal—as I watched a play written by Dr. Frankl. He had written the play shortly after his release from some of the worst of Hitler's concentration camps. Frankl's play movingly presented the idea that life at all levels has meaning—even at the level of deep suffering. Meaning is in fact the real substance of life; it is what makes life something more than mere superficial survival. As I sat in the audience I was moved by the reality of what I was seeing on stage. Truly the audience at that point was less real to me than the players. For the players were presenting life at its apex of significance.

Related to this same idea that we do not always precisely identify reality, Lewis further explained how mere moods and simple circumstances often affect our spiritual beliefs and outlook:

It is always assumed that the difficulties of faith are intellectual difficulties, that a man who has once accepted a certain proposition will automatically go on believing it till real grounds for disbelief occur. Nothing could be more superficial. How many of the freshmen who come up to Oxford from religious homes and lose their Christianity in the first year have been honestly *argued* out of it? How many of our own sudden temporary losses of faith have rational basis which would stand examination for a moment? I don't know how it is with others, but I find that mere change of scene always has a tendency to decrease my faith at first—God is less credible when I pray in a hotel bedroom than when I am in College. The society of unbelievers makes Faith harder even when they are people whose opinions, or any other subject, are known to be worthless.

These irrational fluctuations in belief are not particular in religious belief. They are happening about all our beliefs all day long. Haven't you noticed it with our thoughts about the war? Some days, of course, there is really good or really bad news, which gives us rational grounds for increased optimism or pessimism. But everyone must have experienced days in which we are caught up in a great wave of confidence or down into a trough of anxiety though there are no new grounds either for the one or the other. Of course, once the mood is on us, we find reasons soon enough. We say that we've been "thinking it over": but it is pretty plain that the mood has created the reasons and not *vice versa*.[14]

But there are examples closer to the Christian problem than these, examples that further illustrate how often what we think we believe can be confused with what we *feel* at the moment. Emotion and intellect can be difficult to distinguish between.

There are things, say in learning to swim or to climb, which look dangerous and aren't. Your instructor tells you it's safe. You have good reason from past experience to trust him. Perhaps you can even see for yourself, by your own reason, that it is safe. But the crucial question is, will you be able to go on believing this when you actually see the cliff edge below you or actually feel yourself unsupported in the water? You will have no rational grounds for disbelieving. It is your senses and your imagination that are going to attack belief. Here, as in the New Testament, the conflict is not between faith and reason but between faith and sight. We can face things which we *know* to be dangerous if they don't look or sound too dangerous; our real trouble is often with things we know to be safe but which look dreadful. Our faith in Christ wavers not so much when real arguments come against it as when it looks improbable—when the whole world takes on that desolate look which really tells us much more about the state of our passions and even our digestion than about reality.[15]

Again, Lewis does not condemn but gently explains the sometimes irrational fluctuations we all experience in our faith. Yet once again he does not allow his reader to fall back on the excuse of our humanness with the cop-out of "God will understand." Because we cannot eradicate all our shortcomings and imperfections does not mean we may become passive about them. Here Lewis urges the reader to examine his or her own motives when he says: "For I am sure, after all, whether one of the causes of our weak faith is not a secret wish that our faith should not be very strong. Is there some reservation in our minds? Some fear of what it might be like if our religion became quite real? I hope not. God help us all, and forgive us."[16]

Forgive us God does, for not only does He see our imperfection as a part of our humanity, but He wants us to grow into all we were ever meant to be. He forgives our mixed motives. He is patient with our slowness.

Suzanne sat in my office sobbing because a Christian friend had repeatedly told her she was incapable of changing. In truth, Suzanne has changed so obviously that even the social workers involved with her case have noticed the difference. She no longer becomes so depressed that she fails to feed her two-year-old child or shuts out the child's crying by covering her ears. Suzanne has become a good wife and mother; in fact, she's now better than most. But her friend fails to accept this because she doesn't want to see it. In some smug way she feels more secure in condemning Suzanne for past problems that had arisen more from human imperfection than from any specific sin.

As he considered human imperfection, Lewis saw beyond generalizations and theological discussions. He reached down to the most practical issues we face. And he tackled them with an irresistible sense of humor.

In a letter to his brother, Lewis discussed an incident in which he had become ensnared. His rendering is worth quoting extensively because of its rare humor, its insight into human frailty, and its acceptance of all types of people.

I have a ludicrous adventure of my own to tell. Mme.
Balot is the widow of a M. Balot who died recently. She
had been temporarily insane once during his lifetime;
and tho' there was no serious fear of a relapse, her state of
mind after his death . . . led most of her friends to keep an
eye on her. Mrs. Moore [Lewis's housekeeper] went to see
her pretty regularly. So did the heroine of my story, Mrs.
Moreton . . . "a brave little woman," tho' it is not known
what danger she ever had to encounter. She is a spiritu-
alist, she weighs the babies of poor women, her business
is universal benevolence.

Well, the other night Mrs. Moore suddenly called me
out of the dining room and said, "Mrs. Moreton is here.
She says that Mme. Balot twice tried to commit suicide
today. She has got a taxi here and wants me to go and see
the doctor at the Warneford. We shall have to get a nurse
for Mme. Balot" . . . . I stayed in the taxi while the two
ladies went in to see the doctor . . . . They emerged at last
with a Nurse Jackson and we started off for the Balots'
house. But now the question was what to do? Madame
would certainly refuse to have a strange young woman
thrust upon her for the night for no apparent reason . . . no
one had any authority over her . . . no doctor would certify her as insane . . . . Mrs. Moreton said it was all perfectly simple. She would stay hidden in the Balot garden
all night. Nurse could be put up in the bungalow of a
stranger opposite to madame's house . . . . If only [Mrs.
Moreton] could have a man with her, she confessed, she
would feel less nervous about it. I began to wish I'd stayed
at home; but in the end of course I had to offer. No one
raised the question as to why the nurse had been prevented from going to bed in her hospital in order to be

carried half a mile in a taxi and immediately put to bed in another house totally unconnected with the scene of action, where she could not possibly be of the slightest use. The nurse herself, who was possibly in some doubt as to who the supposed lunatic might be, maintained a stupefied silence. I now suggested as a last line of defence that nothing would be more likely to upset Mme. Balot than to find dim figures walking about her garden all night; to which Mrs. Moreton replied brightly that we must keep out of sight and go very quietly. "We could put our stockings on outside our boots, you know." We were whispering outside a house just down the street, and at this stage a window opened overhead and someone asked me rather curtly if we wanted anything, and if not would we kindly go away. This restored to me some of the sanity which I was rapidly losing, and I determined that whatever else happened, four o'clock should not find me "with my stockings over my boots" in someone else's garden for fear the owner might commit suicide, explaining this to a policeman.

I therefore ruled that we must keep our watch in the road, where, if we sat down, we should be hidden from the windows by the paling (and, I added mentally, would be open to arrest for vagabondage, not for burglary). Several neighbors had now turned up . . . to revel in the excitement and Mrs. Moreton (while insisting on the absolute necessity of letting no one know), gave each newcomer a full account of the situation. . . . I came home, drank a cup of tea, put on a greatcoat, took some biscuits, smokes, a couple of apples, a rug, a waterproof sheet, and two cushions and returned to the fatal spot . . . . Someone had had the rare good sense to leave sandwiches and three thermos flasks, and I found the brave little woman actually eating and drinking when I arrived. Hastily deciding that if I was to lie under the obligations of a man I would assume his authority, I explained that we would be really hungry later on, and authoritatively put a stop to that nonsense.

I settled down. There had been some attempt at moonlight earlier; but it had clouded over and a fine rain began to fall. Mrs. Moreton's feminine and civilian vision of night watches had evidently not included this. She was surprised at it. She was also surprised at its getting really cold; and most surprised of all to find that she was getting really sleepy . . . . If I could have been quit of her society I should have found my watch just tolerable— despite the misfortune of finding my greatcoat pockets stuffed with camphor balls which I flung angrily on the road, and then some hours later forgetting this and trying to eat one of the apples. The taste of camphor is exactly like the smell . . . . However, my story is over now, and when I have added that the crows had been "tuning up for their unseasonable matins" a full half hour before any other bird squeaked (a fact of natural history which I never knew before) I may dismiss Mrs. Moreton from my mind.[17]

Like Lewis, we all encounter annoyances that are trivial in the grand scheme of things. If we allow them to become serious, our methods will appear futile and ineffective. Yet to ignore them, as in the example of Mrs. Moreton, could seem uncaring. And so, we, like Lewis, blunder through. It is somehow reassuring to see Lewis, the man of giant intellect, trapped uselessly in someone else's garden for the night!

Sometimes, however, God can use a seemingly trivial occurrence. For instance, a while back I missed an airplane because of a flat tire. At first I was annoyed. I had an appointment in my home city, with friends planning to meet me, and things to do at home before the next day in the office. Then I realized with delight that I would be isolated in a strange town for an extra day, where I would have hour upon hour to write. Yet the whole scene reminded me afresh of my frequent frustration over plans that are thwarted. Another human frailty, if you please.

Lewis had some additional comforting thoughts on the frustration of work:

> There are always plenty of rivals to our work. We are always falling in love or quarreling, looking for jobs or fearing to lose them, getting ill and recovering, following public affairs. If we let ourselves, we shall always be waiting for some distraction or other to end before we can really get down to our work. The only people who achieve much are those who want knowledge so badly that they seek it while the conditions are still unfavorable. Favorable conditions never come.

Lewis further expounded on his philosophy of work:

> If I say to you that no one has time to finish, that the longest human life leaves a man, in any branch of learning, a beginner, I shall seem to you to be saying something quite academic and theoretical. You would be surprised if you knew how soon one begins to feel the shortness of the tether: of how many things, even in middle life, we have to say, "No time for that," "Too late now," and, "Not for me." But Nature herself forbids you to share that experience. A

more Christian attitude, which can be attained at any age, is that of leaving futurity in God's hands. We may as well, for God will certainly retain it whether we leave it to him or not. Never, in peace or war, commit your virtue or your happiness to the future. Happy work is best done by the man who takes his long-term plans somewhat lightly and works from moment to moment "as to the Lord." It is only our daily bread that we are encouraged to ask for. The present is the only time in which any duty can be done or any grace received.[18]

These comforting words reassured me regarding my own less-than-perfect planning. I, too, am learning that "happy work is best done by the [one] who takes his [or her] long-term plans somewhat lightly and works from moment to moment 'as to the Lord.'"

Lewis extended this common-sense approach to prayer. His thoughts, gleaned from one of his many letters, should relax any Christian who demands a certain routine in his or her daily prayer life.

We all go through periods of dryness in our prayers, don't we? I doubt... whether they are necessarily a bad symptom. I sometimes suspect that what we *feel* to be our best prayers are really our worst, that what we are enjoying is the satisfaction of apparent success, as in executing a dance or reciting a poem. Do our prayers sometimes go wrong because we insist on trying to talk to God, when He wants to talk to us?

Joy tells me that once, years ago, she was haunted one morning by a feeling that God wanted something of her, a persistent pressure like the nag of a neglected duty. And till midmorning she kept on wondering what it was. But the moment she stopped worrying, the answer came through as plain as a spoken voice. It was "I don't want you to *do* anything. I want to *give* you something" and immediately her heart was full of peace and delight.

St. Augustine says, "God gives where He finds empty hands." A man whose hands are full of parcels can't receive a gift. Perhaps these parcels are not always sins or earthly cares, but sometimes our own fussy attempts to worship him in our way. Incidentally, what most often interrupts my own prayers is not great distractions but tiny ones—things one will have to do or avoid in the course of the next hour.[19]

Lewis accepted the psychological foibles of others. In his *Letters to an American Lady,* he spoke of his recipient's impending surgery: "Fear is horrid but there's no reason to be ashamed of it. Our Lord was afraid (dreadfully so) in Gethsemane. I always cling to that as a very comforting fact." And that, in essence, is the very heart of C. S. Lewis's views on imperfection. He was much comforted by his Lord in the midst of the vicissitudes of life. He did not view God as a weapon to use against others. Rather, Lewis reverenced and feared Him. He knew his God too well to fear that He would fail to comfort His children, who try so hard to be perfect, and yet fail.

In *Mere Christianity* Lewis expressed keen insight into this difference between humanness and sin:

When a man makes a moral choice two things are involved. One is the act of choosing. The other is the various feelings, impulses, and so on, which his psychological outfit presents him with, and which are the raw material of his choice. Now this raw material may be of two kinds. Either it may be what we would call normal; it may consist of the sort of feelings that are common to all men. Or else it may consist of quite unnatural feelings due to things that have gone wrong in his subconscious. Thus fear of things that are really dangerous would be an example of the first kind; an irrational fear of cats or spiders would be an example of the second kind. The desire of a man for a woman would be of the first kind; the perverted desire of a man for a man would be of the second. Now what psychoanalysis undertakes to do is remove the abnormal feelings, that is, to give the man better raw material for his acts of choice. Morality is concerned with the acts of choice themselves.

Put it this way. Imagine three men who go to war. One has the ordinary natural fear of danger that any man has and he subdues it by moral effort and becomes a brave man. Let us suppose that the other two have, as a result of things in their subconscious, exaggerated, irrational fears, which no amount of moral effort can do anything about. Now suppose that a psychoanalyst comes along and cures these two: that is, he puts them both back in the position of the first man. Well it is just then that the psychoanalytical problem is over and the moral problem begins. Because, now that they are cured, these two men might take quite different lines. The first might say, "Thank goodness I've got rid of all those doo-dahs. Now at last I can do what I always wanted to do—my duty to the cause of freedom." But the other might say, "Well, I'm very glad that I now feel moderately cool under fire, but, of course, that doesn't alter the fact that I'm still jolly well determined to look after Number One and let the other chap do the dangerous job whenever I can. Indeed one of the good things about feeling less frightened is that I can now look after myself much more efficiently and can be much cleverer at hiding the fact from the others." Now this difference is a purely moral one and psychoanalysis cannot do anything about it. However much you improve the man's raw material, you have still got something else: the real, free choice of the man, on the material presented to him, either to put his own advantage first or to put it last. And this free choice is the only thing that morality is concerned with.

The bad psychological material is not a sin but a disease. It does not need to be repented of, but to be cured. And by the way, that is very important. Human beings judge one another by their external actions. God judges them by their moral choices. When a neurotic who has a pathological horror of cats forces himself to pick up a cat for some good reason, it is quite possible that in God's eyes he has shown more courage than a healthy man may have shown in winning the V. C. [Victoria Cross]. When a man who has been perverted from his youth and taught that cruelty is the right thing, does some tiny little kindness, or refrains from some cruelty he might have committed, and thereby, perhaps, risks being sneered at by his companions, he may, in God's eyes, be doing more than you and I would do if we gave up life itself for a friend.

It is well to put this the other way round. Some of us who seem quite nice people may, in fact, have made so little use of a good heredity and a good upbringing that we are really worse than those whom we regard as friends. Can we be certain how we should have behaved if we had been saddled with the psychological outfit, and then with the bad upbringing, and then with the power, say of Himmler? That is why Christians are told not to judge. We see only the results which a man's choices make out of his raw material. But God does not judge him on the raw material at all, but on what he has done with it. Most of the man's psychological make-up is probably due to his body. When his body dies all that will fall off him, and the real central man, the thing that chose, that made the best or the worst out of this material, will stand naked. All sorts of nice things which we thought our own, but which were really due to a good digestion, will fall off some of us: all sorts of nasty things which were due to complexes or bad health will fall off others. We shall then, for the first time, see every one as he really was. There will be surprises.[20]

As we become increasingly whole psychologically, spiritually, and physically, the potential for choice broadens. With it, so does our responsibility become greater. It all refers back to Lewis's example of war and the man who *couldn't* go and then when he *could* he faced a *moral* choice that then could involve doing right or wrong. At this point sin could enter in, not when the man was unable to make that choice.

In the area of emotions, like love or patience, the lack of feeling or even a negative feeling is not sin, but what we *do* with that feeling involves a moral choice of right or wrong. In areas vital to Christian living Lewis was not only practical but reassuring. How often we try to love and end up failing! To love those we find unlovable, we must pray honestly: "Lord, I don't love so and so, but I am willing to have You love him or her through me." Then, we follow through by *acting* in love. It's F. B. Meyer all over again. As Lewis said:

But though natural likings should normally be encouraged, it would be quite wrong to think that the way to become charitable is to sit trying to manufacture affectionate feelings. Some people are "cold" by temperament; that may be a misfortune for them, but it is no more a sin than having a bad digestion is a sin; and it does not cut them out from the chance, or excuse them from the duty, of learning charity. The rule for all of us is perfectly simple. Do not waste time bothering whether you "love" your neighbor; act as if you did. As soon as we do this we find one of the great secrets. When you are behaving as if you loved someone, you will presently come to love him. If you injure someone you dislike, you will find yourself disliking him more. If you do him a good turn, you will find yourself disliking him less. There is, indeed, one exception. If you do him a good turn, not to please God and obey the law of charity, but to show him what a fine forgiving chap you are, and to put him in your debt, and then sit down to wait for his "gratitude," you will probably be disappointed. (People are not fools: they have a very quick eye for anything like showing off, or patronage.) But whenever we do good to another self, just because it is a self, made (like us) by God, and desiring its own happiness as we desire ours, we shall have learned to love it a little more or, at least, to dislike it less.[21]

Relating to another area where the lines are not always clearly defined, Lewis wrote:

The Christian rule of chastity must not be confused with the social rule of "modesty" (in one sense of that word); i.e. propriety, or decency. The social rule of propriety lays down how much of the human body should be displayed and what subjects can be referred to, and in what words, according to the customs of a given social circle. Thus, while the rule of chastity is the same for all Christians at all times, the rule of propriety changes. A girl in the Pacific Islands wearing hardly any clothes and a Victorian lady completely covered in clothes might both be equally "modest," proper, or decent, according to the standards of their own societies, and both, for all we could tell by their dress, might be equally chaste (or equally unchaste). Some of the language which chaste women used in Shakespeare's time would have been used in the nineteenth century only by a woman completely abandoned.

When people break the rule of propriety current in their own time and place, if they do so in order to excite lust in themselves or others, then they are offending against chastity. But if they break it through ignorance or carelessness they are guilty only of bad manners. When, as often happens, they break it defiantly in order to shock or embarrass others, they are not necessarily being unchaste, but they are being uncharitable, for it is uncharitable to take pleasure in making other people uncomfortable. I do not think that a very strict or fussy standard of propriety is any proof of chastity or any help to it, and I therefore regard the great relaxation and simplifying of the rule which has taken place in my own lifetime as a good thing. At its present stage, however, it has this inconvenience, that people of different ages and different types do not all acknowledge the same standard, and we hardly know where we are. While this confusion lasts I think that old, or old-fashioned, people should be very careful not to assume that young or "emancipated" people are corrupt whenever they are (by the old standard) improper, and, in return, that young people should not call their elders prudes or puritans because they do not easily adopt the new standard.[22]

Lewis concluded with the line that, while not compromising with sin, sets the stage for real acceptance of other people with their, at times, varying standards: "A real desire to believe all the good you can of others and to make others as comfortable as you can will solve most of the problems."

As a little girl I was not allowed to attend the theater. On one occasion I can still remember receiving my parents' reluctant permission to see a Walt Disney movie. But I only half enjoyed it. I sat nervously near the aisle and watched the lights over the exit doors on either side of the theater. As long as they were still burning, I knew that God had not come and taken His own away, leaving me. The conditioning was deep, for until a few years ago theaters still made me edgy.

While many movies are sinful because of what they portray, my childhood was not corrupted by Walt Disney. Indeed, the fantasy and pathos of those stories enriched my early years. Those things that are not directly sinful must be relegated to the individual conscience of the believer. And that will necessarily leave room for imperfection to creep in. For example, there is the matter of temperance—how much TV we watch or how many movies we see. These are issues we must address on a personal level. But "God knows our situation, He will not judge us as if we had no difficulties to overcome. What matters is the sincerity and perseverance of our will to overcome them."[23] If God does not judge, then neither should we judge ourselves or anyone else on the basis of perceived imperfection.

I frequently counsel people who have come from good Christian backgrounds but have turned against God because people in the church had judged where God has not. Or they were rightly criticized, but without love.

Someday, as a church and as individuals, we will have to offer God an explanation for those we have so turned away. In the same way we will have to account for the hurt we have caused our brother or sister who suffered under our intolerance although he or she may not have actually turned away. In the meantime, by acknowledging our own imperfection we can be more accepting of ourselves and of others because of God's love and unconditional acceptance of us. For God has perfect balance, in contrast to our lack of it.

As C. S. Lewis said:

> On the one hand, God's demand for perfection need not discourage you in the least in your present attempts to be good, or even in your present failures. Each time you fall He will pick you up again. And He knows perfectly well that your own efforts are never going to bring you anywhere near perfection. On the other hand, you must realize from the outset that the goal towards which He is beginning to guide you is absolute perfection; and no power in the whole universe, except you yourself, can prevent Him from taking you to the goal.[24]

He continued:

> When a man turns to Christ and seems to be getting on pretty well (in the sense that some of his bad habits are now corrected), he often feels that it would be natural if things went fairly smoothly. When troubles come along—

illness, money troubles, new kinds of temptation—he is disappointed. These things, he feels, might have been necessary to rouse him and make him repent in his bad old days; but why now? Because God is forcing him on, or up, to a higher level; putting him into situations where he will have to be very much braver, or more patient, or more loving, than he ever dreamed of being before. It seems to us all unnecessary; but that is because we have not yet had the slightest notion of the tremendous thing He means to make of us.

I find I must borrow yet another parable from George MacDonald. Imagine yourself as a living house. God comes in to rebuild that house. At first, perhaps you can understand what He is doing. He is getting the drains right and stopping the leaks in the roof and so on: you knew that those jobs needed doing and so you are not surprised. But presently He starts knocking the house about in a way that hurts abominably and does not seem to make sense. What on earth is He up to? The explanation is that He is building quite a different house from the one you thought of—throwing out a new wing here, putting on an extra floor there, running up towers, making courtyards. You thought you were going to be made into a decent little cottage: but He is building a palace. He intends to come and live in it Himself.[25]

Through our own efforts we can be nothing but imperfect. As human beings, though, we are still loved by God, imperfect as we are. And, in the words of C. S. Lewis:

If we let Him—for we can prevent Him, if we choose—He will make the feeblest and filthiest of us into a god or goddess, a dazzling, radiant, immortal creature, pulsating all through with such energy and joy and wisdom and love as we cannot now imagine, a bright stainless mirror which reflects back to God perfectly (though, of course, on a smaller scale) His own boundless power and delight and goodness. The process will be long and in parts very painful; but that is what we are in for. Nothing less. He meant what He said.[26]

G. Campbell Morgan (1863–1945)

G. Campbell Morgan was a British preacher considered by some to be the best Bible expositor of his generation. The following are examples:

Unbelief is the most irrational attitude possible to man. The man who attempts to account for the things in the midst of which he lives by the things in the midst of which he lives, is bereft of reason. I use the expression carefully: the rationality of faith. To me it is infinitely more difficult to believe in this world as I see it—I do not mean as man has often spoiled it, but as it is in itself—its mountains and valleys, its oceans and continents, its magnificent splendours, without a God, than with the God of the Bible accounting for it. I cannot believe that the God in Whom I am bound to believe, Who fashioned the daisy and made a man— I care nothing for the moment about the process—is careless about the man, and not interested in him. If I admit God has some care for human life in any way, I cannot believe He is careless about the highest thing in human life, which is the moral element and capacity. Faith is utterly rational. To try and account for the things that are by the things that are is to work in a vicious circle. It is the man of faith, the man who endures as seeing Him Who is invisible— mark the contradiction and paradox, and face them—seeing Him Who is invisible, Who is the man of rationality. That is the man of reason, that is the man of sanity; that is the man who is not mad.[1]

Why did the men of Antioch call these people Christians? There can be but one answer, a simple answer, and yet including the whole fact. They saw that these people had been with the Christ in spirit, if not in actual personality, and that they had learned of Him. They talked of Christ, lived for Christ, worked for Christ. They had caught His Spirit, they were occupied with His business, and were manifesting Him in character and conduct; and the men of Antioch said, "These people are Christians, men connected with Christ in some way."[2]

A man never finds real freedom of the will until he has found the seat of authority, and has put Christ there as King. Christ knew that. That was His meaning, when He said, "Seek ye first His Kingdom and His righteousness; and all these things shall be added unto you."[3]

So, surely as the Christ life is in us, with merciless, ruthless, and pitiless determination our life will be poured out in unceasing attack upon the strongholds of evil in the city, in the nation, in the home, and everywhere. In the wilderness Jesus said, "Get thee hence, Satan," and He will never cease His work until the enemy is finally cast out. If our life be Christ's life, then we can never sign a truce with evil. We cannot sit down and be indifferent to its presence.

―――――

. . . The Christ life was that of authority over evil. Because Christ has won the battle already, the life of His follower shares His authority. It is most interesting to notice in the study of the life of Jesus that from that wilderness temptation on to the end, He never argued with the devil again. Whenever He came into contact with him, or with the evil spirits, it was with the tone of authority, and the authority was immediately obeyed.[4]

Ruth Bell Graham

ELEVEN

Ruth Bell Graham: Reference Points

A young girl darted out of an appliance store that she and several dozen other people were looting during the 1992 Los Angeles riots. Hesitating at the front of the store, she seemed to be deciding which direction to choose in her escape. At that moment she was confronted by a reporter.

Looking at her armful of stolen goods, he questioned: "Isn't this stealing? Isn't it wrong?"

"I suppose so," she answered hesitantly. Then, as she looked around at her friends and then back at the reporter, her confidence was renewed. "Actually it must not be so wrong," she countered. "Look around you. Everyone is doing it."

This young girl had obviously been taught that stealing was wrong. Perhaps she had learned that from her family or her church. Now her reference point, that standard to which she referred to determine right and wrong, had shifted. Her new reference point of morality became "What is everyone else around me doing?" Because the reference point had changed, her behavior also had changed.

A friend of mine who builds houses defined the term *reference point* as "a starting point for describing any piece of real estate." In her book *It's My Turn,* Ruth Bell Graham, wife of evangelist Billy Graham, wrote a concise piece on the concept of reference points.

There is a small bronze disk on the Meads' ranch in north central Kansas where the thirty-ninth parallel from the Atlantic to the Pacific crosses the ninety-eighth meridian running from Canada to the Rio Grande.

The National Ocean Survey, a small federal agency whose business it is to locate the exact position of every point in the United States, uses the scientifically recognized reference point on the Meads' ranch. So far, no mistakes have been made, and none are expected.

All ocean liners and commercial planes come under the survey. The government can build no dams or even shoot off a missile without this agency to tell its exact locations—to the very inch.[1]

To demonstrate what can happen if such a reference point is *not* used, Ruth Graham provides an apt example.

The State Highway Department in Pennsylvania once set out to build a bridge, working from both sides. When the workers reached the middle of the waterway, they found they were thirteen feet to one side of each other. Alfred Steinberg, writing some time ago in *The Saturday Evening Post*, went on to explain that each crew of workmen had used its own reference point.[2]

Like the situation with the girl looting during the riots, there was no central reference point. We are reminded of 2 Corinthians 10:12: "For we dare not make ourselves of the number, or compare ourselves with some that commend themselves: but they measuring themselves by themselves, and comparing themselves among themselves, are not wise."

To Ruth Graham, our reference point in the spiritual realm is "the Living Word and the Written Word.... It's not a physical place. It's not a certain place in my room or house. It's the Living Word and the Written Word. And I think that's what's happening to our country. We've lost our reference point." In constant communion with that reference point, she lives a day-by-day, moment-by-moment life of "total reliance upon the person of Jesus Christ," to use her daughter Gigi's terminology.

The Graham's eldest daughter, Gigi Graham Tchividjian, bears living testimony to that day-by-day turning to the divine reference point. Says Gigi, speaking of the hard times her mother has faced:

> All these years her immediate reaction has been to throw herself on the Lord and the Scriptures. As a child I can remember her leaving her Bible open in a prominent place, so she could just get a verse every now and then. We found her often by her bed, on her knees. She had her Bible anywhere she was in the house, sometimes even on the ironing board. There would be a verse that she would be gleaning and meditating upon.

The result of the constant turning to her heavenly reference point? "Mother shared with us the sunshine; and she kept the tears and heartache and difficulties from us."

For Ruth, Christ as her reference point started when she was very young. Born of missionary parents in China, she once said: "I can never recall going to sleep at night without hearing gunshots in the countryside around the house."[3] Walking to school, she daily passed a place where, in keeping with a local pagan custom, dead babies were thrown away. Another of her childhood memories is watching a crowd laughing while they beat a mad dog to death. "It contrasted so with the kindness of the Christians I knew, and it made a deep impression."[4]

Of those early days, Ruth confided, "I think God brought me up tough for a good reason, and I'm grateful." She added, "I prayed early on for a tough hide and a tender heart." As a result of that training, when hurtful and controversial things are said about Billy Graham, Ruth's attitude is: "I know who he is and what he is, and what his motives are. And so nothing that anyone else can say about him would, in any way, make me think the less of him."

Yet, in spite of the hard training, her basic memory of that childhood in China remains one of "love, acceptance and fun. Mother ran a tight ship," she said to me. "My mother and daddy both did; but it was a happy home. Lots of singing and lots of laughter and lots of love."

Citing Christmas as an example, she continued:

Christmas was Christmas like you have never seen it over here. We even had candles in the Christmas trees. We didn't have electric lights . . . . I cannot imagine how they had live candles in the Christmas tree without burning the whole house down. But they just went out of their way to make it happy. Yet never once did Santa Claus eclipse Christ. We always knew that it was Jesus' birthday. We had the stockings and all that went with it, but it was Christ's birthday; and it was one of the happiest, happiest days of the whole year.

Reminiscent of Gigi's comments about her mother, Ruth said of her own mother, "I think the greatest tribute to Mother's courage is that we children never sensed fear, and we ourselves never had any fear."[5] In her book *Prodigals and Those Who Love Them*, she cautions: "We must take care, we parents, that we speak less of the problems, the difficulties, the headaches and heartaches and backaches in this work than we do of Him and His glory. Indeed, I question the wisdom of even mentioning the former when the children are small."[6]

Within Ruth Graham's personality is a deep sensitivity and seriousness, balanced by a well-developed sense of humor. As a child, her love for God was so intense that at the end of each day she would kneel by her bed and pray that God would let her die for Him, a prayer that was quickly countered by her sister Rosa: "Please, God, don't listen to her."[7] By the time Ruth had reached her teens, her sole desire was to be a missionary in Tibet. Her dedication to the will of God is reflected unmistakably in a poem she wrote before leaving China for college in the United States.

> *Spare not the pain*
> *Though the way I take*
> *Be lonely and dark,*
> *Though the whole soul ache,*
> *for the flesh must die*
> *though the heart may break.*
> *Spare not the pain, oh,*
> *spare not the pain.*

In contrast to the dedicated, serious side of her personality, Ruth's sense of humor has been a great balancing factor in her life. Among her family and friends she is known for her practical jokes. On the day the young Billy Graham came to visit her, dressed in white from head to toe and carrying in his pocket a gold engagement ring, Ruth, unaware of his intentions, chose that day to play a practical joke. With the help of a friend, she blacked out her front teeth, allowed her long hair to hang loose and donned a frumpy, flowered housedress, that was at least two sizes too big. Barefoot, she set off down the road to meet Billy.

Driving along the dusty road, Billy stared at what he would later call the "snaggle-toothed" mountain girl, who in turn stared back at him. Finally recognizing her, he opened the car door numbly and then began to laugh. Near dusk, at the top of a mountain, undaunted, he gave her the ring.[8]

The incident had a humorous climax, but few marriages have had more serious impact on the world. To most of the world, Billy Graham is seen as having a more significant impact for God on the twentieth century than almost any other human being. God has used him in a miraculous way. Yet behind the influence of the Billy Graham ministries has been the support and force of a very special woman of God. In 1942 Ruth wrote:

> *Lord, common things*
> *Are all I've ever asked*
> *Of Thee.*

But Ruth Bell Graham has lived a remarkably uncommon life. The little girl who prayed to be a martyr, and the young woman who asked only for a common life, was granted neither request. God said no to both prayers. What a blessing it is that God does not always say yes. What God did give this young woman, however, was an authentic sense of how to follow Him in a day-by-day fashion. Always His Word and His Person have been her reference point.

About the time Ruth Bell left China, she wrote down a list of the qualities she wanted in a husband—in spite of the fact that she had decided to remain single and be a missionary!

If I marry:

He must be so tall that when he is on his knees, as
    one has said, he reaches all the way to Heaven.
His shoulders must be broad enough to bear the bur-
    den of a family.
His lips must be strong enough to smile, firm enough
    to say no, and tender enough to kiss.
Love must be so deep that it takes its stand in Christ
    and so wide that it takes the whole lost world in.
He must be active enough to be gentle and great
    enough to be thoughtful.
His arms must be strong enough to carry a little child.[9]

Later, before Ruth and Billy were married, she aptly described
her future counterpart:

> *God, make me worthy to be his wife:*
> *as cliffs are made, so make me strong,*
> *a help for him when things go wrong.*
> *Clear as the dew, Lord, make my mind,*
> *clear as the dew, and just as kind;*
> *and make me a refreshment, too,*
> *a quiet encourager, like You;*
> *I'll laugh with him in face of tears,*
> *in face of worries and of fears;*
> *brave to be and do and bear,*
> *both quick to yield, and glad to share.*
> *Remind him, God, through coming days*
> *how warm is my love for him always.*
> *His head's held high as he faces life;*
> *God, make me worthy to be his wife.*

The standards for both were high. But they were God's standards. Furthermore, those standards have been possible to fulfill because there is an intensely practical, commonsense element in their view of marriage.

In her book *It's My Turn*, Ruth gives a simple example of this common sense, as well as some good advice for a successful marriage. One day when she stopped at the home of an elderly couple from their church, the husband asked Ruth, " 'Would you like to know the secret of our happy marriage?' 'Of course I would.' He led me into their study, where there stood two cluttered rolltop desks; I was surveying these with genuine interest when he explained, 'I never disturb her desk. And she never disturbs mine.' "

As a couple, the Grahams balance each other out in the area of temperament. Ruth is positive, while Billy tends to worry. From the perspective of a daughter, Gigi succinctly sums up the differences between her parents: "Daddy walks in the room, and tension follows him. Mother walks into the room, and peace follows her." Says Ruth more simply: "Some people are born worriers."

Both Gigi and her mother refer to Billy Graham as "Puddleglum," the Marsh-wiggle in *The Silver Chair* by C. S. Lewis. For those who have not read the *Chronicles of Narnia*, or who do not remember Puddleglum, a typical interchange between Puddleglum and his friends reads like this:

> "Good-by, dear Puddleglum," said Jill going over to the Marsh-wiggle's bed. "I'm sorry we called you a wet blanket."
>
> "So'm I," said Eustace. "You've been the best friend in the world."
>
> "And I do hope we'll meet again," added Jill.

"Not much chance of that, I should say," replied Puddleglum. "I don't reckon I'm very likely to see my old wigwam again either . . . ."

With insight into the true character of Puddleglum, Jill concludes: "Puddleglum! You're a regular old humbug. You sound as doleful as a funeral and I believe you're perfectly happy. And you talk as if you were afraid of everything, when you're really as brave as—as a lion."[11]

With similar optimism, Ruth Graham concluded: "I'm married to a Puddleglum. And yet he turns out to be the most sterling character I've ever known."

Ruth relates an amusing anecdote regarding her own Puddleglum:

> We landed at the Miami airport. Bill had to stay, while I was to fly home. He checked the weather and learned it was not good in Atlanta, Georgia, where I would have to change planes for Asheville, North Carolina.
>
> "You probably won't be able to land," he predicted. "If not, I don't know where you will go—probably on to New York City. But if they try to land, I hope you make it; Atlanta is one of the busiest airports in the United States. And if you do, I'd advise you to spend the night in a motel—if you can get a room, which I doubt—as a lot of planes will be grounded and the motels will be full. In that case, rent a car, if you can get one, and drive home. But drive carefully because . . . ."
>
> You guessed it . . . "You could have a wreck."[12]

According to Gigi, both of her parents are intense and high-strung, but in different ways. "Mother's always thinking of something, always doing something. Sitting on a plane with her last fall, my husband leaned over and said, 'Gigi, look at your mother. You're just like her. She's always doing something. She's always writing notes or reading something.'"

Of her father's lifelong determination to live with eternity's values in view, Gigi reflected:

> I have been with him and watched him change his mind about something. And it's not because he's just changing his mind. It's because his first reaction was, "No, I can't do it." Then he starts to think more about it. He begins to change because he realizes that from Eternity's point of view he might never have an opportunity to speak to this person again. I think Daddy really looks at things from Eternity's perspective . . . . He always tries to remind us: "How would you look at this from Eternity?"

Because their reference point is Jesus Christ, Ruth and Billy's very different lives have blended together in a union that has lasted. They have learned to enjoy their similarities and complement their differences. No one who talks to Ruth Graham for any length of time can fail to realize the depth of love that this very public, yet intensely private couple have for each other.

In a particularly moving and sensitive poem of Ruth's, she portrays the quiet, perceptive kind of relationship that in many ways is the epitome of real love between two human beings.

> *Cradle her within your arms*
> *when evening falls*
> *after the wearying day;*
> *secure her in tenderness*
> *that she may sleep*

> *her tiredness away.*
> *Passion is a gift from God,*
> *but when the body aches*
> *with weariness, one longs*
> *for quiet love. It takes*
> *so little to restore the soul,*
> *so little to renew:*
> *just gather her within your arms,*
> *let her sleep close to you.*

Whether the issue relates to differences of temperament in a marriage, clinical depression, prodigal children, or hormonal imbalances, when Ruth Graham discusses emotional pain there is a delightful absence of the "Confess your depression" mentality. Indeed, she sounds a great deal more like a favorite writer of hers, F. W. Boreham, when he comments: "Humanity is a strange tangle; and no man can say where the work of the doctor ends and the work of the minister begins."[13]

It is also quite clear that Ruth has suffered and that she understands the depth to which pain can go.

> *Don't talk to me yet;*
> *The wound is fresh,*
> *The nauseous pain*
> *I can't forget*
> *Fades into numbness*
> *Like a wave,*
> *Then comes again.*
> *Your tears I understand,*
> *But grief is deaf,*
> *It cannot hear the words*
> *You gently planted*

> *And tried to say,*
> *But . . .*
> *Pray . . .*

Yet, characteristically, she always goes on. After a prolonged bout of depression during her pregnancy with her youngest child, Ned, Ruth stated, "I'm glad I had that, because it helps me to understand how people feel. It was just nine months of a depression and then as soon as he was born it was over." Truly putting her Christian beliefs into shoe leather, she added, "Thank God that David wasn't always on a perpetual high. What would we do without the Psalms?"

So often we miss God's blessing when we are depressed or anxious, because rather than seeking His comfort in the midst of the feelings, we are busy blaming ourselves for being human. In a poem she wrote in 1980, Ruth speaks of God's kindness in the *middle* of feelings of depression.

> *Sunk in this gray*
> *depression*
> *I cannot pray.*
> *How can I give*
> *expression*
> *with no words*
> *to say?*
> *This mass of vague*
> *foreboding*
> *of aching care*
> *love with its*
> *overloading*
> *short-circuits prayer.*
> *Then in this fog*

of tiredness
this nothingness, I find
a quiet, certain, knowing
that He is kind.

It is difficult for me as a counselor to deal with some of the extreme views so frequently put forth by certain Christians. Some who want God's reference point for morality, purity, or holiness seem frequently to ignore His standard on love and compassion. Others who go to an opposite extreme speak of a cheap kind of love that demands little in the way of holiness.

Most of us have difficulty understanding other people's pain unless it is a pain we too have experienced. We who are prone to depression will likely empathize with others who suffer from depression. We may, however, be less tolerant of those who struggle with anxiety. We are far more willing to excuse another's frailty, and even their sin, if it is our own frailty or sin.

While there are times when God allows us as Christians to suffer in some particular way so that we will better understand the problems of others, because of Christ in me I can also take His compassion and understanding for that which I may *never* experience. Ruth Graham has done a remarkable job of combining high standards with deep compassion in the most difficult areas of life. Her desire to do so started early and is reflected in a poem she wrote from school in Korea in 1934:

"Inasmuch" a cup of water
offered one in Jesus' name,
"Inasmuch" a gentle handclasp
treating one and all the same,
"Inasmuch" a single penny
dropped in some poor beggar's palm,

"Inasmuch" a piece of clothing
just to keep a body warm,
"Inasmuch," so said the Master
(though the very least he be),
"Inasmuch as done to someone
you have done it unto me."

Even when failure or sin is involved, while Ruth maintains a high standard for Christian living, at the same time she holds a higher standard than most for the necessity of acting in love and refusing to give up. She once commented to a Sunday school class she was teaching, "When a person seems at his worst, we should demonstrate Jesus' love the most. When a child falls, you don't avoid or scold him. You help him up and comfort and encourage him."[14] Isn't that precisely what Christ did?

Parenting is an area where Ruth Graham offers advice that is sound and yet realistic. Many Christians sneer at the notion of quality time devoted to children by parents who work outside the home. Such people assume that any such mother has chosen to abdicate her parental role in favor of making more money. There are such parents, it is true. But most mothers would prefer to raise their own children.

Comments Ruth: "I think children are wise enough to know when a parent is working because they want a second car or a finer home or more things, or when they're working because they absolutely have to keep bread on the table.... They'll understand whether their parents put them first or possessions first." With reassurance to those who feel continually guilty because they literally don't have enough time to spend with their children, she adds, "I think it's not the quantity of time you spend with your child. It's the quality of it.... Close, loving companionship: they'll remember that rather than a whole day of indifference."

Similarly, with reference to prodigals, Ruth speaks of unconditional love, the kind not earned but freely offered: "Prodigals need to know that they are loved at all times, and no matter what happens, that they are welcome home." In a personal reference she added, "We made it a point to keep the contact open to where they could make long-distance calls collect.... God loves us unconditionally, and He allows us to call Him person to person and collect any time." Repeatedly, there is recognition of that divine reference point. In this instance it is loving, not as the world loves, but as God does. Sometimes we look pretty good when we compare ourselves to others. But He is our Standard, not our friends or those whom we observe around us.

With her insightfulness she goes on to say: "I think a mother hurts more when one of her children is hurting. I think the mother suffers as much, if not more, than the child does." During such times she emphasizes that those are the times when prayer is vital. "When you can't sleep it's a great time to pray. We need to pray for those we love and encourage them. And I don't think there's any room for bitterness. I think bitterness is something we really need to watch against when someone has been really unkind or unfair."

Furthermore, what other people think is not nearly as important as what happens to the prodigal or to the one who is not prodigal at all, but who, like David of old, is simply downcast. Gigi feels that her mother's poems more than her prose reveal her soul. Certainly that soul, and the souls of a great multitude of those who deal with prodigals, are revealed in the following poem:

> *They felt good eyes upon them*
> *and shrank within—undone;*
> *good parents had good children*
> *and they—a wandering one.*

> *The good folks never meant*
> *to act smug or condemn,*
> *but having prodigals*
> *just "wasn't done" with them.*
>
> *Remind them gently, Lord,*
> *how You*
> *have trouble with your children,*
> *too.*

On the topic of bitterness as it relates to people in general, when a friend of hers found out that her husband had been cheating on her for over half of their married life, she asked Ruth: "How do you deal with bitterness?" Ruth realized that the friend had been so deeply wounded that it was like a deep abscess. "You have to allow time for an abscess to come to a head before you can lance it," she said to me. "I think the bitterness is like the pus," she continued. "Once you lance it and the pus is drained off, then the healing can begin. It's a slow process, but it is an important process."

In putting her faith into shoe leather, Ruth can be intensely practical. When others might sermonize, she offers advice in concise statements that are profound in their wisdom. Once again in a conversation about prodigals and the frustration people feel in trying to convince their children to come back to the Lord, she commented, "Something that helped me tremendously when it finally dawned on me was that we take care of the possible and trust God for the impossible." Speaking of someone else who had sought her advice, she added, "I had the feeling that this poor woman was trying to do God's work for Him instead of her own. I think sometimes we do that. We just wade around trying to do the impossible."

After I had written these words, I spent some time with two young people about whom I care a great deal. We talked about their struggles, and I longed to see them happy in their newfound relationship. Then I realized that I was trying to arrange everything for them. I thought of that word *impossible* and realized that I was endeavoring to do just that. None of us can impose ourselves into the life of another and make the problems go away. Even if we could, none of us have the time and energy to live our own life along with even one other person's. We can listen and advise. But the individual must make the changes. And God in that person must be the motivator and the power to enable such changes. That does not imply that the situation I encountered is impossible for God. Simply, it means that I have done all I can to help. I have done, to the best of my knowledge and ability, the possible. Now I must leave the impossible to Him.

Ruth Graham's practical wisdom does not end when the issues become heavy and controversial. For isn't God the God of the impossible? I once shared my concern over a young man who had refused to accept Christ as Savior and then in a drunken stupor drove his motorcycle into a pole and died. In speaking of the godly parents who were distraught, I asked: "What would you say to them?" She answered honestly, "I don't know," but then added something that I found to be of great help. "I remember a little couplet I heard somewhere. I do not know where it came from. I do not know who wrote it. But it said: 'Between the saddle and the ground, mercy sought and mercy found.'" Then, with conviction, she added: "So many parents don't live to see their prayers answered. But I'm convinced God will answer our prayers .... We don't know what happens in that last split second .... I really think that we cannot begin to comprehend the mercy of God."

How deeply simple words of hope such as these can become part of our everyday thinking, even for a child. As we were watching the news one evening the death of a famous person was announced. With the announcement came the statement that the person had no belief in God. I made a simple statement of regret that it was sad to think of someone dying without knowing God. A soft voice at my side said quietly, "But between the saddle and the ground, mercy sought and mercy found." It was my eight-year-old granddaughter.

Of the suicide of a young man, Ruth was realistic about the family: "They'll go through it, but they'll never get over it." Yet when confronted by the reality of those who insist that Christians who kill themselves will go to hell, her response was immediate: "That's baloney! God knows when a person is pushed beyond endurance. And I love this saying: 'God did not call him home, but God welcomed him.'" When I shared that with a patient not long ago, visible waves of relief swept over his face, and he was comforted.

Death faced in God's timing is not always easy, even for the Christian. Many years ago I remember hearing the famous preacher J. Sidlow Baxter say that he didn't fear death itself but that he certainly didn't look forward to the process. His realism comforted me more than if he had promised that for the Christian the process would be pure joy. It's not always so; we all know that. And to think that somehow we must make it a happy time in order to honor God makes it even more difficult. A poem Ruth wrote in 1974 balances the extremes of abject fear and the attitude that somehow the experience of death must be made pleasant in order to honor God:

> *"Death, be not long.*
> *Death, be not hard,"*
> *we prayed.*
> *But days stretched year-like*
> *and when death came, God*

it was not made
easy as we had prayed.
Quiet, but not easy.

Forgive all my complaints;
For precious to You
Is the death of Your saints.

Unknown to most, Ruth Graham's practical wisdom extends far beyond words. She is a doer, and no task is too menial for her to perform. To her the concept of the cup of cold water is quite literal. On a simple level, when I expressed an interest in reading an author who is a favorite of hers but whose works are hard to locate, I shared my plan to initiate a search in used bookstores. This was before the days of the Internet. To my surprise, a few days later three of the man's books arrived in the mail, dispatched in haste while Ruth was rushing to prepare for a trip. Such an act is typical of her thoughtfulness and generosity.

But to Ruth the cup of cold water extends far beyond a simple act of kindness to actions that go back to Christ's example and teaching on this earth. A man named Arthur Radcliffe, who taught horticulture in North Carolina, later managed a flower shop and served as an usher in the Montreat Presbyterian Church. Around the time Ruth started teaching her Sunday school class, the man was placed in a nursing home in Greensboro, North Carolina. By this time Radcliffe was in his seventies.

Miserable due to his separation from the plants and soil he loved to work, he fled and landed at Ruth's door. " 'I'm not going to let the highway patrol take me back!' he declared, his voice rising. 'I'll die before I'll go back to that nursing home.' Then he begged, his eyes gleaming. 'Why don't you just let me die right here in this old cabin you got at the end of the road?' "[15]

Ruth fixed up the cabin, and Radcliffe moved in. Two years later he died, after having worked his beloved earth once again.

At times poor families have experienced having their houses repaired and food and clothing provided. Yet always the dignity of the individual involved is preserved. Their permission is asked rather than having help forced upon them.

In one particular situation, after asking a terminally ill father whether he would accept help, Ruth obtained the clothing sizes of all his children. Then, on Christmas Eve, she sent her husband and children down the mountain to deliver clothes, along with some toys. Later, when the same man was being ignored by hospital staff, in spite of his pain and difficulty breathing, Ruth put in a call that made the place buzz with activity. The patient ended up under the care of a private nurse and a doctor. Dying, he whispered: "I want you to see that all my debts are paid. And I want my children raised as Christians."[16] To that man it was crystal clear that all this love found its source in a profound personal relationship with Jesus Christ, a relationship he wanted for his children.

One of Ruth Graham's most touching poems relates back to a long-term, ongoing relationship with a woman in London. A characteristic of our Lord is that, while He is always a gentleman who declines to intrude or force Himself upon people, He doesn't give up on people either. In that way, too, He is to be our reference point.

Ruth first met Meg during one of Billy's crusades in England. Meg had a drug problem, and through the years she experienced problems ranging from lesbianism to promiscuity and pregnancy. Ruth has prayed for Meg, met with her in coffee shops when she has been in England, and encouraged her in letters.

Early in their relationship, Meg had sadly commented, "I wish I had a mother like you."[17] Ruth's relationship is probably the closest Meg has ever come to being mothered.

On the plane after a seemingly futile encounter with Meg, Ruth wrote:

> *Perhaps*
> *she will land*
> *upon that Shore,*
> *not in full sail,*
> *but rather*
> *a bit of broken wreckage*
> *for Him*
> *to gather.*
>
> *Perhaps*
> *He walks those Shores*
> *seeking such*
> *who have believed*
> *a little*
> *suffered much*
> *and so*
> *have been washed Ashore.*
>
> *Perhaps*
> *of all the souls redeemed*
> *they most adore.*

The end result of finding our reference point in the person of Jesus Christ is that those around us see Christ living through us. Gigi said of her mother, "When we went through the hard times, the first thing we saw her do was grab a Bible." That private reference point has issued forth into a public example that Christianity really does work.

Gigi told me of a time when her mother was visiting her in Paris, France, while Billy was in some other part of the world. A family crisis arose that was disturbing and needed attending to. Gigi had already planned a dinner party with some friends her mother had not yet met. Yet when Gigi offered to cancel the dinner, feeling that the stress on her mother would be too great, Ruth insisted she proceed with her plans. When the guests arrived, in Gigi's words, "We just had a good time and they left."

Months later the friends told Gigi that the impression "that came from your mother that night and that just stayed with us was her peace." Ruth had once again turned to her reference point and found her way.

Ruth shared with me an incident in which, while one of her teenaged sons was going through a period of rebellion, he worked in an office in which a younger man was treating an older employee rudely and unfairly. Yet the older man remained longsuffering and saintly in his behavior. He never retaliated, never answered back. "He was just his sweet, gracious Christian self. He had no idea . . . of the effect his actions were having on the seventeen-year-old prodigal who was quietly watching." She concluded, "God lets us be treated rudely, unpleasantly, or have difficult things happen to us from time to time so that the world can see how we react to them." What we show to the world by our reaction to suffering becomes part of the specific meaning of our own individual suffering. How to find that meaning in the first place is by continually finding our reference point in Jesus Christ.

A statement that is characteristic of Ruth Bell Graham, and one that she seems to refer to frequently, is "Make the least of all that goes and the most of all that comes. And keep looking forward. Don't look backwards." The statement reflects a contentment found only in those who, in Augustinian terms, have found their repose in Him. It reflects a cup-half-full attitude rather than a cup half empty.

In reference to the death of her own parents, Ruth comments: "It's one thing to remember; it's another thing to wallow in grief—that is wrong. When I lost both of my parents, I missed them but I wouldn't have them back for anything... I know where they are and am just thankful for the memories, and I just keep going on."

Ruth not only has always made the best of what comes but she has a unique sense of humor and can occasionally be a practical joker. Both Gigi and Ruth told me about a very unusual dinner at the Graham home. The menu included bean soup. Now, bean soup was not in itself an unusual entree, except that one guest was not served bean soup. His soup only *looked* like bean soup. In actuality he was served *tadpole* soup, complete with muddy water and live tadpoles. As the guest attempted to capture a frisky "bean" from his bowl, to his surprise the "bean" swam away! Serving tadpole soup, along with Ruth's adventurous attempts at hang-gliding and motorcycling, are behaviors that are delightfully inconsistent with the stereotypical view of a preacher's wife. When Gigi first told me about the tadpole soup incident, I wasn't sure I could take her seriously. Somehow to envision a dinner, with guests, at the Graham home with tadpoles swimming around in the soup was hard to imagine. Eventually, I cautiously asked Ruth, "Did you really serve tadpole soup?" Without hesitation she said, "Yes."

"Were they alive?" I countered.

"Oh yes," she affirmed.

"So they really were alive," I repeated.

"Oh yes. When he went after his little meatball it swam away," she added.

This sense of humor has undoubtedly played a big part in preserving an otherwise serious woman who has in her own right made an impact on the world.

The Grahams live in a place they have called Little Piney Cove in a log cabin in the mountains of North Carolina. When retired heavyweight boxer Muhammad Ali visited in the fall of 1979, he said to the press, "I thought he lived on a thousand acre farm. . . . And we drove up to this house made of logs; (it was) the kind of house a man of God would live in."[18] He graciously declined Billy's invitation to spend the night there.

In the fall of 1975 Ruth wrote:

> We bought this cove
> when coves were cheap,
> and flatland scarce,
> and mountains steep.
> But not once
> were we told
> That here, in autumn
> all the poplars
> turn to gold.
>
> Oh, it was cheap
> (beyond belief)
> but autumn makes me feel
> a thief.

In contrast, right after the Grahams were married, Billy Graham took a pastorate outside of Wheaton, Illinois, without talking to his new bride about it. He not only accepted the position, but also chose an apartment without consulting her. As Gigi said, "When she got there she found this dreary, dingy, horrible little apartment. But she made do the best she could." Then she found some red fabric and fixed it on the wall with a light shining on it so that "she could pretend it was a fireplace on dreary nights . . . and she could sit with a cup of tea or coffee."

According to Ruth, "it was a piece of bright, red Chinese embroidery . . . and I hung it on the wall and we had a floor lamp that I shined on it to give it an illusion of a fireplace because I didn't have one. I just love a fireplace in cold weather," she added. "It's pretty. It's company."

To quote once again from Frank Boreham: "There is a magic that turns prisons into palaces and crusts into dainties. There is a wonder that wraps a man about, and thenceforth no humiliation can degrade him, no banishment can exile him, no poverty can make him poor, and no death can destroy him."[19]

To make the best of what is has been a life long pattern for Ruth. Explained Gigi, "She never complained. As soon as Daddy walked out the door, with tears in her eyes she would turn around and say: 'Okay, let's prepare for his homecoming.' And we would turn around and do a project: cleaning the attic, building a treehouse, or whatever."

"Make the least of all that goes and the most of all that comes" does not result in the eradication of pain in this life, but it does lead to contentment. For Ruth Bell Graham life always goes on. But underneath that going on, there is a constant referral to the person of Jesus Christ, a constant taking of time to "indulge herself in the Lord."[20] Perhaps it is impossible to be anything but content when you walk moment by moment, hand in hand, with the King of kings.

Cloud of Witnesses

Hebrews 12:1

"Therefore, indeed, seeing that we also have encircling us so great a cloud of witnesses, stripping off every incumbrance and the easily entangling sin, with endurance let us be running the race that is lying before us."[1]

—JOSEPH BRYANT ROTHERHAM

Are we to think of all these as spectators in an amphitheatre looking down upon those who were contestants in the arena below? It seems to me it is not so easy to decide this question as some have thought. Our English word "witness" can be used in two very distinct senses. It may mean to behold, or on the other hand simply to bear testimony. It would seem as though the original word here used has distinctly the latter sense, so that those of whom we have read in [Hebrews] Chapter 11 are really testimony-bearers to the power of faith. On the other hand, the apostle clearly seems to indicate that there is a sense in which we are surrounded by a great cloud of spectators who apparently are looking down upon us, while themselves witnessing to the grandeur of faith. But in any case, it is intended to be a message of encouragement to those who are still in the place of testing.[2]

—H. A. IRONSIDE

If Only

Hebrews 12:1

"Compassed about
with a great cloud . . ."
the Scriptures say;
If only I could hear,
one shout, the distant roar
of that great crowd,
just some small word
aloud . . .
aloud . . .
to cheer my way.

— RUTH BELL GRAHAM
Minneapolis, October 22, 1980

We have, lying around us, "so great a cloud of witnesses"
(ver. 1). "We" are running, like the competitors in the
Hellenic stadium, in the public view of a mighty concourse, so
vast, so aggregated, so placed aloft, that no word less great
than "cloud" occurs as its designation . . . . True, the multi-
tudinous watchers are unseen, but this only gives faith another
opportunity of exercise; we are to treat the Blessed as seen, for
we know that they are there, living to God, one with us,

fellows of our life and love. So let us address ourselves afresh to the spiritual race, the course of faith.

I thus explain the "witnesses" to mean spectators, watchers, not testifiers. The context seems to me to decide somewhat positively for this explanation. It is an altogether pictorial context; the imagery of the foot-race comes suddenly up, and in a moment raises before us the vision of the stadium and its surroundings. The reader cannot see the course with his inner eyes without also seeing those hosts of eager lookers-on which made, on every such occasion, in the old world as now, the life of the hour. In such a context nothing but explicit and positive reasons to the contrary could give to the word "witnesses," and to the word "cloud" in connection with it, any other allusion. True, these watchers are all, as a fact, evidential "witnesses" also, testifiers to the infinite benefit and success of the race of faith. But that thought lies almost hidden behind the other. It is as loving, sympathetic, inspiring lookers-on that the old saints, from Abel onwards, are here seen gathered, thronging and intent, around us as we run.

. . . We ask, and ask in vain, what is the medium through which these observers watch us, the air and light, as it were, in which their vision acts: what is their proximity to us all the while; to what extent they are able to know the entire conditions of our race. But all this leaves faith in peaceful possession of a fact of unspeakable animation. It tells the discouraged or tired Christian, tempted to think of the unseen as a dark void, that it is rather a bright and populous world, in mysterious touch and continuity with this, and that our forerunners, from those of the remotest past down to the last-called beloved one

who has passed out of our sight, know enough about us to mark our advance and to prepare their welcome at the goal.[4]

—HANDLEY C. G. MOULE

TWELVE

Living Within an Eternal Perspective

It was in Mexico that I realized most fully—and for the first time in my life—that a whole host of situations in life cannot be eradicated. When I was a child, going to a doctor meant to me that a person would become well. Then a little friend of mine died from polio, even though her father was a doctor. When I was in my teens I was injured in an automobile accident. As I waited for the ambulance, I remember a kind man bending over me, saying, "We never think that this can happen to us." And I didn't think it could. But it had. And as I lay there I kept experiencing flashes of thought that this had to be just a nightmare and that I would soon wake up.

Yet throughout my early life I held tenaciously to the notion that a problem could always be conquered, eliminated, done away with. Injustice could be abolished if we worked hard enough. The "impossible" just took a little longer, as the saying goes. Disillusionment came at times when my theory failed, but I rationalized that with a little more work my next attempt would be successful.

Somehow when I was in Mexico the beginning of realism broke through upon my thinking. It's not that I became less idealistic. For more than ever I believe that God can indeed do the "impossible" and that there is no person alive in whom God cannot perform miracles.

But now my idealism is at last becoming temperate. Each time I stayed for any length of time in that tropical climate I was totally defeated by the onslaught of mosquitoes and my allergy to them. Coming from Southern California, where heat is artificially eliminated by air-conditioned cars, homes, and stores, I now found myself in a much hotter climate, grasping gratefully for purified ice cubes. I looked around and saw hunger that was not satisfied, animals that suffered without the intervention of a Society for the Prevention of Cruelty to Animals, death unsoftened by funeral homes, and desperate lives that could not be altered significantly.

In the United States we have developed easy answers for many problems. The government subsidizes much poverty and takes care of us, to a degree, in old age. We have access to instant food, microwave ovens, immediate news coverage from all points in the world, sophisticated medical treatment and, in general, many comforts that much of humankind cannot dream of. Yet even for us, and at times especially for us, the basic problems of humanity, such as loneliness, physical pain, depression, and anxiety, cannot be obliterated. To believe otherwise is to be disillusioned.

Many times we mistakenly believe that greatness implies the eradication of problems. In the lives of the people in this book, we have clear examples that such is not the case. For them, pain as well as pleasure ebbed and flowed throughout their lives.

So-called victorious Christian living is not found in the elimination of problems. It is to be found in handling problems with all the resources we can gather—of physical well being, emotional growth, and the all-sufficiency of God.

It is a profound relief to know that we are in the good company of such an illustrious group of people, who, in spite of problems and suffering, have learned to cope with life and to become truly great, both in the eyes of people and of God.

One paraphrase of Hebrews 12:1 reads, "Since we have such a huge crowd of men of faith watching us from the grandstands, let us strip off anything that slows us down or holds us back... and let us run with patience the particular race that God has set before us" (TLB). Amy Carmichael believed that this "huge crowd of men of faith" are literal witnesses, that from Heaven they literally observe us, support us, encourage us.

Much theological debate has centered around this verse, but I, for one, agree with Amma. The "particular race" that God has set before me has been partially focused and motivated by the thought that I have the support of such people. Their encouragement would not be so great, however, if they had in their lifetimes eradicated all pain and problems. They would not have seemed like real, flesh-and-blood persons. But because they were great and yet mortal, I can garner inspiration and hope from their lives.

Tonight once again I walked down by the ocean and watched the tide as it moved relentlessly in and out over the smooth shoreline. The softness of the rocky beach was evidence of the fact that the tide always does go back and forth. It never stays and never fails to return. So it is with our feelings. Painful or joyful, they do not stay. They leave, only to return. And part of the gracefulness of maturity is to acknowledge this fact. For no matter how painful circumstances may become, the feelings neither remain unmitigated nor can they be eradicated. Pain in one form or another invariably returns, but only for a time. What remains forever is the One God and the host of heavenly beings who surround us with love and care. His presence does not guarantee the elimination of need, whether that need be emotional, spiritual, or material. But He does guarantee that our needs will be met, one way or another.

As Hudson Taylor began the seemingly impossible task of evangelizing inland China, he was warned: "You will be forgotten.... With no committee or organization before the public, you will be lost sight of in that distant land. Claims are many nowadays. Before long you may find yourselves without even the necessities of life!"

"I am taking my children with me," was the quiet answer, "and I notice it is not difficult to remember that they need breakfast in the morning, dinner at midday, and supper at night. Indeed, I could not forget them if I tried. And I find it impossible to think that our heavenly Father is less tender and mindful of his children than I, a poor earthly father, am of mine. No, He will not forget us!"[1]

Hudson Taylor's God is our God. He alone, along with heaven's forces, remains the ultimate source of all our going on.

EPILOGUE

Duties are ours, events are the Lord's. When our faith goeth to meddle with events, and to hold a court (if I may so speak) upon God's providence, and beginneth to say, "How wilt Thou do this or that?" we lose ground. We have nothing to do there. It is our part to let the Almighty exercise His own office, and steer His own helm. There is nothing left to us, but to see how we may be approved of Him, and how we may roll the weight of our weak souls in well-doing upon Him who is God Omnipotent.

—SAMUEL RUTHERFORD

NOTES

Chapter 1 —Living in Our Tension-Filled World

[1]Dr. Joseph Fabry, *The Pursuit of Meaning*, (Saratoga, CA: Institute of Logotherapy Press, 1987), 9.

Chapter 2—Divine Spending Money

[1]F. B. Meyer, B.A., D.D., *Our Daily Homily*, Vol. IV, Isaiah–Malachi (New York: Fleming H. Revell Company, 1899), 169.

[2]W. Y. Fullerton, D.D., *F. B. Meyer, A Biography* (London: Marshall, Morgan and Scott Ltd., n.d.), 8.

[3]F. B. Meyer, *Peace, Perfect Peace: A Portion for the Sorrowing* (Westwood, NJ: Fleming H. Revell Company, 1892), 28.

[4]F. B. Meyer, Ibid., 38–40.

[5]Gloria Steinem, *Revolution from Within* (Boston: Little, Brown and Company, 1992), 153.

[6]C. S. Lewis, *Mere Christianity* (New York, Macmillan Publishing Company, Inc., 1964), 160.

[7]F. B. Meyer, *Exodus, Vol. 2, Chapters 1–20* (London: The Religious Tract Society, n.d.), 223.

[8]F. B. Meyer, Ibid., 147.

[9]F. B. Meyer, *Christian Living* (New York: Fleming H. Revell Company, 1892), 80–81.

[10]George Matheson, "Make Me a Captive, Lord," *Keswick Hymn-Book* (London: Marshall, Morgan and Scott, Ltd., n.d.), 38–39.

[11]F. B. Meyer, *Steps into the Blessed Life* (Philadelphia: Henry Altemus Co., 1896), 127.

[12]F. B. Meyer, Ibid., 47.

[13]F. B. Meyer, *Light on Life's Duties* (Chicago: Bible Institute Colportage Association, 1895), 123.

[14]C. H. Spurgeon, *Sermons*, Vol. II (New York: Funk and Wagnall's Company, n.d.), 147.

[15]C. H. Spurgeon, *Sermons*, Vol. XI, Sermons Preached at the Metropolitan Tabernacle (New York: Funk and Wagnall's Company, n.d.), 81.

[16]G. K. Chesterton, *The End of the Armistice* (London: Sheed and Word, 1940), 18.

[17]Amy Carmichael, *Candles in the Dark: Letters of Amy Carmichael* (Fort Washington, PA: Christian Literature Crusade, 1982), 9.

[18]Amy Carmichael, Ibid., 59.

Chapter 3—Found Faithful

[1]Francis Thompson, "Hound of Heaven," poem.

[2]John Donne, "Batter my heart, three-personed God," sonnet.

[3]Henry and Mary Guinness, interview on Geraldine Guinness Taylor of CIM, 6/9/92.

[4]Henry and Mary Guinness, Ibid.

[5]Interview with Ruth Bell Graham.

[6]Amy Carmichael, Gold Cord (Fort Washington, PA: Christian Literature Crusade), 28.

Chapter 4—F. B. Meyer: Putting Faith Into Shoe Leather

[1]W. Y. Fullerton, D.D., F. B. Meyer, A Biography (London: Marshall, Morgan and Scott Ltd., n.d.), 59–60.

[2]W. Y. Fullerton, Ibid., 61.

[3]W. Y. Fullerton, Ibid.

[4]W. Y. Fullerton, Ibid, 9.

[5]W. Y. Fullerton, Ibid.

[6]W. Y. Fullerton, Ibid.

[7]F. B. Meyer, Light on Life's Duties (Chicago: Bible Institute Colportage Association, 1895), 41–42.

[8]F. B. Meyer, The Christ-Life for the Self-Life (formerly A Castaway) (Chicago: Moody Press, n.d.), 126.

[9]F. B. Meyer, Ibid., 58–59.

[10]F. B. Meyer, The Future Tenses of the Blessed Life (Chicago: Fleming H. Revell Company, n.d.), 120–21.

[11]F. B. Meyer, Ibid., 116–117.

[12]F. B. Meyer, David: Shepherd, Psalmist, King (Chicago: Fleming H. Revell Company, 1895), 52.

[13]F. B. Meyer, The Present Tenses of the Blessed Life (London: Marshall, Morgan, and Scott, 1953), 11.

[14]W. Y. Fullerton, F. B. Meyer, 33.

[15]W. Y. Fullerton, Ibid.

[16]W. Y. Fullerton, Ibid., 37.

[17]W. Y. Fullerton, Ibid., 182–183.

[18]W. Y. Fullerton, Ibid.

[19]F. B. Meyer, Steps into the Blessed Life (Philadelphia, Henry Altemus Co., 1896), 78.

[20]F. B. Meyer, Ibid., 74–75.

[21]F. B. Meyer, Ibid., 76–78.

[22]F. B. Meyer, Ibid., 114–115.

[23]F. B. Meyer, Ibid., 106–107.

[24]F. B. Meyer, Ibid., 306.

[25]F. B. Meyer, Ibid., 82.

[26]F. B. Meyer, Ibid., 69.

[27]F. B. Meyer, Ibid., 60.

[28]F. B. Meyer, Ibid., 272–273.

[29]F. B. Meyer, *The Prophet of Hope: Studies in Zechariah* (Grand Rapids: Zondervan Publishing House, 1952), 126–127.

[30]W. Y. Fullerton, *F. B. Meyer*, 184.

[31]F. B. Meyer, *The Christ-Life for the Self-Life*, 125.

[32]F. B. Meyer, *Steps into the Blessed Life*, 165.

[33]F. B. Meyer, *Peace, Perfect Peace: A Portion for the Sorrowing* (Westwood, NJ: Fleming H. Revell Company, 1997), 80.

[34]F. B. Meyer, *David: Shepherd, Psalmist, King*, 182–83.

[35]F. B. Meyer, Ibid., 183–185.

[36]F. B. Meyer, *Our Daily Homily*, Vol. 5 (Chicago: Fleming H. Revell Company, 1899), 229.

[37]F. B. Meyer, *Our Daily Homily*, Vol. 4, 249.

[38]F. B. Meyer, *Peace, Perfect Peace*, 52–53.

[39]F. B. Meyer, Ibid., 54–56.

[40]W. Y. Fullerton, *F. B. Meyer*, 129.

[41]W. Y. Fullerton, Ibid., 213.

[42]W. Y. Fullerton, Ibid., 215.

[43]W. Y. Fullerton, Ibid., 148.

Chapter 5—Amy Carmichael: Triumph in Suffering

[1]Amy Carmichael, *Gold Cord* (Fort Washington, PA: Christian Literature Crusade, n.d), 195.

[2]Frank Houghton, *Amy Carmichael of Dohnavur* (Fort Washington, PA: Christian Literature Crusade, n.d.), 195.

[3]Amy Carmichael, *Toward Jerusalem* (Fort Washington, PA: Christian Literature Crusade, 1961), 94.

[4]Amy Carmichael, *Kohila* (Fort Washington, PA: Christian Literature Crusade, n.d.), 129.

[5]Amy Carmichael, Ibid., 129–130.

[6]Amy Carmichael, Ibid., 131–132.

[7]Amy Carmichael, *Gold by Moonlight* (Fort Washington, PA: Christian Literature Crusade, 1960), 48.

[8]Amy Carmichael, Ibid., 46.

[9]Amy Carmichael, *Kohila*, 97.

[10]Amy Carmichael, *Rose From Brier* (Fort Washington, PA: Christian Literature Crusade, 1972), 18–19.

[11]Amy Carmichael, *Candles in the Dark* (Fort Washington, PA: Christian Literature Crusade, 1981), 54.

[12]Amy Carmichael, *Gold by Moonlight*, 74–75.

[13]Interview with Dr. Nancy Robbins.

[14]Interview with Dr. Nancy Robbins.

[15]Interview with Dr. Nancy Robbins.

[16]Amy Carmichael, *Gold Cord*, 268.

[17]Amy Carmichael, *Kohila*, 139.

[18]Amy Carmichael, Ibid., 134.

[19]Amy Carmichael, Ibid., 135.

[20]Amy Carmichael, Ibid., 136.

[21]Amy Carmichael, Ibid., 135.

[22]Interview with Dr. Nancy Robbins.

[23]Bruce L. Shelley, *Transformed by Love: The Vernon Grounds Story*, (Grand Rapids, MI: Discovery House Publishers), 152.

[24]Amy Carmichael, *Gold Cord*, 169–170.

[25]Amy Carmichael, *Gold by Moonlight*, 93.

[26]Amy Carmichael, Ibid., 101–102.

[27]Amy Carmichael, *Ponnammal* (Fort Washington, PA: Christian Literature Crusade, 1950), 108–109.

[28]Amy Carmichael, *Rose From Brier*, 112–113.

[29]Frank Houghton, *Amy Carmichael*, 189.

[30]Frank Houghton, Ibid., 373.

[31]Interview with Dr. Nancy Robbins.

[32]Amy Carmichael, *Gold by Moonlight*, 36.

[33]Interview with Dr. Nancy Robbins.

[34]Interview with Dr. Nancy Robbins.

[35]Amy Carmichael, Ibid., 38.

[36]Amy Carmichael, *Gold Cord*, 69–70.

[37]Amy Carmichael, *Rose From Brier*, xii.

Chapter 6—Charles Spurgeon: Living With Depression

[1]Amy Carmichael, *Gold Cord* (Fort Washington, PA: Christian Literature Crusade, 1957), 268.

[2]Helmut Thielicke, John W. Doberstein, trans., *Encounter with Spurgeon* (Grand Rapids: Baker Book House, 1975, © 1963 by Fortress Press), 214.

[3]Richard E. Day, *The Shadow of the Broad Brim* (Valley Forge: Used by permission of Judson Press), 175.

[4]Richard E. Day, Ibid., 85.

[5]Richard E. Day, Ibid., 96.

[6]Richard E. Day, Ibid., 185.

[7]Richard E. Day, Ibid., 197.

[8]Richard E. Day, Ibid., 198.

[9]Richard E. Day, Ibid., 173.

[10]Richard E. Day, Ibid.

[11]Richard E. Day, Ibid., 177–178.

[12]C. H. Spurgeon, *Sermons*, Vol. 11 (New York: Funk & Wagnall's, n.d.), 80.

[13]Helmut Thielicke, John W. Doberstein, trans., *Encounter with Spurgeon*, 218–222.

[14]Bruce L. Shelley, *Transformed by Love: The Vernon Grounds Story*, (Grand Rapids, MI: Discovery House Publishers, 2002), 37.

[15]Bruce L. Shelley, Ibid., 228.

[16]Bruce L. Shelley, Ibid., 87-88.

[17]Os Guinness, *In Two Minds: The Dilemma of Doubt and How to Resolve It*, (Downers Grove, IL: InterVarsity Press, 1976), 90–91.

[18]C. H. Spurgeon, *The Metropolitan Tabernacle Pulpit*, 36 (1890): 134.

[19]C. H. Spurgeon, *The Metropolitan Tabernacle Pulpit*, 56 (1910): 398–399.

[20]C. H. Spurgeon, *The Metropolitan Tabernacle Pulpit*, 57 (1890): 266.

[21]Elizabeth Ruth Skoglund, *Bright Days, Dark Nights: With Charles Spurgeon in Triumph Over Emotional Pain* (Grand Rapids, MI: Baker Books, 2000), 31.

[22]W. E. Vine, *The Epistle to the Hebrews: Christ All Excelling*, (London: Oliphants Limited, 1952), 44.

[23]Sigmund Freud, quoted by Sackler, M.D., et al. in "Recent Advances in Psychobiology and Their Impact on General Practice," *Inter. Record of Med.* 170:1551 (1957).

[24]Bruce L. Shelley, *Transformed by Love: The Vernon Grounds Story*, (Grand Rapids, MI: Discovery House Publishers, 2002), 147-148.

[25]Helmut Thielicke, John W. Doberstein, trans., Ibid., 222–223.

[26]Charles H. Spurgeon, *Treasury of David* (Grand Rapids: "Taken from *Treasury of David*, by C. H. Spurgeon, edited by David Otis Fuller. © 1940, 1968 by David Otis Fuller. Used by permission of Zondervan Publishing House"), Vol. 1, 110.

[27]Charles H. Spurgeon, Ibid., Vol. 3., 108.

[28]Charles H. Spurgeon, *New Park Street Pulpit 1858*, Vol. 4 (London: Banner of Truth Trust, 1964), 400–461.

[29]Helmut Thielicke, John W. Doberstein, trans., *Encounter with Spurgeon*, 216.

[30]Ernest W. Bacon, *Spurgeon: Heir of the Puritans* (Grand Rapids: William B. Eerdmans Publishing Co., 1968), 78.

[31]Helmut Thielicke, John W. Doberstein, trans., *Encounter with Spurgeon*, 217–218.

[32]Helmut Thielicke, John W. Doberstein, trans., Ibid., 11.

[33]Helmut Thielicke, John W. Doberstein, trans., Ibid., 215.

[34]Charles H. Spurgeon, *Treasury of David*, Vol. 2, 3–4.

[35]Richard E. Day, op. cit., 178.

[36]Richard E. Day, Ibid., 179.

[37]Charles H. Spurgeon, *The Metropolitan Tabernacle Pulpit*, 32 (1886): 344.

[38]Charles E. Spurgeon, op. cit., Vol. 2, 463.

[39]Charles E. Spurgeon, Ibid., 254, 257.

[40]Charles E. Spurgeon, *The Saint and His Savior* (London: Hazell, Watson & Viney Ltd., 1895), 35.

[41]Charles H. Spurgeon, *Treasury of David*, Vol. 2, 254.

[42]Charles E. Spurgeon, *New Park Street*, 460.

[43]Charles E. Spurgeon, op. cit., 251, 254.

[44]Richard E. Day, op. cit., 226.

[45]Richard E. Day, Ibid., 113–114.

[46]Richard E. Day, Ibid., 115.

[47]Richard E. Day, Ibid., 227.

[48]Ernest W. Bacon, op. cit., 167.

Chapter 7—Hudson Taylor: Drawing on God's Provision

[1]Dr. and Mrs. Howard Taylor, *Hudson Taylor's Spiritual Secret* (Chicago: Moody Press. Used by permission, China Inland Mission, Robesonia, PA), 120.

[2]Dr. and Mrs. Howard Taylor, Ibid., 33–36.

[3]Dr. and Mrs. Howard Taylor, Ibid., 37.

[4]Dr. and Mrs. Howard Taylor, Ibid., 43.

[5]Colin M. Turnbull, *The Mountain People* (New York: Simon and Schuster, 1972), 292.

[6]George Müller, *The Life of Trust* (New York: Thomas Y. Crowell Company, Pub., 1898), 481–487.

[7]Dr. and Mrs. Howard Taylor, *Hudson Taylor in Early Years: The Growth of a Soul* (London: The China Inland Mission, 1921. Republished as *Biography of J. Hudson Taylor*, OMF Books, Littleton, CO, © 1965.), 399–400.

[8]Dr. and Mrs. Howard Taylor, *Hudson Taylor and the China Inland Mission: The Growth of a Work of God* (Newington Green, London: Lutterworth Press, 1958), 476.

[9]Dr. and Mrs. Howard Taylor, Ibid., 32.

[10]Dr. and Mrs. Howard Taylor, Ibid., 314.

[11]Dr. and Mrs. Howard Taylor, Ibid., 315.

[12]Dr. and Mrs. Howard Taylor, Ibid., 316.

[13]Dr. and Mrs. Howard Taylor, *Hudson Taylor's Spiritual Secret*, 195–196.

[14]Dr. and Mrs. Howard Taylor, Ibid., 196–197.

[15]Dr. and Mrs. Howard Taylor, *Hudson Taylor and the China Inland Mission: The Growth of a Work of God* (London: China Inland Mission, 1958. Republished as *Biography of J. Hudson Taylor*, OMF Books, Littleton, CO, © 1965.), 176.

[16]Dr. and Mrs. Howard Taylor, Ibid., 204.

[17]Dr. and Mrs. Howard Taylor, Ibid., 290–291.

[18]Dr. and Mrs. Howard Taylor, Ibid., 291.

[19]A. J. Broomhall, *Hudson Taylor and China's Open Century: Book Seven, It Is Not Death To Die* (London: Hodder and Stoughton, Ltd., 1989), 516–517.

Chapter 8—Geraldine Taylor: Divine Renewal

[1]Joy Guinness, *Mrs. Howard Taylor: Her Web of Time* (London: China Inland Mission, n.d.), 93.

[2]Joy Guinness, Ibid., 94.

[3]Walter A. Elwell, ed., *Evangelical Dictionary of Theology* (Grand Rapids: Baker Book House, 1984), 934.

[4]Joy Guinness, *Mrs. Howard Taylor: Her Web of Time*, 36.

[5]Joy Guinness, Ibid., 201.

[6]Joy Guinness, Ibid., 124.

[7]Amy Carmichael, *Toward Jerusalem* (Fort Washington, PA: Christian Literature Crusade, 1961), 95.

[8]Joy Guinness, *Mrs. Howard Taylor: Her Web of Time*, 322.

[9]Gigi Graham Tchividjian, *Weather of the Heart* (Portland, OR: Multnomah Press, 1991), 42–43.

[10]Joy Guinness, *Mrs. Howard Taylor: Her Web of Time*, 279.

[11]Dr. and Mrs. Howard Taylor, *Hudson Taylor and the China Inland Mission: The Growth of a Work of God* (London: China Inland Mission, 1958), 528.

[12]Joy Guinness, *Mrs. Howard Taylor: Her Web of Time*, 199.

[13]Joy Guinness, Ibid., 198.

[14]Geraldine Taylor, Foreword to H. Grattan Guinness, *A Father's Letter* (London: China Inland Mission, n.d.), 6.

[15]Geraldine Taylor, Ibid., 6–7.

[16]H. Grattan Guinness, *A Father's Letter*, 9.

[17]H. Grattan Guinness, Ibid., 10–11.

[18]H. Grattan Guinness, Ibid., 12–13.

[19]H. Grattan Guinness, Ibid., 16–18.

[20]Joy Guinness, *Mrs. Howard Taylor: Her Web of Time*, 198–199.

[21]Phyllis Thompson, *D. E. Hoste: A Prince with God* (London: China Inland Mission, n.d.), 48.

[22]Phyllis Thompson, Ibid., 101.

[23]Phyllis Thompson, Ibid., 130–131.

[24]Phyllis Thompson, Ibid., 80.

[25]Phyllis Thompson, Ibid., 81.

[26]Phyllis Thompson, Ibid., 116.

[27]Mrs. Howard Taylor, *Behind the Ranges: Fraser of Lisuland, Southwest China* (London: China Inland Mission, 1956), 84.

[28]Mrs. Howard Taylor, Ibid., 87.

[29]Mrs. Howard Taylor, Ibid., 89.

[30]Mrs. Howard Taylor, Ibid., 89–90.

[31]Mrs. Howard Taylor, Ibid., 91.

[32]Mrs. Howard Taylor, Ibid., 134.

[33]Mrs. Howard Taylor, Ibid., 135.

[34]Mrs. Howard Taylor, *Pastor Hsi: Confucian Scholar and Christian* (London: China Inland Mission, 1949), 49.

[35]Mrs. Howard Taylor, Ibid., 240.

[36]Mrs. Howard Taylor, Ibid., 242.

[37]Mrs. Howard Taylor, Ibid., 291.

[38]Dr. and Mrs. Howard Taylor, *Hudson Taylor and the China Inland Mission: The Growth of a Work of God*, 509–510.

[39]Dr. and Mrs. Howard Taylor, Ibid.

[40]Dr. and Mrs. Howard Taylor, Ibid., 511.

[41]Dr. and Mrs. Howard Taylor, Ibid., 515.

Chapter 9—Isobel Kuhn: A Platform of Testing

[1]Isobel Kuhn, *In the Arena* (Chicago: Moody Press, 1958), 33.

[2]Isobel Kuhn, Ibid., 142.

[3]Isobel Kuhn, Ibid., 150.

[4]Isobel Kuhn, Ibid.

[5]Isobel Kuhn, Ibid., 221.

[6]Isobel Kuhn, Ibid.

[7]Isobel Kuhn, Ibid., 212.

[8]Isobel Kuhn, Ibid., 213.

[9]Isobel Kuhn, Ibid., 220.

[10]Isobel Kuhn, Ibid.

[11]Isobel Kuhn, Ibid., 9.

[12]Isobel Kuhn, Ibid., 8.

[13]Isobel Kuhn, Ibid., 35.

[14]Isobel Kuhn, *Green Leaf in Drought-Time* (Chicago: Moody Press, 1957), 7.

[15]Carolyn L. Canfield, *One Vision Only* (Chicago: Moody Press, 1959), 60.

[16]Carolyn L. Canfield, Ibid., 61.

[17]Carolyn L. Canfield, Ibid., 61–62.

[18]Isobel Kuhn, *Precious Things of the Lasting Hills* (Chicago: Moody Press, 1963), 42–43.

[19]Isobel Kuhn, *Nests Above the Abyss* (Philadelphia: China Inland Mission, 1947), 183–184.

[20]Isobel Kuhn, *Precious Things*, 42.

[21]Isobel Kuhn, Ibid., 41.

[22]Isobel Kuhn, Ibid., 42.

[23]Isobel Kuhn, Ibid., 43–44.

[24]Isobel Kuhn, *Stones of Fire* (Chicago: Moody Press, 1960), 9.

[25]Ellice Hopkins, as quoted by Isobel Kuhn, Ibid., 147.

[26]Isobel Kuhn, *Ascent to the Tribes: Pioneering in North Thailand* (Chicago: Moody Press, 1956), 164.

[27]F. B. Meyer, as quoted by Isobel Kuhn, *In the Arena* (Chicago: Moody Press, 1958), 184.

[28]Isobel Kuhn, *In the Arena*, 194.

[29]Isobel Kuhn, Ibid., 215.

[30]Isobel Kuhn, *Green Leaf in Drought-Time*, 45.

[31]Isobel Kuhn, *In the Arena*, 216.

[32]Amy Carmichael, as quoted by Isobel Kuhn, Ibid., 216.

[33]Isobel Kuhn, Ibid., 216.

[34]Oswald Chambers, as quoted by Isobel Kuhn, *Green Leaf in Drought-Time*, 111.

[35]Isobel Kuhn, *By Searching* (Robesonia, PA: OMF Books, 1959), 63–64.

[36]Isobel Kuhn, *In the Arena*, 65.

[37]Isobel Kuhn, *Precious Things*, 33.

[38]Isobel Kuhn, *By Searching*, 67–68.

[39]Isobel Kuhn, Ibid.

[40]Isobel Kuhn, *Nests Above the Abyss*, 206.

[41]Isobel Kuhn, *Green Leaf in Drought-Time*, 29–30.

[42]John Stott, *Life in Christ* (Wheaton, IL: Tyndale House Publishers, Inc., 1991), 83–84.

[43]Isobel Kuhn, *Green Leaf in Drought-Time*, 57–58.

[44]Isobel Kuhn, Ibid., 93.

[45]Isobel Kuhn, Ibid., 94.

[46]Samuel Rutherford, as quoted by Carolyn L. Canfield, *One Vision Only*, 186.

[47]Amy Carmichael, *Candles in the Dark: Letters of Amy Carmichael* (Fort Washington, PA: Christian Literature Crusade, 1982), 59.

Chapter 10—C. S. Lewis: Dealing With Imperfection

[1] C. S. Lewis, *The Problem of Pain* (New York: the Macmillan Company ©1943, 1945, 1952. Used by permission, William Collins Sons & Co., Ltd., London), 9.

[2] C. S. Lewis, Ibid., 18.

[3] C. S. Lewis, Ibid., 105.

[4] C. S. Lewis, *Mere Christianity* (New York: Macmillan Publishing Company, Inc., 1964. Used by permission, William Collins Sons & Co., Ltd., London), 109.

[5] C. S. Lewis, *A Grief Observed* (New York: The Seabury Press, 1963), © 1961 by N. W. Clerk. Reprinted by permission Harper & Row Publishers, Inc., 36.

[6] C. S. Lewis, Ibid., 43.

[7] C. S. Lewis, Ibid., 8–9.

[8] C. S. Lewis, *Mere Christianity*, 180–182.

[9] C. S. Lewis, *Surprised by Joy* (Orlando, FL: Harcourt Brace Jovanovich, Inc., 1956), 21.

[10] C. S. Lewis, *Reflections on the Psalms* (Orlando, FL: Harcourt Brace Jovanovich, Inc., 1964), 28.

[11] C. S. Lewis, *The Weight of Glory* (Grand Rapids: William B. Eerdmans Publishing Company, 1965), © by the executors of the Estate of C. S. Lewis, 1967. Used by permission, William Collins Sons & Co., Ltd., London, 40–41.

[12] C. S. Lewis, Ibid., 14–15.

[13] C. S. Lewis, *Christian Reflections* (Grand Rapids: William B. Eerdmans Publishing Company, 1974). Used by permission, William Collins Sons & Co., Ltd., London, 39.

[14] C. S. Lewis, Ibid., 42.

[15] C. S. Lewis, Ibid., 43.

[16] C. S. Lewis, Ibid.

[17] W. H. Lewis, ed., *Letters of C. S. Lewis* (Orlando, Florida: Reprinted by permission Harcourt Brace Jovanovich, Inc., 1975), 118–120, © 1966 by W. H. Lewis and executors of C. S. Lewis.

[18] C. S. Lewis, *The Weight of Glory*, 52.

[19] C. S. Lewis, *Letters to an American Lady* (Grand Rapids: William B. Eerdmans Publishing Company, 1967), 73.

[20] C. S. Lewis, *Mere Christianity*, 84–86.

[21] C. S. Lewis, Ibid., 116.

[22] C. S. Lewis, Ibid. 88–89.

[23]C. S. Lewis, Ibid., 92.

[24]C. S. Lewis, Ibid., 172.

[25]C. S. Lewis, Ibid., 174.

[26]C. S. Lewis, Ibid., 174–175.

Chapter 11—Ruth Bell Graham: Reference Points

[1]Ruth Bell Graham, *It's My Turn* (Old Tappan, NJ: Power Books, Fleming H. Revell Company, 1973), 173.

[2]Ruth Bell Graham, Ibid.

[3]John Pollock, *A Foreign Devil in China: The Story of Dr. L. Nelson Bell* (Minneapolis, MN: World Wide Publications, 1971), 113.

[4]John Pollock, Ibid., 203.

[5]John Pollock, Ibid., 113.

[6]Ruth Bell Graham, *Prodigals and Those Who Love Them* (Colorado Springs, CO: Focus on the Family, 1991), 76.

[7]Patricia Daniels Cornwell, *A Time for Remembering: The Story of Ruth Bell Graham* (New York: Harper and Row Publishers, 1983), 18.

[8]Patricia Daniels Cornwell, Ibid., 71.

[9]Ruth Bell Graham, poem, as quoted in Ibid., 39.

[10]Ruth Bell Graham, *It's My Turn*, 72.

[11]C. S. Lewis, *The Silver Chair* (New York: Collier Books, Division of Macmillan Publishing Co., Inc., 1976), 207.

[12]Ruth Bell Graham, *It's My Turn*, 62–63.

[13]Frank W. Boreham, D.D., *Mountain in the Mist* (London: The Epworth Press, 1933), 174.

[14]Ruth Bell Graham, as quoted in Patricia Daniels Cornwell, *A Time for Remembering*, 179–180.

[15]Ruth Bell Graham, as quoted in Patricia Daniels Cornwell, Ibid., 158.

[16]Ruth Bell Graham, as quoted in Patricia Daniels Cornwell, Ibid., 160.

[17]Ruth Bell Graham, as quoted in Patricia Daniels Cornwell, Ibid., 172.

[18]Ruth Bell Graham, as quoted in Patricia Daniels Cornwell, Ibid., 121.

[19]F. W. Boreham, *Mountains in the Mist*, 130.

[20]Patricia Daniels Cornwell, *A Time for Remembering*, 140.

Chapter 12—Living Within an Eternal Perspective

[1]Dr. and Mrs. Howard Taylor, *Hudson Taylor's Spiritual Secret* (Chicago: Moody Press, used by permission, Littleton, CO, OMF), 124.

Notes for Vignettes

No Scar?

[1]Amy Carmichael, *Toward Jerusalem* (Fort Washington, PA: Christian Literature Crusade, 1961), 85.

D. Martyn Lloyd-Jones

[1]D. Martyn Lloyd-Jones, *Authority* (London: InterVarsity Fellowship, 1958), 29.

[2]D. Martyn Lloyd-Jones, Ibid., 21.

Andrew Murray

[1]Amy Carmichael, *Though the Mountains Shake*, 12–13.

Frances Ridley Havergal

[1]Frances Ridley Havergal, poem, as quoted in Joy Guinness, *Mrs. Howard Taylor: Her Web of Time* (London: China Inland Mission, 1952), 368.

[2]Frances Ridley Havergal, *My King* (London: James Nisbet and Company, Ltd., 1878), 30–32.

Handley C. G. Moule

[1]H. C. G. Moule, *Thoughts on Union With Christ*, as quoted by Amy Carmichael, *If* (Fort Washington, PA: Christian Literature Crusade, 1960), 34.

[2]Amy Carmichael, *Gold by Moonlight* (Fort Washington, PA: Christian Literature Crusade, 1960), 34.

Dwight L. Moody

[1]S. Spurgeon, as quoted by A. P. Fitt, *The Life of D. L. Moody* (Moody Press, n.d.), 45.

[2]A. P. Fitt, *The Life of D. L. Moody*, 5.

Brother Lawrence

[1]Brother Lawrence, *The Practice of the Presence of God (Being Conversations and Letters of Nicholas Herman of Lorraine)*, (Westwood, NJ: Fleming H. Revell Company, 1957), 6–7.

H. A. Ironside

[1]H. A. Ironside, Litt. D., *Addresses on the First Epistle to the Corinthians* (Neptune, NJ: Loizeaux Brothers, Inc.), 353–354.

Arthur T. Pierson

[1]Arthur T. Pierson, *The Bible and Spiritual Life* (London: James Nisbet and Co., Ltd., 1908), 376–377.

[2]Dr. Arthur T. Pierson, "Christ Our Wisdom from God," *The Ministry of Keswick,* edited by Herbert F. Stevenson (Grand Rapids: Zondervan Publishing House, 1963), 114.

George MacDonald

[1]Lewis, C. S., *George MacDonald: An Anthology* (Simon & Schuster: New York, 1996), xxxii.

[2]Rolland Hein, *The World of George MacDonald* (Wheaton, IL: Harold Shaw Publishers, 1978), 60.

[3]Rolland Hein, Ibid., 148–149.

[4]Rolland Hein, Ibid., 77.

[5]George MacDonald, *Diary of an Old Soul* (Minneapolis, MN: Augsburg Publishing House, 1975), 25.

G. Campbell Morgan

[1]G. Campbell Morgan, D.D., *Hosea: The Heart and Holiness of God* (Westwood, NJ: Fleming H. Revell Company, 1994), 105–106.

[2]G. Campbell Morgan, *The Life of the Christian* (London: Pickering & Inglis Ltd., n.d.), 11.

[3]G. Campbell Morgan, Ibid., 65–66.

[4]G. Campbell Morgan, D.D., Ibid., 54.

Cloud of Witnesses (Rotherham, Ironside, Graham, Moule)

[1]Joseph Bryant Rotherham, *Emphasized Bible*, New Testament (Grand Rapids: Kregel Publications, 1992), 232.

[2]H. A. Ironside, Litt. D., *Hebrews, James, Peter* (Neptune, NJ: Loizeaux Brothers, 1932), 150–151.

[3]Ruth Bell Graham, "If Only" poem.

[4]Handley C. G. Moule, D.D., *Messages from the Epistle to the Hebrews* (London: Elliot Stock, 1909), 81–83.

NOTE TO THE READER

The publisher invites you to share your response to the message of this book by writing Discovery House Publishers, Box 3566, Grand Rapids, MI 49501, USA. For information about other Discovery House books, music, or videos, contact us at the same address or call 1-800-653-8333. Find us on the Internet at http://www.dhp.org/ or send e-mail to books@dhp.org.

ABOUT THE AUTHOR

*E*lizabeth Skoglund has authored more than 30 books, including these books by Discovery House Publishers: *Secrets of the Second Half: Living Well for the Rest of Your Life;* and *Gifts from the Hearth: Your Guide to the Art of Hospitality.* The author is a licensed marriage, family, and child counselor in private practice in Burbank, California, and is a regular guest on radio and television talk shows.

You may learn more about Elizabeth Skoglund on her Web site, called *Netmenders.* The site features inspirational excerpts from Charles Haddon Spurgeon, family recipes (many gleaned from *Gifts from the Hearth*), and a clear explanation of what it means to be a Christian.

The Web address is www.elizabethskoglund.com.